The Dreaming & Other Essays

W.E.H. Stanner

EasyRead Large

Copyright Page from the Original Book

Published by Black Inc. Agenda,
an imprint of Schwartz Media Pty Ltd
37–39 Langridge Street
Collingwood VIC 3066 Australia
email: enquiries@blackincbooks.com
http://www.blackincbooks.com

Introduction © Robert Manne 2010
First edition published 2009
Essays © Retained by Patricia Stanner

ALL RIGHTS RESERVED.
No part of this publication may be reproduced, stored in a retrieval system, or transmitted in any form by any means electronic, mechanical, photo-copying, recording or otherwise without the prior consent of the publishers.

The National Library of Australia Cataloguing-in-Publication entry:

> Stanner, W. E. H. (William Edward Hanley), 1905-1981
>
> The dreaming & other essays / W.E.H. Stanner ; introduction by Robert Manne.
>
> 2nd ed.
>
> ISBN: 9781863955171 (pbk.)
>
> Includes index.
>
> Aboriginal Australians--Social life and customs. Aboriginal Australians--Government relations. Australia--Race relations. Australia--Colonization--History.
>
> 305.89915

Book design: Thomas Deverall
Typeset by J&M Typesetting Pty Ltd
Index by Michael Ramsden

Printed in China by Guangzhou Xin Yi Printing Co., Ltd.

TABLE OF CONTENTS

W.E.H. Stanner: The Anthropologist as Humanist	ii
Durmugam: A Nangiomeri (1959)	1
The Dreaming (1953)	85
Caliban Discovered (1962)	121
'The History of Indifference Thus Begins' (1963)	165
The Aborigines (1938)	230
Continuity and Change among the Aborigines (1958)	280
The Boyer Lectures: After the Dreaming (1968)	337
The Yirrkala Land Case: Dress-Rehearsal (1970)	456
Aborigines and Australian Society (1972)	502
Aboriginal Humour (1956)	546
Concluding Thoughts from 'Aborigines in the Affluent Society' (1973)	575
Publication Details & Acknowledgements	581
Back Cover Material	584
Index	587

Published by **Black Inc. Agenda**
Series Editor: Robert Manne

Other books in the Black Inc. Agenda series:

Whitewash: On Keith Windschuttle's Fabrication of Aboriginal History ed. Robert Manne

The Howard Years ed. Robert Manne

Axis of Deceit Andrew Wilkie

Following Them Home: The Fate of the Returned Asylum Seekers David Corlett

Civil Passions: Selected Writings Martin Krygier

Do Not Disturb: Is the Media Failing Australia? ed. Robert Manne

Sense & Nonsense in Australian History John Hirst

The Weapons Detective Rod Barton

Scorcher Clive Hamilton

Dear Mr Rudd ed. Robert Manne

Goodbye to All That? On the Failure of Neo-Liberalism and the Urgency of Change eds. Robert Manne and David McKnight

W.E.H. Stanner: The Anthropologist as Humanist

Robert Manne

Several years ago I began reading widely on the Australian Aborigines. No author I encountered seemed as important as W.E.H. Stanner; no book as wise or deep as his *White Man Got No Dreaming.* I soon discovered that not only had this volume of his essays been out of print for decades; even attempts to locate and buy a second-hand copy proved fruitless. The publisher at Black Inc., Chris Feik, came to share my enthusiasm for Stanner. At his suggestion, we decided to publish this collection. We believed that just as the novels of Patrick White or the poetry of A.D. Hope should be available to each new generation of Australian readers, so too should the essays of W.E.H. Stanner.

Stanner was born in Watsons Bay in 1905. While working as a journalist, he went to the University of Sydney in 1928. Although Stanner initially intended to read economics, a new direction emerged after an encounter with the first Professor of Anthropology in any Australian university, the flamboyant Englishman A.R. Radcliffe-Brown. Stanner proved himself a first-class anthropology student. In circumstances that created considerable bitterness, Radcliffe-Brown left Sydney in 1931. He was eventually replaced as Professor of Anthropology by the Anglican minister A.P. Elkin. Under his supervision and that of a longtime academic patron, Raymond Firth, Stanner researched and wrote his master's thesis. Originally he intended to conduct his fieldwork in the East Kimberleys. Rumours arrived, however, of the existence of what Stanner once sardonically described as 'the wild unspotted savage' around Daly River in the Northern Territory. He went there instead. His thesis on culture contact in the Daly River region was completed in 1934.

Already Stanner was aware, even in a region as remote as this, of the collapse of what he would later call

Aboriginal High Culture. He understood that the old men who were acting as his informants on language and belief were doing so 'in the hope that something of their knowledge would be preserved'. Stanner also became acquainted with the miserable social circumstance of the Aborigines. Living as they did on a 'rotting frontier, with the smell of old failure, vice, and decadence', they were by now reliant on the goodwill of the English and Chinese peanut farmers, themselves scratching out a meagre income in a situation of almost unimaginable harshness, who supplied the Aborigines with the stimulants—tobacco and tea—they could no longer bear to be without. Much later, Stanner reflected on the curious quality of his own response to this tragedy at this time. In his private letters, he wrote movingly on the plight of the Aborigines. In his public reports, he wrote without affect. 'The tone of my comments,' he recalled in 1968, 'is rather reminiscent of the flat, emotionless remark that Spencer and Gillen had made thirty years earlier when they said that "...taking all things into account, the black fellow has not perhaps any particular reason to be grateful to the white man."' Reflection on the oddness of his own initial response to the situation he observed on the Daly River provided Stanner with a first clue about the peculiarity that lay at the heart of Australian national identity, the systematic obliteration in national memory of what the British settlers had done to the Aborigines.

Having successfully completed his master's thesis, and having spent some time working for the New South Wales Premier, Bertram Stevens, Stanner gathered further materials in the Daly River–Port Keats region for a doctoral dissertation. As no opportunity to complete a doctorate existed in Australia, he was encouraged by Elkin to travel to England and by Radcliffe-Brown, after he arrived at Oxford, to go to the London School of Economics to study under the eminent and demanding Bronislaw Malinowski. Stanner's career now became rather complicated, even messy. In 1937, he worked very briefly for Richard Casey, an Australian representative at the

Imperial Conference, and also in Geneva at the League of Nations. Having contemplated joining the anti-fascist side in the Spanish Civil War, despite political dislike of the communist-controlled International Brigades, he moved instead to the foreign desk of *The Times.* During this time, Stanner wrote a series of impassioned essays—the flatness of affect had by now completely lifted—on the plight of the Australian Aborigines, the most important of which, 'The Aborigines', is included in this volume. Unable to find any anthropological position in Australia, Stanner moved to a research post in the British colony of Kenya and returned to Australia only after the outbreak of war. Rejected for military service because at thirty-four he was regarded as too old, he was appointed first to the new Ministry of Information and then to civilian posts with Menzies's and then Curtin's Army Ministers, Percy Spender and Frank Forde. In 1941 Stanner seriously considered standing for parliament on the non-Labor side. After the fall of Singapore in February 1942, for the only time in history, Australians feared foreign invasion. Stanner was by instinct a military man. He seems to have greatly relished his appointment as Major, then Colonel, in command of the bush commando unit, the North Australia Observer Unit, whose surveillance and reconnaissance duties stretched from Cape York to the West Kimberleys. Far less to his taste was his next appointment, to the fabled Alf Conlon's secretive Army Directorate of Research in Melbourne, from where Stanner left for London, to work on General Blamey's staff, and later to British North Borneo. Following demobilisation, Stanner turned his anthropological attention to the cultures of the South Pacific and also, as founding Director of an Institute of Social Research in Uganda, to colonial East Africa.

Stanner won his first permanent university post at the newly established Australian National University in 1950. He was by now in his mid-forties. This position gave him the chance to return to the work he had been taken from for almost fifteen years: the study of religion and cultural change chiefly among the Murinbata people. Stanner made field trips to the Daly River and Port Keats region in 1952, 1954 and 1957. In 1958, he travelled to the Fitzmaurice River—a transcendent and harrowing experience, where he discovered luminous rock art and lost three stone, which has been beautifully described by Melinda Hinkson in a recent volume. He returned in 1959, but this time with the help of a helicopter. During this time Stanner began writing what many anthropologists regard as his most important work, a complex series of articles on Aboriginal religion for the scholarly journal *Oceania*. But he also began on a series of essays and lectures for nonspecialist audiences, the most important of which are included in this volume. These essays and lectures represent one of the true bravura performances in the intellectual history of Australia.

In 1953 Stanner wrote, as a 'jeu d'esprit' for a gathering of the Canberra Fellowship of Australian Writers, a talk on the Aboriginal world view, 'The

Dreaming', which soon became a standard text for a generation of American undergraduates. It is a triumph of empathetic anthropological imagination. In 1956, as another amusement for the Canberra writers' group, he put together a wonderfully perceptive account of the character and social function of Aboriginal humour, which at the time he did not even consider worth publishing. In 1958 Stanner delivered a lecture to an audience of scholars, 'Continuity and Change among the Aborigines', which offered by far the most penetrating and devastating non-indigenous critique of the reigning and virtually unchallenged Hasluck policy of assimilation that had been written until that time. The following year he published for a major American anthropological anthology 'Durmugam: A Nangiomeri', an unforgettable portrait of a warrior's noble but ultimately unsuccessful attempt to hold back the waves of cultural change on the basis of fierce fidelity to tradition and the force of moral character. Stanner wrote this essay with 'a passion'. 'He was such a man. I thought I would like to make the reading world see and feel him as I did.' It is the finest essay by an Australian I have ever read. In the early 1960s, Stanner turned his attention to historical anthropology: in 1962, in 'Caliban Discovered', to a savage indictment of the blindness of the Europeans to the miraculously adaptive culture they stumbled upon in the Antipodes; and, in 1963, in 'The History of Indifference Thus Begins', to a forensic account of Governor Phillip's Aboriginal policy—his well-intentioned but hopelessly muddled incomprehension about the ruin he was visiting on the Aborigines.

In 1968 Stanner was invited to deliver the ABC's Boyer Lectures. In them he brought together all the themes of his essays and his talks—the persistence of what Stanner now called 'the great Australian silence' concerning the Aboriginal dispossession; the gradual penetration of contemporary consciousness by what he called 'the anthropological principle', which had almost dissolved the old Western certainties about cultural superiority and inferiority and cleared the way for an 'appreciation of difference'; the belated recognition in Australia of the genius and the strangeness of the indigenous culture the British had so light-heartedly and thoughtlessly set about destroying; the emerging possibilities of a racial composition if we could only see that *'our'* problem with the Aborigines was less important than *'their'* problem with us; the arrogance and certain failure of the policy of assimilation, which was inviting the Aborigines to relinquish what it was that made them a distinctive people, or, in Stanner's biting phrase, which was asking them to 'un-be'; and, finally and tentatively, the question which came more and more to obsess him, the possibility of an historic act of reconciliation through a willingness to contemplate some new deal over the question of the ownership of land.

Despite their unfailing quality, Stanner's earlier essays and lectures had reached only small audiences in Australia. For his public influence, the Boyer Lectures, which were printed seven times under the title *After the Dreaming,* were to prove decisive. The great Australian historian Keith Hancock, whose lapidary line in *Australia* about the fatal incompatibility of a hunter-gatherer and a pastoral economy had been so persuasive for so long, now wrote to Stanner to tell him how deeply he had been moved by the lectures. Stanner's friend, the former Governor of the Reserve Bank, Nugget Coombs, told him that in his opinion the lectures 'had more influence [on Aboriginal affairs] than any other utterance' in Australian history. After becoming acquainted with Stanner through the lectures, the solicitor advising the Yolngu people of the Northern Territory, Frank Purcell, invited Stanner to act as anthropological adviser in Australia's first common-law native-title case. And when the man who was to become the most important historian of the dispossession, Henry Reynolds, read the lectures in 1969, the idea he encountered there—'the great Australian silence'—provided him with the inspiration for his life agenda. Ann Curthoys has recently argued, reasonably enough, that the influence of the lectures cannot be explained without taking into account a particular historical moment and political context. Yet even she does not dispute the fact that, in the history of non-indigenous Australian public conscience, Stanner's Boyer Lectures of 1968 occupy a central place.

In all previous Australian generations, as Henry Reynolds demonstrated in *This Whispering in Our Hearts,* some isolated individuals or groups had grasped the meaning of the dispossession. They were, however, surrounded by an atmosphere of general indifference or worse. During the 1960s and 1970s, for the first time in Australian history, moral consciousness awoke for very many members of an entire non-indigenous generation. Evidence of this awakening was everywhere to be seen. In 1961, the Commonwealth Government supported the idea of establishing the Australian Institute of Aboriginal Affairs. Stanner was a pivotal but eventually disillusioned player, as John Mulvaney has recently shown. In 1964, the Australian Social Science Council supported the research of Charles Rowley, who eventually produced the ground-breaking trilogy *The Destruction of Aboriginal Society, Outcasts in White Australia* and *The Remote Aborigines*. In 1967, the referendum ceding power to the Commonwealth in Aboriginal affairs passed with 90 per cent popular support. In 1968, the Holt Government formed an advisory three-man Council of Aboriginal Affairs—Stanner, Barrie Dexter and Nugget Coombs. And in 1972, with the election of Whitlam, for the first time in Australian history, a government placed Aboriginal affairs, including land rights, at the centre of its agenda. After this government was defeated, some of the most important pro-Aboriginal members of this generation—Nugget Coombs, Charles Rowley, Judith Wright and W.E.H. Stanner—formed a committee calling for a Treaty with the Aborigines. In the year of Stanner's death, 1981, two of the most powerful historical works on the dispossession were published, Henry Reynolds's seminal *The Other Side of the Frontier* and Judith Wright's haunting saga of her Queensland pastoral family and its crimes, *The Cry for the Dead.*

For the first generation of non-indigenous Australians who had heard a whispering in their hearts, the most eloquent voice, the most authoritative teacher, had unquestionably been W.E.H. Stanner. It is interesting to ponder why.

***

Stanner was an admirer of the achievement of the pioneers of rigorously scientific Australian Aboriginal anthropology, such as Lorimer Fison and A.W. Howitt or Walter Roth or Sir Baldwin Spencer and Frank Gillen. And yet, as he wrote, what had been written by previous anthropologists who had worked amongst the Australian Aborigines 'did not square' with his experience. He had also learned a great deal, as he acknowledged, from his two teachers, Radcliffe-Brown and Malinowski. But there was something about their work that left him unsatisfied and uneasy. 'We have to avoid Radcliffe-Brown's effort of making human, man-made facts seem non-human,' he wrote to one of his friends, 'and we have to grasp more of the creative and aspirational side of man than Bronislaw Malinowski did. How odd the scheme of "primary and derived needs" now seems!' 'A scholarly rigour is one thing: another thing altogether is to use logic and method to dehumanise what one studies.' What Stanner thought was needed was something he called a 'humanistic anthropology'. The writing of such anthropology was at the very centre of his achievement.

One of the staples of the earlier anthropology had been very detailed descriptions of traditional rituals. Yet never were these anthropologists able to disguise the mixture of fascination and tedium they experienced in the presence of these 'primitive' ceremonies. The following characteristic passage comes from a Spencer and Gillen description of an initiation ceremony.

> No loud talking was allowed, and everyone looked as solemn as possible. The Churinga [sacred object] having been at last unpacked—for in these ceremonies

everything is done with the utmost and, to the onlooker, often exasperating deliberation—they were taken up one by one by the Alantunja [totemic chiefs], in whose charge they were, and after a careful examination of each he pressed them in turn against the stomach of one or another of the old men present.

Compare this with Stanner's description of the *Punj* ceremony of the Murinbata people, buried in a dense monograph on Aboriginal religion in the journal *Oceania*.

> The principals at *Punj* cluster for the opening phase in a compact circle. The formation is one in which physical association is intimate. The men sit flank to flank, with knees often crossing, and with arms often flung around the shoulders of neighbours ... While at song the celebrants vie rather than compete ... The men's faces take on a glow of animation and tender intent. At the last exclamatory cry—*Karwadi yoy!*—everyone shouts as if with one voice. An observer feels that

he is in the presence of true congregation, a full sociality at a peak of intimacy, altruism and unison.

What is significant here is the contrast between the impoverishment of meaning of Spencer and Gillen's detached pseudo-scientific laboratory observations and the richness of what Stanner is able to see and to convey with his inwardness, his enlivened imagination and attentiveness, or what social scientists, following Dilthey and Weber, would come to call his *verstehen.*

But there was more to Stanner's achievement than a capacity for empathetic understanding. Unlike his predecessors, Stanner rejected the view of history as material and moral progress through stages, from primitive hunter-gatherer society to sophisticated industrial civilisation. He thought the earlier anthropologists, who had looked down upon the Aborigines as a 'child-race', had done a great human disservice in seeing the Aborigines as people of the Stone Age or as forming the chrysalis of civilisation. Stanner's achievement depended on the entire absence in his sensibility of this kind of condescension. For him, the Aborigines were a contemporary and a successful and a specialised people. He was also convinced that contempt for human difference, the division of cultures into primitive and advanced, worthy and unworthy, was a characteristic disease of modernity. This contempt revealed, he once argued, 'the decay of the old sense of humankind in the European tradition that allowed Herodotus to write in a neighbourly way of strange peoples, and made him think Cambyses mad for scorning Persian and Egyptian religious rites.' As Conor Cruise O'Brien has shown in *The Great Melody*, the greatest conservative in the English tradition, Edmund Burke, was a courageous defender of the Indian culture and way of life, which had been threatened by the behaviour of the British East India Company. Stanner's deepest instincts were those of a Burkean conservative.

One of the main ambitions of Stanner's practice of humanistic anthropology was to make perspicuous the mindset of indifference and contempt the British settlers had come to feel about the indigenous peoples they encountered in Australia and, as he once put it, 'to evoke public interest in the Aborigines' life-fate'. To achieve this end, he chose not direct political pamphleteering, which he came to regard as futile, but a strategy of indirection, the composition of anthropologically informed public essays and talks, through which he hoped to help non-indigenous Australians come belatedly to understand who the Aboriginal people were and are, and the depth of both the social tragedy and the cultural loss—as early as 1938 Stanner wrote of the 'wealth of mythology, rich in its imaginative feeling [that] has been allowed to die unrecorded with unkempt old men in their squalid camps on the fringes of so many country towns'—that had occurred since the arrival of the British.

Stanner began his attempt at building understanding with the concept at the heart of the Aboriginal world view: the Dreaming. The Dreaming was for the Aborigines, as Stanner explained in one of his most brilliant neologisms, 'everywhen'. It was 'a kind of narrative of things that once happened; a kind of charter of things that still happened; and a kind of *logos* or principle of order transcending everything significant for Aboriginal man.' Because he understood that 'the worst imperialisms are those of preconceptions', with one poetic turn of phrase after another Stanner strove to reveal to non-indigenous Australians a frame of mind and a metaphysic about as distant from the European as it was possible to be. For the Aborigines, he once wrote, life was 'a joyful thing with maggots at the centre'. At the heart of their religion was 'a celebration of a dependent life which is conceived as having taken a wrongful turn at the beginning, a turn such that the good life is now inescapably connected to suffering'. The Aborigines had 'stopped short of, or gone beyond, a quarrel with the terms of life.' Their core, stoical virtue, 'abidingness', was 'equilibrium ennobled'. They were not merely a people without a concept of 'time' or 'history' but an 'ahistorical' people, a people without yearnings for the return of a Golden Age or the hope of salvation in the future. Although theirs was not a rigid or inflexible culture, for them changelessness was both the desired and the anticipated state of the world. All this had difficult real-world implications for the relations between the two contemporary peoples who now lived alongside each other in Australia. 'The Dreaming and the Market,' Stanner wrote, 'are mutually exclusive. What is the Market? In its most general sense it is a variable locus in space and time at which values—the values of anything—are redetermined as human needs make themselves felt from time to time. The Dreaming is a set of doctrines about values—the value of everything—which were determined once for all in the past.'

When the British arrived in Australia, they were, in general, blind not only to the spiritual character but also to the social achievement of the people they encountered. It was another ambition of Stanner's anthropology to make this achievement clear. Decades before the idea became generally accepted, Stanner spoke of Aboriginal society as touched by 'genius' and as a 'marvel' of successful adaptation to environment. Perhaps 500 'congeries' or more of nomadic peoples with spiritual links of utmost intimacy to their clan-estates had 'humanised' the continent 'from end to end', in a pattern that Stanner likened to a vast spider's web, with crisscrossing trading pathways that he likened to a lattice. The only animal they tamed was the 'wild dog' which, as Stanner put it, they 'gentled into human service'. The tools they carried with them were not simple but 'simplified', honed perfectly to the task. Their ethos was based on strict dealings of reciprocity and egalitarianism, although old men were more powerful than the young and men more powerful than women. The Aborigines were a fierce warrior people. However, hierarchical structures of political authority and wars of territorial conquest or of tribal extermination were entirely unknown. Even over the battlefield at its most apparently ferocious, 'an invisible flag of prudence waved'. The life of the hunter-gatherer people was no doubt harsh and Spartan but in no way reminiscent of the Hobbesian portrayal of life in the state of nature—'solitary, poor, nasty, brutish and short'. For those who were tempted to believe this nightmare resembled the reality of Aboriginal life, Stanner proposed they spend a night in an Aboriginal camp and 'experience directly the unique joy in life which can be attained by a people of few wants, an other-worldly cast of mind and a simple scheme of life which so shapes a day that it ends with communal singing and dancing in the firelight.' 'Joy' and 'jollity' are two of the words most commonly encountered in Stanner's writing on the Aborigines. Stanner's serious academic writing was dense and complex. It was really only in the essays of the kind collected in this volume that he allowed himself the freedom to write about the Aboriginal life he had observed with lyricism and ease. In 'Aborigines and Australian Society' there is a wonderful, extended ideal-typical analytic narrative of the initiation ceremony. In 'Durmugam: A Nangiomeri' there is a vivid account of a fearsome Aboriginal battle Stanner had observed in 1932. Towards its conclusion, rather unexpectedly, there is also a beautiful evocation of the first idyllic years of Aboriginal childhood when tradition is intact. 'Aboriginal culture leaves a child virtually untrammeled for five or six years. In infancy, it lies in a smooth, well-rounded *coolamon* which is airy and unconstraining, and rocks if the child moves to any great extent. A cry brings immediate fondling. A child may still cry at three as a sign that it wants something—water, attention, carrying. Its dependence on and command of both parents is maximal, their indulgence extreme. To hit a young child is for them unthinkable.'

***

Stanner's humanistic anthropology was as much concerned with analysis of the behaviour of the British during the long dispossession as it was with Aboriginal culture. All the materials for the coming tragedy could, he thought, be seen in the first three years of Governor Phillip's muddled and incoherent rule, where an early romanticism of the noble-savage kind had quickly turned to violence, indifference and contempt. While Stanner did not question Keith Hancock's aphorism about the fatal incapacity of a hunter-gatherer and a pastoral economy to co-exist, his explanation of the reason why the impact proved so fatal was complex. In part, he argued that as British settlement spread over the continent on the basis of the 'mania' for land, a basic pattern was repeated (although also, with experience on both sides, foreshortened): initial contact, conflict, violence, the inevitable triumph of the stronger group, dispossession, disease, demoralisation, death. Yet, in large parts of Australia, he thought a different explanation for the fatal impact of the British was required. Stanner was greatly influenced by Elkin's argument about the emergence among the Aborigines of what he had called 'intelligent parasitism'. With his own eyes, Stanner observed how the search for stimulants had proven as irresistible to the Aborigines as the spice trade had once been for medieval Europeans. He also understood that once European material goods became available, many

Aborigines chose to abandon traditional life in exchange for a cultivated dependency and 'a constant or increasing supply of food for a dwindling physical effort.' Stanner once said he knew of no example where Aborigines who had become reliant on European goods had returned to the rigours of a hunter-gatherer life. He was also aware that even though the association of Aborigines with their lands possessed an intimacy and force beyond European understanding, in many parts of Australia, including those areas he knew best, Aborigines had voluntarily left their homelands in the search for the new material goods. 'I had seen a man, revisiting his homeland after an absence, fall on the ground, dig his fingers in the soil, and say: "O, my country". But he *had* been away, voluntarily; and he was soon to go away *again* voluntarily.' And yet, despite all this, Stanner could not accept the view of Hancock, and of almost all Australians of his own and earlier generations, that the fatal impact of the pastoral economy on a hunter-gatherer people and the subsequent threat of the destruction of Aboriginal society was a kind of morally neutral fact. The destruction of Aboriginal society was not merely the consequence of British settlement but its price.

How had the British settlers responded to this tragedy? Ann Curthoys is wrong to imply that Stanner was unaware that in the 19th century some historians among the settlers had expressed sympathy for the Aborigines. 'A gleaning of the records of 1820–50,' he once wrote, 'produces scores of sorrowful expressions of regard for the "real welfare of that helpless and unfortunate race"'. But what he insisted upon was that these expressions were, even at that time, overwhelmed by expressions of contempt and indifference to their fate, which was almost invariably regarded as inevitable extinction. In the second half of the century, feelings grew even more brutal and coarse. 'Few national histories can have afforded a more blazing and odious rationalisation of ugly deeds.' More than once Stanner allowed Anthony Trollope's famous statement, in his 1873 *Australia and New Zealand*, to stand as a representative summary of what he took the opinion of the settler majority to have been at this time. 'Their doom is to be exterminated; and the sooner their doom is accomplished—so that there be no cruelty—the better it will be for civilization'.

Yet Stanner also knew that as a Christian and a civilised people it was not easy for the British settlers to acknowledge what they had done. Stanner was fascinated by the other very common 19th-century belief, captured in the line of Percy Russell's poem—'Her shield unsullied by a single crime'—that in the birth of the Australian nation no sin had been committed. Rather than acknowledge complicity in the destruction of Aboriginal society and consequent remorse, it was far easier for Australians either to avert their gaze—'sightlessness' was one of Stanner's favourite words—or to claim, as had the Reverend G.A. Wood, 'that the cause of the extinction lies in the savage himself and ought not to be attributed to the white man.'

All this helped Stanner come to understand the characteristically 'apologetic' quality of Australian history writing which, as he once put it, 'sticks out like a foot from a shallow grave'. In turn, this led him to an understanding of that 'cult of forgetfulness practised on a national scale', which he called 'the great Australian silence'. This silence did not begin in innocence, as 'a simple forgetting of other possible views', as Stanner seemed almost to suggest in his cautious formulation in the Boyer Lectures. It arose rather, as he argued constantly elsewhere, in the systematic strangulation of national conscience. 'Whatever happened,' he asked in characteristic timbre in a letter to a close friend, 'to the Australian social conscience on the way to the 20th century?' In the anthropological exploration of non-indigenous Australia, Stanner's 'great Australian silence' was perhaps the most important discovery ever made. It provided the most vital clue to the puzzle at the heart of Australian national identity.

***

Stanner commented either directly or indirectly on the evolution of policy towards the Aborigines in the remote regions of Australia from the mid-1930s to the late 1970s. Before World War II, during the policy era of protection and immurement on supposedly guaranteed reserves, Stanner could see nothing but noble and worthless sentiment, 'almost unbelievably mean finances', and a general indifference to the eventual extinction of the Aborigines, which was still widely regarded as their unavoidable fate. There was, he wrote, no suggestion of 'urgency or even complexity' in the vapid resolutions of the first-ever meeting of Aboriginal administrators in Canberra in 1937. Yet 'the extinction of the Aborigines' was 'only inevitable if we allow it to be so.' Sincerity on this matter would be tested by a very simple question: 'How much will you spend?'

Stanner was hardly more flattering about the first fruit of the 'positive policy' suggested in 1934 by his teacher, A.P. Elkin—'assimilation'—where, for the first time explicitly, eventual extinction was no longer assumed. At a time when it took real courage to stand against the tide, Stanner was by far the most important non-indigenous critic of assimilation. For Stanner, assimilation was an impertinence, an invitation to Aborigines to shed their distinctive identity and to pass through a doorway to one or another European, supposedly superior, way of life. Among the many hundreds of Aborigines of his acquaintance, he argued on one occasion, there was only a tiny handful who aspired to a European style of life or regarded it as superior. Virtually everyone he knew wanted to combine elements of the Aboriginal and the European cultures and then not according to decisions made by others but through choices they themselves would make. Assimilation was also, he thought, extraordinarily naïve from the sociological and the psychological points of view. Its fundamental assumption, that Aborigines could relatively easily be treated primarily as individuals and not as tightly bonded members of a network of kinship groups, was simply false. Nor was it possible to think that even if Aboriginal culture had altogether broken down into an individual identity that an integrated European identity would then somehow magically rush in to fill the vacuum. It was far easier to destroy an identity than to create something new and solid in its place. It was not even true that assimilation was working from the material point of view. After a decade and a half of assimilation, he argued in 1968, 'the gap' between indigenous and non-indigenous life prospects was continuing, if anything, to grow wider.

In the essays, Stanner's critique of assimilation is cogent. His alternative vision of what was possible for the contemporary Aborigines in the remote regions of the centre and the north (he wrote little of those in the townships or the south) is more difficult to grasp. No one was more aware than Stanner of the extent to which the traditional life had broken down, or more clear-sighted about the dangers that, as a consequence, lay ahead. In the 1950s, Stanner returned to the Daly River– Port Keats region after an absence of some fifteen years. Among the young men he found that gambling and manipulative cunning had taken hold. The old men were now refusing to pass on vital religious knowledge to a generation who treated it with derision. Stanner encountered one old man who, in an act of symbolic personal suicide, was 'killing his dreaming'. At this time, Stanner believed that while Aboriginal High Culture had, in many parts, broken down almost irreparably, a Low Culture residuum—kinship ties, marriage laws, magic, initiation—would nonetheless hold firm. Towards the end of his life even that assumption seemed not so clear. In one of his late essays, 'Aborigines and Australian Society', he asks his readers to ponder the problems for what he called 'the lost generation' of Aboriginal youths who were now entering manhood without passing through any rite of initiation.

As a matter of fundamental justice, Stanner supported land rights for Aborigines. Barrie Dexter has recently revealed that it was Stanner who was responsible for suggesting that Whitlam, in one of the most eloquent gestures in recent Australian history, pass soil into the hands of Vincent Lingiari as a symbol of the new era. Although he rarely used the word in his writing, Stanner seems to have given his support to the post-assimilation policy of self-determination, whose most important theorist, architect and enthusiast was his close friend and political collaborator, Nugget Coombs. After some initial misgivings, Stanner also gave his support to the idea of a Treaty, on the grounds that a symbolic recognition of the injustice that had been dealt the Aborigines might be of fundamental significance in the course of Australian history. Yet Stanner did not pretend to know the future of the Aborigines. He was not even, he said, sufficiently foolish or wise to be certain that anything he had done would ultimately prove of benefit to them.

With a thinker like Stanner it is tempting to speculate about what he would have made of the present, troubled situation of Aborigines in the remote regions of Australia. Although this temptation is best avoided, for we can of course never know, there is perhaps at least one clue in the words at the conclusion of his last major essay. A German scholar had recently arrived at the bleak conclusion that the Aborigines, as a distinctive people, were now destined to 'progress into nothingness'. Stanner regarded this kind of supposedly realistic pessimism as foolish, dangerous and indefensible. 'In the past we were wrong—in some respects grotesquely wrong—about the Aborigines. We thought that they could not possibly survive; that they had no adaptive capacity; that there was nothing in their society of other than antiquarian interest; that there was nothing of aesthetic value in their culture. We could be as wrong about the future.'

***

The principles governing the choice of essays in this collection and the order in which they appear require a few words of explanation. Towards the end of his life, Stanner chose the essays he wanted for the anthology *White Man Got No Dreaming.* All of the essays we have chosen appeared there except for 'Aboriginal Humour', which was published shortly after his death. In this selection, a few essays Stanner chose have been omitted—one because it is rather technical, others because of repetition or because the political circumstances that occasioned them have been long forgotten. In *White Man Got No Dreaming,* the essays appeared in the order of their writing. In this collection we decided on a different logic. The volume begins with Stanner's masterpiece, 'Durmugam: A Nangiomeri'. The order of the chapters then follows not the dates of the essays' composition but the movement of history and shifts in collective sensibility: the Aboriginal world view before the impact of Europe; European fantasies about primitive peoples before and during the settlement of Australia; the portent of tragedy during the first three years of the settlement—1788 to 1791; the meaning of that tragedy by the time of the settlement's 150th anniversary—1938; the reigning illusions and Stanner's piercing of them at the high point of the era of assimilation—1958; the beginning of the change of heart—1968; the emergence of the legal struggle for native title—1970; and the intimation of a new time of troubles in the era of self-determination—1973. It concludes with Stanner's timeless whimsy on Aboriginal humour and his final salutary warning about the limits of pessimism.

Some personal thanks are due. I am grateful to Patricia Stanner for her gracious support for this project; to John Morton for his help in finding the cover photo; to Adam Shaw for his painstaking editorial work; to the publisher at Black Inc., Chris Feik, for his invaluable advice throughout; and, as always, to the founder and proprietor of Black Inc., Morry Schwartz, for his enthusiasm, generosity and support.

MAIN REFERENCES

Diane E. Barwick, Jeremy Beckett and Marie Reay (eds.), *Metaphors of Interpretation: Essays in Honour of W.E.H. Stanner*, Australian National University Press, Canberra, 1985.

Melinda Hinkson and Jeremy Beckett (eds.), *An Appreciation of Difference: W.E.H. Stanner and Aboriginal Australia,*

Aboriginal Studies Press, Canberra, 2008.

W.E.H. Stanner, *On Aboriginal Religion,* Oceania Monographs, University of Sydney, Sydney, 1966.

W.E.H. Stanner, *White Man Got No Dreaming: Essays 1938–1973,* Australian National University Press, Canberra, 1979.

Durmugam: A Nangiomeri (1959)

One wintry afternoon in 1932 on the Daly River in North Australia I saw that some of the men in an Aboriginal camp near my own had painted themselves garishly with earth-pigment. I knew this to be a sign of impending trouble but no one would give me any clear idea of what was to come. At about three o'clock the men began to go unobtrusively downriver, and some women and older children drifted off in the same direction. Each man carried a *womerah* or spear-thrower and a handful of mixed spears but this fact, in itself, meant little for in those days every male Aboriginal went armed on the shortest journey. Curiosity overcame any fear that I might be unwelcome if I followed so I made haste after them as soon as I could. By the time I made my camp and stores as secure as possible the party was lost to sight in the timber. I had to cast about a good deal to find the right direction, but eventually the sound of a distant uproar led me out of the savannah and on to the edge of a clearing where I could see more than one hundred men, my friends among them, locked in noisy battle.

    I stood awhile at the edge of the clearing to take the measure of what was happening, for I had not before seen a large-scale fight. The human scene had a savage, vital splendour. The pigments daubed on the men's bodies gleamed harshly in the late afternoon light. The air was filled with flying spears, each making a brief flicker of light as it sped. Some of the overshot missiles slithered with a dry rattle into the timber nearby. One pair of eyes could scarcely take in all that was happening at once. A distracting and continuous din came as much from spectators, of whom there were again over one hundred, as from combatants.

    The men were ranged in two groups, one whitened, one yellowed, each in a very rough formation of line, about sixty paces apart. Scarcely for a moment did the lines hold form. Some men, alone or supported, were running forward to throw their spears, others back to retrieve spent weapons or snatch new ones from supporters, others from side to side in challenge to a succession of enemies. Sometimes a solitary man on each side would stand with the others in echelon on both flanks. Old men, capering with excitement on the sidelines, would suddenly run to the battle line to throw spears, and then go back to their former posts. Women, with fistfuls of spears, would come without apparent fear into the danger area to offer the weapons to their menfolk, at the same time shouting in shrill execration of the enemy. On both sides great shows of anger, challenge and derision were being made. Some men would range up towards the enemy and contort their faces hideously; some, the older, would chew their beards and spit them out; some would bite on the small dilly-bags worn as neck-ornaments or stuff their loin-cloths into their mouths; here and there one would turn and, with gesticulations of insult, poke his anus towards the other line. Only the light duelling spears were in use but I saw one powerful Aboriginal, on what seemed to be the weaker side, run abruptly from the middle of the fight to wrestle fiercely with supporters to gain possession of their heavy, iron-bladed spears. They would not yield them, and sought to pacify him. He returned to continue fighting with the light spears.

The patterns and canons of the fighting eventually showed themselves through the aggregate moil. The struggle could be seen to resolve itself into discontinuous phases of duels between pairs of men with supporters. I could identify various pairs hurling spears at each other and, at the same time, see eddies of movement as others came to support them, so that something like a battle of masses would thus develop. This led to much cross-movement, and a veering of the heat of battle from place to place in the line as principals here became supporters there when an associate or kinsman came under heavy attack. Later, the principals would resume a phase of their own duels.

In trying to sort out the encounters of pairs, my eyes were drawn and held by an Aboriginal of striking physique and superb carriage who always seemed pinned by an unremitting attack. He seemed, as far as any individual could, to dominate the battlefield. He was so tall that he stood half a head above the tallest there. His muscular power was apparent in his bulk but it was the grace and intensity of his fighting which captured my attention. His favourite posture was to fling arms and legs as wide as possible as though to make himself the maximum target. Having drawn and evaded a spear he would often counter with a dexterity and speed remarkable in so large a man. His fluent movements in avoiding injury—an inclination of the head, a sway of the body, the lifting of an arm or leg, a half turn—always seemed minimal. I saw his spears strike home several times. As they did, the roars of exultation from his own side, and of rage from the other, would bring a rally to both. He himself stayed unwounded through the afternoon after a peerless display of skill and courage.

The battle died, as if by agreement, towards sundown and some of the antagonists began to fraternise, others to drift away. No one had been mortally hurt though many had painful flesh-wounds. There was some talk of continuing the fight another day. As I moved about making my enquiries, the tall Aboriginal came smilingly across and asked me in a most civil way if I had liked the fight. I asked him who he was and he told me that he was Durmugam, a Nangiomeri, and that Europeans called him Smiler. I then realised that here was the man widely believed by Europeans to be the most murderous black in the region, and whose name I had heard used with respect and fear.[1]

His appearance at this moment was truly formidable. The glaring ochre, the

---

[1] Durmugam was named after a locality on the seacoast in the territory of the Murinbata, the western neighbours of the Nangiomeri. In Murinbata, the name is Dirmugam, and has been borne by several men. Possibly Durmugam's mother conceived when she was visiting the Murinbata. This seems likely, for a man of the Nangor or Point Pearce clan captured her sister in marriage, and the place Dirmugam is in Nangor territory.

tousled hair above the pipe-clayed forehead band, the spears, and something opaque in his eyes made him seem the savage incarnate. He stood at least 6 feet 3 inches, and must have weighed a sinewy 180 pounds. But his voice was musical, his manner easy, and his smile disarming. I was much taken with him. I noticed particularly how smoothly contoured was his body, how small his feet, how sensitive and finely boned his hands. Other men present were more heavily muscled but none had so large and so finely moulded a physique. His carriage was perfect, and he walked very erect, with head held high, and with quick, purposeful steps. Yet there was nothing truculent or overbearing about him.

We had a brief but pleasant conversation, at the end of which he said that I should make my camp upriver at The Crossing, near him. I promised that some day I should do so and that we would then talk further.

We did not meet again for several weeks. The next occasion was another intertribal gathering, the initiation of a young boy, a member of the Maringar tribe which was at violent enmity with the Nangiomeri. The bad feeling had been suppressed, after the Aboriginal fashion, for a necessarily intertribal affair. On this occasion I was warmly welcomed, not tolerated. The blacks seemed touched that I had walked several times to their distant camps with bags of flour and other gifts, and went to pains to see that I was honoured, even to the point of taking me within the screen which hid the act of circumcision from the throng. Durmugam too was within the screen, seated with three others—all, by rule, classificatory wife's brothers of the initiate—so that their legs made a floor between the boy and the ground.

I saw little of Durmugam during the great events of the ceremony—the vigil of the night, after a warning spear told of the boy's return from isolation, the spectacular, serpentine rush of the boy's abductors from afar soon after dawn; the massed, chanting escort to Mununuk, the camp of the hosts, the rite of sorrow as the boy was passed from kin to kin to be fondled before circumcision; and later, the healing by fire and the presentation of valuables and insignia. But, as night came on, and the preparations for dancing and festivity were in hand, Durmugam joined me at one of the fires. I soon began to feel that we could become friends. I could not fault his manner and found him to be quick to see the drift of questions. When he pointed out some of the ceremony's features which I had missed, I began to see him as a new main informant, always one of the most exciting moments of fieldwork.

This particular ceremony had been conducted in the style of Dingiri, which is the name of a mythical ancestor. It is also a term denoting a direction of travel during initiation, a type of dance, a style of decoration, and a set of songs set to a fashion of music. Later, Durmugam told me the myth of Dingiri, the tired hunter who sat singing until he turned to stone. The symbolism is obscure and perhaps the only function of the myth is to give historic credibility to the song and the movements of the dance, which is filled with small intricacy to test the skill of any dancer.

I had already learned that Durmugam was a notable dancer. He flung himself into this dance with zest and gaiety. He must have been at his best but even so he was outclassed by Tjimari, a restless wanderer from the distant Murinbata tribe. Where Durmugam had grace and skill, Tjimari had polish and a set of artful tricks which made each dance end in a furore. He would introduce a comical contrast of position and expression, prolong a stance so that it seemed absurd even to my eye, or use some form of caricature too subtle for me to grasp. But the roar of appreciative laughter from the watchers told its own story. I could see no mortification or jealousy in Durmugam or the other dancers. The performances are competitive in a sense but the prestige men gain through them does not seem necessarily to depreciate others.

Durmugam and Tjimari made an interesting comparison. Both were notable men in their own ways. Tjimari was at least Durmugam's equal with fighting weapons, though only half his size. He was so extraordinarily agile that it was almost impossible to hit him with spear, fist, or stick. He claimed to be able to dodge bullets as easily. Since he was deadly accurate with a spear, no one liked to fight him, for it meant being wounded without being able to give wounds in return. Tjimari (or to give him his European name, Wagin, probably a corruption of 'wagon') traded on this skill, and took upset with him wherever he went. He was the first Aboriginal I ever met and, over a quarter of a century, I found him to be a fascinating mixture—a liar, a thief, an inveterate trickster, a tireless intriguer, an artist of high ability, and a man of much if inaccurate knowledge. In the 1930s he was the main *agent provocateur* of the Daly River. The police suspected him, rightly, of using the knowledge gained in court and gaol to instruct other blacks in the limits of police powers. He was adept in playing white against both white and black. Whenever he made a request one had to ask oneself what was Tjimari's 'angle', for there was bound to be one. Some Aborigines said he was a warlock, and he himself told me how he had cut open a woman at Port Keats and had taken some of her abdominal fat. I established the truth of this independently. Late in life, Tjimari became the friend and confidant of Roland Robinson, the Australian poet, who greatly admired his intelligence, knowledge, and imaginative gifts but took a somewhat sentimental view of other aspects of his character. I thought him an arch-manipulator, with wit and charm but no principles, and ready for any villainy that paid. Durmugam was no manipulator, and had a rocklike steadiness that Tjimari lacked. I feel that he had a deeper and more passionate conviction than Tjimari of the rightness of Aboriginal ways. I sometimes felt compassion for Durmugam; for Tjimari, much less frequently, and then mainly because he too typified the vital will of the blacks to make something of the ruined life around them.

In the second half of the dry season I moved upriver to be nearer the Nangiomeri. I had first wanted to learn something of the Mulluk Mulluk and Marithiel-Maringar clusters, which were some distance west by north of The Crossing. Thereafter I saw Durmugam almost daily until my expedition was over. He would come soon after dawn to help Melbyerk, my Mulluk Mulluk follower, fetch wood and water for the day. We would then settle down after breakfast for discussions, usually with other Aborigines present, which not uncommonly went on into the night, unless there was business to take us afield—places to visit, ceremonies to see, or game to kill. I was soon compelled to spend part of almost every other day hunting because of the pressure on my food supplies. Each day was something of a battle to keep unwanted natives from settling nearby to live on me. They were peaceable but as persistent as running water. I was importuned at every turn for tobacco, tea, sugar, and flour in that order of preference. I will say this for Durmugam, that he was never importunate or greedy. He would occasionally ask for tobacco when he was hard up for a smoke, but that was all. He and Belweni, an influential and surly Wagaman who would never work for any European but was the prince of cadgers, or Djarawak, a Madngella whose voice had the whine of the professional beggar, were men from different worlds of personal dignity. There are many Aborigines too proud to beg though they will exploit a claim to the full.

The hunting excursions were by no means a waste of time. I learned through them many things much better seen or shown than told. Durmugam was naïvely vain of his skill with spear and gun, and by indulging him I learned not only much about Aboriginal ecology but also about motives which powerfully drive the blacks to parasitism. The life of a hunting and foraging nomad is very hard even in a good environment. Time and again the hunters fail, and the search for vegetable food can be just as patchy. A few such failures in sequence and life in the camps can be very miserable. The small, secondary foodstuffs—the roots, honey, grubs, ants, and the like, of which too much has been made in literature—are relished titbits but not staples. The Aborigines rarely starve but they go short more often than might be supposed when the substantial fauna—kangaroos, wallabies, goannas, birds, fish—are too elusive. The blacks have grasped eagerly at any possibility of a regular and dependable food supply for a lesser effort than is involved in nomadic hunting and foraging. There is a sound calculus of cost and gain in preferring a belly regularly if only partly filled for an output of work which can be steadily scaled down. Hence the two most common characteristics of Aboriginal adaptation to settlement by Europeans: a persistent and positive effort to make themselves dependent, and a squeeze-play to obtain a constant or increasing supply of food for a dwindling physical effort. I appreciated the good sense of the adaptation only after I had gone hungry from fruitless hunting with rifle, gun, and spears in one of the best environments in Australia.

The blacks vary greatly in their hunting skills. Durmugam was very good with the fish-spear but less skilful than at least one other Nangiomeri, a slightly-built youth with a marvellous ability to judge the depth and speed of fish in spite of the refracted image. Where Durmugam was unsurpassed was in the use of the so-called 'shovel' spear. This spear, the main hunting and fighting weapon, may be as much as ten feet long. It is bamboo-shafted and has a lanceolate blade laboriously rubbed down from iron fence-droppers or heavy-gauge roofing. It is not suitable for distances much over sixty paces and, being long and heavy, its efficacy is a function of the strength of the thrower's arm, aided of course by his skill. It was Durmugam's great strength which gave him his superiority by enabling him to give the spear greater force and range. One European who had employed him as a sleeper-cutter told me that he had lifted and carried an ironwood log (which weighs up to 85 pounds a cubic foot) too heavy for three white men, manual workers in their prime.

I never saw Durmugam use the spear against men or game. After he learned that my scent was too strong, my white skin too visible, and that I made too much noise to let us both get within throwing distance, he gave up any attempt to show me his prowess. Several times he came back with a kill when, rubbed with mud to deaden his scent, he went on alone carrying only his spear and *womerah.* More often we hunted with firearms, I with a Winchester .32, he with my Browning repeater gun, the mechanism of which fascinated him. He could not use the rifle well, the fine sights evidently being beyond him, but he was an excellent set-piece shot with the gun.

On the hunt, we walked in file, he in the lead. He never went behind me with a weapon of any kind, though I had not asked him to refrain. He was ceaselessly watchful in the bush for the smallest movement, and saw game long before I did. He often grew irritated if I could not pick up targets to which he was looking or pointing. Once, unable to restrain himself, he snatched my rifle from my hands to fire at a wallaby I could not see. Having missed, he was ashamed, and embarrassed by his breach of good manners. Ordinarily, he was courteous in speech and conduct. He addressed me as *maluga,* not a

Nangiomeri word, but one from a dialect to the south, and meaning something like 'elderly sir' (though I was ten years his junior). He never spared the pace while walking (all Aborigines find this difficult and irritating) but if I flagged would turn back and offer to carry things for me. He would break off projecting twigs which might injure me, or hold obstructing branches to one side, or point silently with gun or spear at obscure impediments. When we halted he would often pluck an armful of leaves or grass for me to lie on, and would scuff a place clear with his feet. It was always he who drew the water and fetched the wood. If wildfowl had to be retrieved he would strip and plunge without ado into waters frequented by man-eating crocodiles. True, such services were a convention of black man and white together in the bush, and many other natives performed them for me just as well, but his merit was that he made them seem a courtesy.

Over this period my knowledge of him and confidence in him deepened to the point at which I knew I could safely ask him to tell me about the murders. He did so with what seemed full candour, with no trace of vainglory on the one hand or regret on the other. Wagin, who had himself taken two lives, was no less open, but he also claimed to be 'a good man now'.

The talk around Europeans was that six, nine, eleven, or some other good round number of murders, were this one man's work. He was supposed to have a monumental cunning in disposing of the bodies, or in otherwise concealing his crimes. Durmugam admitted to taking four lives. The admission was made at a time when he was in real danger of the law, a fact he well knew. I could discover no evidence of other crimes and it seems inherently improbable that, had there been, he would have denied them. If his record of blood is to be considered in an estimate of his personality one should also know something of the social context of which he was in some sense a product and in which the killings took place.

Durmugam's camp, about a quarter of a mile from mine, was on the property of a European farmer for whom he and his wives worked for part of each year. There were two other farms, one owned by a Chinese, over the river and a mile or more away. Downriver were six other farms, the nearest being three miles away. The police station was six miles farther on. This scattered community then constituted the Daly River 'settlement' as it was called. It was linked by a rough track with two sidings on the Darwin-Alice Springs railway at Adelaide River and Brock's Creek, respectively sixty and seventy miles away.

The settlers, among whom were two Chinese, were with two exceptions rough, uneducated men with bush backgrounds. They had known little comfort throughout their lives and were inured to hardship and poverty. Each grew a yearly crop of peanuts, sown in the December rains and harvested at the beginning of the dry season. They lived in shanties with earthen floors, and the bare minimum of crude furnishings. Equipment, methods, and life on these farms were so starkly simple that one often felt the year might almost as well have been 1832. The world depression had hit hard. The farmers thought themselves lucky to get sixpence a pound for their crops. They kept going, rarely seeing money, on credit from the distant Darwin stores, and eked out a life on bread, tea, and the simplest condiments which would make tolerable bush-foods supplied by natives. Wallaby stew was the staple dish. Most of them went hatless, bootless, and shirtless. One or two had decrepit tractors, but the others used horse-drawn ploughs to keep perhaps twenty acres in production. The sandy soil, the opulent weed growth, pests, a parching winter, and a deluge of summer rain were in conspiracy to offer good crops only when there was a glut elsewhere, and bad crops with a frequency guaranteed to keep them in debt.

Each farm had its attached group of Aboriginal workers and hangers-on, who were paid nothing but were given a meagre daily ration of the foods which the farmers themselves ate, together with a small allowance of tobacco. Once a year, if the farmers were not destitute, the work-teams were given a handout of the daily commodities and a few articles of clothing. Pitiably small as this real income was, it attracted far more natives than could be employed. Each one at work had others battening on him as adhesively as he on his employer.

All of these men were hard on their natives, some brutally so, but perhaps not much more so than they were on themselves. They supposed that their lives would be insupportable if they lost the physical dominance, and this may very well have been so. They and the Aborigines were mutually dependent, desperately so, and no love was lost on either side. The settlers also feuded among themselves, in most cases over the supposed enticement of their more dependable labourers of whom, at this time, there were very few. Unskilled labourers were plentiful enough, within the limits set by the total numbers (the population was about 300) and by the tribal jealousies which I shall mention later, but most of the Aborigines were feckless and likely to wander away at whim, usually when most needed for agricultural tasks that could not wait. Dependable men and women able to do unsupervised work were few indeed, and the loss of one from a farm was a serious blow. No agreement about poaching could be depended on, and some of the sophisticated blacks played one employer against another.

The Aboriginal women, single or married, were eager for associations with Europeans and Chinese. While ready enough for casual affairs, they tried by any and all means to make semi-permanent or permanent attachments. Their menfolk, with few exceptions, not only did not object but often pushed them to such service, which always led to a payment of tobacco, sugar, and tea, and might lead to a steady real income if it could be turned into a squeeze-play against a captured protector. The moment a settler became attached to or dependent on a native woman her close kin and affines put in an appearance, and every artifice and pressure was used to make themselves part of the protector's estate. The same thing tended to happen even with male employees. A single man would have at least classificatory brothers, a married man a set of consanguines and affines, to put him under pressure. Each farm was thus in fact or in Aboriginal prospect the locus of a group of natives who made it, or wanted to make it, the centre of their lives. Around them again was a circle of other Aborigines using every device of kinship, friendship, and trade to draw on the yield. Since, by Aboriginal definition, almost every European and Chinese was concupiscent, any stranger entering the area was likely to be pestered.

Durmugam did not offer his women to me on any occasion, and prudence made me let his past in this respect go without inquiry. However, I saw no sign in him or in any other Aboriginal that continence in a European was thought a moral virtue, or that sexual use of their women led to a loss of repute. The continent man who had much to do with the blacks was like a brother or father, and there was a strong sense that they had a claim on his goods. The concupiscent man was like an affine on whom the claim was even more strong.

The murders of two Europeans, one immediately before and one soon after my first visit, had backgrounds of this kind. The male kin of women who had gone with the men felt they had been bilked of due payment.

The river seemed to me a barbarous frontier—more, a rotted frontier, with a smell of old failure, vice, and decadence. I had at first no clear idea of how sombre its history had been since the first effective penetration by Europeans and Chinese after the late 1870s. It was with the utmost surprise that I began to piece together the story of how, over half a century, enterprise after enterprise had failed. A sugar plantation, a Jesuit mission, a copper smelter, a Government experimental farm, and a planned settlement of 'blockers' or small farmers, to say nothing of one essay after another by individual fortune hunters, all attracted by absurd optimisms, had failed miserably.

I should have known all this before going, but all my interest had been in the Kimberleys. Radcliffe-Brown, my teacher, had asked me to go to Turkey

Creek but when he left Sydney for Chicago late in 1931 a chance meeting with Gerhardt Laves, the linguist, persuaded me to change the plan. Laves told me of half a dozen unstudied tribes, and of scores of *myalls,* i.e. wholly uncivilised natives, who spoke no English, on the Daly River. Turkey Creek faded from sight; I had to see the unspotted savage; I had to be there when the dry season opened; there was not even time to comb the general literature and I knew the anthropological literature; that was enough. It was not enough, when I arrived in Port Darwin, to allow me to assess the innocent misinformation which some of the authorities gave me. Yes, they said, it was truly *myall* country; I would have to look to my skin and possessions; there had been murders and robberies; it was on the fringe of the last unknown part of the North. Nothing I was told was actually incorrect. The trouble was that in capital and province the sense of history was shallow; there was no grasp whatever of the chaos of the past; and there was no understanding of the welter which contemporary life had become for the surviving Aborigines.

Each enterprise after the 1870s had drawn more Aborigines towards the river and had made them more familiar with Europeans and more dependent on their goods. Each failure had led those now dependent to wander elsewhere to look for the new wealth and excitements—to Pine Creek, Brock's Creek, the Victoria River, even to Darwin itself. In places where no European had ever set foot, or was to do so for many years, a demand had grown up for iron goods, tobacco, tea, sugar, and clothes. There was also a hankering for a sight of such marvels as houses, machines, vehicles, firearms, and bells, one of the most alluring things of all. Unrest and covetousness had drawn in people from tribes on the outer marches, the Moiil and Fitzmaurice rivers, the Wingate and Macadam ranges. Whole tribes—like Durmugam's Nangiomeri—had migrated, and large tracts had thus been emptied decades before the authorities or settlers were aware of it. Some of the small tribes of the Daly (Kamor, Yunggor) had ceased to exist. Those members who had not died from new diseases (such as measles, influenza, tuberculosis, and syphilis), or from bullets, or from debauchery by grog and opium, or in the jealous battles for possession of which Durmugam had been a childish witness, had been dispersed by migration or else absorbed into larger tribes on which they had claims by contiguity, kinship, friendship, or affinity. The Marimanindji, Marinunggo, and Madngella were among the tribes which went this way. The dwindling in total numbers, so far as they were visible on the Daly, had been concealed by the inward drift. The Marithiel, Maringar, Mariga, and Maritjavin were already on the river when I arrived, except for a few parties still out in the blue. There were then no more tribes to come, except the Murinbata of Port Keats, and all that held them away was the opening of the Sacred Heart Mission by Father Docherty in 1935. The authorities, in all good faith, could well imagine that the hinterland was still densely populated, for the Daly River seemed to keep on breeding *myalls* continuously.

Durmugam was about 37 years of age when I first met him in 1932. He had been born about 1895 at Kundjawulung, a clan-country of the Nangiomeri, about seventy miles south of The Crossing. About the turn of the century the Nangiomeri had been made restless by tales of the wonders to be seen at the new goldmine at Fletcher's Gully, which lay about half way to The Crossing. In this region of many small tribes, the Nangiomeri were blocked from the Daly River, so they went instead to Fletcher's Gully. Once there, they and the western Wagaman, who accompanied them, never returned to their own country. Durmugam's father died at the mine; how, he does not know. The mine failed and his mother and mother's brother took him on to the Daly; what new circumstances made this possible, so soon after the earlier impasse, he cannot say. He remembers only two things clearly of his earliest days on the Daly, where his mother died at the copper mine—endless, bloody fights between the river and the back-country tribes, and numbers of drink-sodden Aborigines lying out in the rain. The few police records which have survived make both memories seem credible enough. Between 1898 and 1911 the police inquired into seventy-three sudden deaths, sixty-two of them Chinese, two Aboriginal. Among the genial causes were murder, suicide, accident, alcoholism, lightning, snakebite, fever, and syphilis. But any anthropologist would find indirect genealogical proof that scores, if not hundreds, of Aborigines must have died prematurely from unrecorded causes.

Durmugam was a product of this background. He remembers little of his patrikin or matrikin, though he was 'grown up' by his mother's brother. One of his bitternesses is that his mother's brother did not tell him anything of the secret male culture of the Nangiomeri. He had to learn this as a man from other tribes which shared it, or had known of it, and he felt there was some element of shame in such a thing. He cannot give a sequential or, indeed, a fully coherent account of how or where he spent his formative years. He seems to have drifted about the region with other Nangiomeri, and with some

Wagaman, whose language he understands, sometimes living a truncated Aboriginal life in the bush, sometimes a life not unlike that of the Daly River in the 1930s, or working for a succession of Europeans. Some were good men, he says, meaning generous and kindly men. To find a job, when he liked, for as long as he liked, was never difficult: his physique, manner, and general steadiness were in his favour and, unlike many Aborigines of his generation, he did not succumb to opium or alcohol, though he had tasted both, and he liked bushwork. He was never in trouble with the police, and he pleased himself where he went. He married a Nangiomeri girl who died, without children. A turning point came in his life when, in the middle of the 1920s, he met an energetic, vital European, who gave him work at a variety of jobs—mining, building construction, sleeper-cutting. At the end of the decade this man went to the Daly River to try his fortune as a farmer. Durmugam joined forces with him and, apart from a few interruptions, remained in permanent association with him. It was there that I found him.

Although all this had been, in one sense, central to Durmugam's life, in another sense it had been peripheral. On several occasions, probably during the first world war, of which he knows nothing beyond the fact that it occurred, he had followed up the trade routes which still link the Daly tribes with those of the Victoria. These visits for adventure and trade, in company with other youthful Nangiomeri and Wagaman, were the most decisive and formative events of his life. On the Victoria, he was initiated into the secret rites of the older men. He learned of the religious cult of Kunabibi which Sir Baldwin Spencer had noted in 1914. He was given his first bullroarers. He began to learn too of the lost secret life of the Nangiomeri. He was also 'placed' immutably in a fixed locus in the system of eight subsections which, in tribes possessing it, is fundamental to the local organisation, the conception of descent, the practices of marriage, residence, and inheritance, and acts reflexively on the sacred culture. In other words, he came for the first time into intimate association with an Aboriginal High Culture.

As he told me of these experiences, in the sequence of his lifestory, it was as though his mind and heart had suddenly unified. His expression was rapt, his mood earnest, and he seemed filled with passionate conviction. There was no mistaking his gratification when I showed, by a grasp of principles and details, especially of the subsection system, that I really knew what he was talking about. From that time on he treated me as one who understood—the phrase is the Aborigines' own. I found myself assigned to the Djangari subsection, that is, as Durmugam's wife's brother.

It was not altogether clear to me at the time, though it is now, that after the failures of the plantation, the mission, and the copper smelter, and over the time when Durmugam was growing up, the weakened tribes had settled down in a protracted tertiary phase of adaptation. I mean by this one of systematic effort to turn to their greater advantage the more or less stable routines imposed on them once the primary stage of contact was over. Many of the preconditions of the traditional culture were gone—a sufficient population, a self-sustaining economy, a discipline by elders, a confident dependency on nature—and, with the preconditions, went much of the culture, including its secret male rites. What was left of the tradition amounted to a Low Culture—some secular ceremonies, magical practices, mundane institutions, and rules-of-thumb for a prosaic life. I found indisputable physical evidences of a regional High Culture—ovoid, circular and linear piles of man-arranged stones, deep earth-excavations, and some other signs, to say nothing of fragmentary memories of rites evidently last celebrated before the turn of the century. There had been nothing of equivalent force to destroy the High Culture of the Victoria River tribes at this stage and, at the time when Durmugam encountered it, there had been a vivification by the spread of the cult of Kunabibi.

In the 1920s a widespread conviction had grown up on the Daly River that their own culture-hero, Angamunggi, the All-Father, a local variant of the almost universal Rainbow Serpent, had deserted them. Before I heard a word of Kunabibi I had been told that Angamunggi had 'gone away'. Many evidences were cited that he no longer 'looked after' the people: the infertility of the women (they were in fact riddled by gonorrhoea), the spread of sickness, the dwindling of game among them. The cult of Kunabibi, the All-Mother, thus came at a beautifully appropriate time. The cult assumed the local form of a cult of Karwadi, by which name the bullroarer, the symbol of the All-Mother, had been known in the days of the All-Father. Karwadi became the provenance of the mixed but connected elements which I term the new High Culture. It was this that the young Nangiomeri brought back from the Victoria—a secret wisdom, a power, and a dream shared by no one else on the Daly River. It is clear that these young men were fired, and also felt under some kind of command.

Durmugam was one of a group of three who seem to have set about remodelling their lives and their culture. He was not the leader; it would be more accurate to say that he was the secular force of the movement. And it is here that a connection with his killings is to be sought.

That the cult was at a peak could be seen from the fact that it was spreading intertribally in my early days on the river. Collectively, however, the Marithiel and Maringar remained aloof. The secular plight of the Aborigines was also at its worst, for the bottom had fallen out of the white economy on which they were dependent. There was much disenchantment with Europeanism and constant friction with the farmers. I should think that no scrap of European prestige remained. I found an unshaken belief that Aboriginal ways were right, even on the level of the Low Culture. But the Aborigines were in chains: they could not bear to be without the narcotic tobacco and the stimulating tea; any woman could be bought for a fingernail of one or a spoonful of the other. Their still complex economy also demanded the hardware and softgoods obtainable from Europeans alone. And an increasing difficulty in getting bush food bound them to parasitism on a settlement where the farmers themselves often had barely enough to eat.

In these circumstances the cultivation of a great secret and its expressive rite was, for the Aboriginal men at least, a compensatory outlet. What the women thought did not matter. The secret was guarded as closely as possible, and the euphemism 'Sunday business' or 'big Sunday' came into use to explain to Europeans the nature of the affair which often took men away for a month at a time. I learned of the cult in 1932, not at first from Durmugam, though he confirmed the knowledge and gave me an outline description, but I was required to wait until 1934, on my second visit, before I was invited to attend. I presumed that the delay was deliberate. Durmugam and Belweni, with the knowledge of their leader, used a variety of artifices to make sure of my discretion and goodwill before inviting me to cross the river to Ngurbunmumu, the secret dancing-ring. They told me that I was the only European they had allowed to do so. The farmers of course knew of the existence of the rite but were either uninterested or thought it wiser to look the other way.

It is my hypothesis that the Kunabibi-Karwadi cult belongs to the great family of movements which, for want of better names, have been called 'messianic' or 'nativistic', although it is probably a distinct species, or at least a very uncommon variety. It is reversionary, mystical, and religious, as well as magical, and is concerned with preserving the continuity of life. At the same time it is in intelligible series with the conventional initiations. The implicit theme of fertility, the sexual symbolisms, and the summoned presence of the All-Mother, are natural images of life and continuity. In all important respects the essential constitution of the cult is comparable, at the level of family likeness, with the Melanesian 'cargo' movements. The differences may be explained by the postulates and ontology of Aboriginal culture.

I could discover no evidence that the local Europeans were right in attributing all Durmugam's killings to the cult. Only one, I believe, was so connected. My facts were drawn from Durmugam himself, and from other natives, not long after the events. Since that time there has been a tendency in other tribes to believe that offences against Karwadi underlay all the killings. It is an *ex post facto* rationalisation: an attempt to adduce a moral justification based on canonised values.

One Lamutji, a Marithiel, had been given a bullroarer by Durmugam as a symbol of admission to membership in the secret circle. Lamutji had promised a substantial payment, a necessary condition of possession, and a condition that the donor had to enforce if, at the very least, his own safety were not to be in danger. When, after five years, Lamutji had paid nothing in spite of many reminders, Durmugam decided to kill him at the first opportunity. He ambushed the bilker in a jungle near the river and transfixed him from behind with a shovelspear. Lamutji recognised Durmugam before dying and was told why he had been killed. Durmugam then pierced the body with sharp stakes and pinned it in the mud below tide level. On the bank, he left a few traces of Lamutji, obliterated his own tracks, and cleverly simulated the marks of a crocodile to give the impression that this had been Lamutji's fate. The body was never found. Durmugam came under instant suspicion, but he kept silent or denied all knowledge, and the police evidently felt unable to act. On the facts as Durmugam told them, this was the only murder connected with the cult.

He killed Waluk, a Marimanindji who was as powerful and formidable a man as Durmugam himself, in talion for the death of a brother who had sickened and died after a visit by Waluk. The Marimanindji was alleged to have taken the victim's kidney-fat by physical, not mystical, means. Durmugam's uncle publicly alleged that he had seen an incision in his nephew's side and had seen Waluk with a tin containing human fat and red ochre. Durmugam, with an accessory, followed Waluk to a quiet place, deceived him as to the purpose of the visit, and then killed him with a shovel-spear when a good opportunity came. The body was left where it lay. Again, evidently, no good basis for police action could be found.

His third and fourth victims were also Marimanindji, an old man named Barij and his son Muri. A classificatory brother of Muri had killed an old man in a camp fracas at which Durmugam was present. The murderer, Mutij, fled and was later arrested by a party of natives under the control of police-trackers, then the conventional police method of apprehending criminals. Durmugam was a member of the party. Mutij was sent to gaol for seven years. The Nangiomeri then held a divination to find out who had been Mutij's secret prompter. The spirit of the dead man is alleged to have named Barij and Muri as guilty of prime agency. In fact, Barij had done nothing in the fracas and Muri had only run to the aid of his threatened brother, which is a brother's duty. Durmugam and accomplices lured the two men to a quiet place after a kangaroo-hunt, lulled them into a false security, and killed them. Durmugam was arrested but an error of procedure led to his release from custody after five months. He believes he served a gaol sentence expiating the offence. I was told that he wept over this affair, and he once said to me that he had been egged on by others—a standard self-exculpation of the Aborigines. This was the nearest I ever heard him come to an expression of regret.

The word 'murder' is pejorative and begs a question at issue in these events. Were any of the killings lawful homicide in Aboriginal customary law?

All the river tribes believed in mystical agency and in the mystical discovery of it. All practised and acted on the outcome of divinations. Durmugam acted within an established custom and under an acknowledged sanction in killing Barij and Muri. The custom was universal but the sanction had no necessary force in another tribe and, in any case, the Marimanindji were few and decadent. Mutij's real and Durmugam's imagined imprisonment seemed to end the matter. There seemed to be no further consequences. The killing of Waluk worked out differently. All tribes believed in the mystical power of the warlock, and a number of persons were actually cut open for their fat, which was thought to have life-giving and protective properties. A public accusation was, so to speak, a formal indictment, but I never heard of anyone's confessing to his guilt. I could not establish whether Durmugam's uncle made his accusation before or after Waluk's death. But Waluk's kin at once challenged Durmugam. He fought against them three times at just such a fight as I described earlier. Once he was wounded as he stood alone while three men threw spears at him simultaneously, and there the matter seemed to end. Durmugam had fulfilled the obligation of brotherhood and had met in full the juridical demands of the victim's kin. I would say that he acted within the canons of the ruling Low Culture.

The killing of Lamutj was a duty inherent in Durmugam's membership of the cult. He had to kill or risk his own life. The deep secrecy, the artifices of mystification, and the ominous sanctions of the cult were meant to maintain the value of the main symbol, the bullroarer. The Nangiomeri were very nervous about swinging a bullroarer by its haircord lest the cord break and damage the venerated object. They disliked using them as percussion-sticks in song, for the same reason. They believed that if the original donors in the Victoria River tribes heard of such accidents, they would seek the deaths of the men responsible. Each member of the cult had an equity in maintaining the valuation of the bullroarer, and each was not only ready, but obliged, to kill a man who damaged the value, or the symbol itself. As I have said, the Marithiel as a whole did not share the High Culture, indeed, had rejected it, but many individuals like Lamutji were flirting with it and were covetous of the new bullroarers. His kin claimed that they wanted Durmugam's life and many threatened to take it, but no one did anything about it. In their eyes the killing was an unjustifiable murder; in Nangiomeri eyes it was a justifiable homicide. If Durmugam's duty coincided too neatly with his personal interest, the same might be said of many honoured men in history.

***

In 1932, two intertribal coalitions existed which were in acute conflict. The surface of life was, for the most part, peaceable enough but under the surface something like a state of terror existed. All the talk was of warlockry and poison. The death of any man or male child (females did not count) was thought to be evidence of the human use of dark powers, and a divination usually followed, with a plot of talion. No one dared to walk about alone. To do so invited speculation about evil motive, or risked the assassin's spear. An unescorted woman was usually raped. Men, even within eyeshot of their camps, carried a *womerah;* it suggested pacific intention but gave them a means of returning a spear. If they went any distance they carried a spear as well. The camps were fenced in with wire-netting or scraps of roofiron. No one slept close enough to the fence to be within reach of a warlock's arm.

These fears and tensions were almost exclusively between the two intertribal coalitions. Durmugam had an unconquerable hatred of the Marithiel and Maringar. So too did Melbyerk, the most intelligent and detached Aboriginal I have known. Neither Nangiomeri nor Mulluk Mulluk would intermarry with the hated tribes, and I am nearly sure they did not trade. They needed each other at initiations and they would then intermingle, but cautiously, and fights were always likely to occur. When I saw Durmugam in 1958, there was no longer much talk of warlocks and poison but his hatred had, if anything, grown. The Nangiomeri epithets could not express his sentiments. He spoke in English about those 'bloody f-----g bastards of Moiils', even falling into the vulgar European error of lumping both tribes together as 'Moiils' whereas a generation before they had been lumped together as 'Brinkens'.

European law on the river had been feeble, fitful, and sometimes a brutal thing. The police administration sometimes used the station as a penalty-post for men without futures in the force. In general, there was no dependable resort at law for Aborigines suffering by felony, misdemeanour, or tort. Many of the police-trackers had served gaol sentences for felonies. The blacks, for the most part, had to look to their own justice.

Thus, in 1932, there was no effective European law interposed between the warring coalitions. The white farmers kept a minimum of discipline and in some sense the farms were sanctuaries too. At night, natives would often come out of the darkness and ask to sleep nearby, leaving when daylight came. It was unnecessary to ask for an explanation. Marabut, my main Marithiel informant, was too frightened to leave if kept inadvertently after sundown. Belweni, the Wagaman, was thrown into consternation by a footprint he could not recognise. Melbyerk, when on the southern or 'Brinken' bank, would try to defecate at night so as to be within the glow of my campfire. A group of saltwater blacks who came to one initiation sat sleepless, under my own eyes, throughout the whole night. There were, of course, men of greater courage. Durmugam would willingly walk for me the sixty miles to Stapleton or Adelaide River carrying mail in a cleft stick (these were still days of unsophistication) and would do so alone.

I often asked other Aborigines what they thought of Durmugam. The most common observation was that he had 'a hot belly', was a man of passion. His face suggested rather dignity, strength, and self-possession. While in no sense stony, it was not kindly. There was no trace of brutality or coarseness, but not of great sensibility either—simply a calm, strong face without any excess. He was the authentic Australian in having a rather broad, flat nose and craggy brows, but even these were refined by Aboriginal standards. His lips were moderately full, his mouth shapely, his ears small, his jawline clean, and his chin fairly well-formed. Sometimes his eyes left one a little uncertain what to think: they were heavy lidded, perhaps a trifle protuberant, and could wear a hooded and brooding look. This impression may have been only an effect of the Aboriginal iris or of the eye diseases from which he was a constant sufferer. I always thought that the smile which had earned him his European name, and was never very far away, was a good index of his most constant temper.

His mind was inclined to be slow and heavy-working. He needed ample time to weigh any question put to him. If pushed he showed perplexity rather than irritation. One felt that his mind worked well only on familiar and unhurried lines, but there was more to it than mental slowness. He had a prudent, judicious quality too. I often waited for minutes in silence while he thought over something. At such times a variety of expressions would show naïvely in his face; he would come several times to the brink of speech only to pause; finally, almost always with a half-smile, he would speak. the quality of his observations usually made up for their slowness. I never proved that he misled me, and found him correct on innumerable occasions. He had a feeling for the truth, whereas Tjimari had none. Durmugam would be very open if he made mistakes and offer the correction candidly. This probity of mind made him invaluable on matters of theoretical significance. Unlike many Aborigines, he had great mental stamina. He was also gifted, exceptionally so, in making simple visual demonstrations of things. Eventually, I turned one of his demonstrations (in which sticks were used as counters and stick-movements as signs of marriage, parentage, residence, and descent) into a model for teaching the theory of the subsection system, much as the Aborigines teach it.

I saw no more of him, after 1935, until the winter of 1952. He was then about 57, white-haired, with failing eyesight, but still erect and still a striking figure of a man. But many things had changed greatly: the farmers were, if not prosperous, no longer poor; the blacks were on wages and very money-conscious; all had European clothes and in their camps, some now reasonably well built, one could find gramophones, torches, kitchenware, even bicycles; some of the younger people, though unable to read, were fond of looking at comic papers and illustrated magazines; the old men had lost authority; and, although I did not have time to make proper inquiry, I had the impression that the traditional culture was on its last legs. There had been no 'big Sunday' for some years; the High Culture had not prospered; many of the young men openly derided the secret life; the coalitions now mattered only to those with long memories.

Durmugam was much more difficult to talk to, though still courteous. Many troubles were coming upon him, and he brooded on them so much that I found it hard to keep his mind on other matters. The young men were starting to make overtures to his wives, but he could never catch them. I tried to persuade him, if he did, not to use undue violence, since I had no wish to see him hang or languish in gaol. He promised to be cautious and made himself a bamboo stick loaded with heavy wire. He was filled with angry contempt for the young men of the day. 'They can throw a spear,' he said, 'but can they *make* one? Can they find their own food in the bush?' He told me of a conversation with one youth who was deriding the bullroarer. Durmugam told him that it might cost him his life. The youth said, with a shrug, 'If I live, I live; if I die, I die.' I asked Durmugam what he said then. Durmugam said: 'I said, "Well, f—you."' The use of English for expression in such crises had become common in the area. It was a means of appeal to a wider world, a new code, and a new scale of values.

I met Durmugam again in 1954. His general mood had worsened as his troubles had grown. I noted too, for the first time, an element of desperation and pessimism for the future. At the same time, there were signs of antipathy in him towards Europeanism and a deepening attachment to the old Aboriginal ways. He said several times, almost angrily, 'the blackfellows have their own laws'. Between talks about his own troubles, we went over most of my original notes. They emerged almost unaltered, but I found him able to make more powerful abstractions than twenty years before. He no longer came so freely to me, though I had camped on the same spot; he had to sit, brooding, in his own camp, waiting for the next attempt to take his women.

The last time I saw him, in 1958, only a few months before writing this, he told me that great shame had come upon him and that he would be better dead. His favourite wife, the youngest of four, had run away with the son of his first wife, a great humiliation to a man still alive, although in the old law the youth might have inherited her. A married daughter, living for the time being with him, had been abducted by a youth whom Durmugam had befriended all his life. The girl had taken her daughter, the apple of Durmugam's eye, as well. Another wife, the second youngest, had been sexually assaulted, a traditional penalty, by a number of men, mainly Maringar, on the ground that she had illicitly seen a bullroarer in Durmugam's camp—a pretext, he said vehemently, a lie. Would he, who knew the dangers, be likely to have a bullroarer there? They were all hidden in the bush.

He appealed to me for advice and help. The women, he said, were his, given him by their fathers in the proper way. The blackfellows had their own laws; he had broken none, but the young men had; and the European seemed not to care, to be on their side. Was this right? The young men were 'flash' (out of hand, conceited), not listening to anyone, not caring for anything. Much trouble would come from this, trouble for everyone. He grieved over the unfilial conduct of his son. Who ever heard of a son running away with his mother? Who ever heard of a son helping another man to abduct a married sister? Why would no one help him? The police, he said, would do nothing; they had told him no one had broken the Europeans' law; and, if he hurt or killed anyone, they would send him to Fanny Bay (the gaol), or hang him. He said repeatedly: 'My belly is like a fire. My brain never stops. It goes round and round.'

He had received, or thought he had received, a promise of help from the remote Welfare Department, for he kept speaking of it—a promise to ban the young men from the river and to have the women and child returned. To the Aborigines a promise (of which they have a verbalised concept) is a contract. A broken promise is to them iniquitous.

I listened, with all compassion, to the story. I promised, but without much hope, to intercede with the authorities on his behalf. His case had already been pleaded, to no obvious avail, by two other Europeans. One was his employer, the other a Catholic priest who had been until recently the local Protector of Aborigines. Both had seen that Durmugam's natural rights had suffered, that the injustices were compounding, and that an issue had arisen for the administration of the new policy of 'assimilation'.

The policy of assimilation is meant to offer the Aborigines a 'positive' future—absorption and eventual integration within the European community. Does it involve a loss of natural justice for the living Aborigines? No one answers. Cases like Durmugam's are irritating distractions from loftier things. The policy assumes that the Aborigines want, or will want, to be assimilated; that white Australians will accept them on fair terms; that discrimination will die or can be controlled; that, in spite of the revealed nature of the Aborigines and their culture, they can be shaped to have a new and 'Australian' nature. The chauvinism is quite unconscious. The idea that the Aborigines might reject a banausic life occurs to no one. The unconscious, unfocused, but intense racialism of Australians is unnoticed. The risk of producing a depressed class of coloured misfits is thought minimal, although that is the actual basis from which 'assimilation' begins.

It would be too far to one side of my purpose here to examine the new policy in detail. The aspirations are high; the sincerity is obvious; everyone is extremely busy; a great deal of money is being spent; and the tasks multiply much faster than the staffs who must do the work. In such a setting a certain courage is needed to ask if people really know what they are doing. I have space only for a simple question, which is closely connected to Durmugam's life and problems.

There is such a thing as Aboriginal customary law. It is in radical conflict with European law in almost every respect. Our notions of tort and crime, of procedures of arrest and trial, of admissible evidence, and so on do not fit with theirs. Only by extremely high abstraction can the two systems be brought together at all, and then only in a way which is almost useless administratively. The Aboriginal system has *in part* widely broken down and cannot be restored. It broke down for a number of reasons. Among them, certainly, was a contempt among Europeans of all classes for all things Aboriginal. To the older generations of Australians it seemed an impossible idea that there could be anything in the Aborigines or in their tradition to admire. The contempt has perhaps almost gone. In its place one finds, surprisingly widely, both interest and solicitude. But old contempt and new solicitude have a common element: a kind of sightlessness towards the central problems of what it is to be a blackfellow in the here-and-now of Australian life. For this reason hundreds of natives have gone through, and will go through, the torment of powerlessness which Durmugam suffered.

Australia has nothing like the system of local administration which exists in New Guinea, where officials with both executive and judicial powers live in and control given districts. Even if there were, no code of law or regulations exists which is based on Aboriginal problems in their own right. It is very doubtful if a European court would recognise an Aboriginal marriage as a fact of law. The same is so of most of the other things of life which, to a blackfellow, make life worth the living. For example, the totally inalienable link between a man and his clanestate, a man's right to hunting tracts, his right to claim material wealth from the husband of his sister or daughter—all these, and a dozen others, are a world away from European minds. The occasional welfare officers whom the Aborigines see are not magistrates, and in any case have no code to guide them. The local scene thus tends to be anarchic. If grievance leads to crime then police and magistrates act as might be expected. They may allow a vague sense—it cannot be other than vague—of the Aborigines' special problems to mitigate their decisions, but their canons are essentially European. The whole system actually rests on a pretence, rather, on a set of pretences, or fictions about facts. One of them is likely to prove ruinous: the fiction that the Aborigines' interest in their rights, as they define them, can safely be ignored while plans are perfected for the greater good which Europeans have in mind. What is produced is a two-sided dissatisfaction among the blacks: a growing rancour among themselves and a projection of the hostility upon Europeans. A strong counterforce against assimilation is thus growing within the anarchy which surrounds the Aboriginal pursuit of women, goods, and egoistic satisfaction in the modern period.

The Aboriginal tradition permits polygyny. All Durmugam's marriages had had Aboriginal sanction. His possession and enjoyment had never been challenged by native or European authority. No statute or common law of the Commonwealth had ever been held explicitly to apply. The Roman Catholic Mission (the second, established in 1955) did not seek to interfere, since Durmugam was not Christian and did not wish to be. Tribal institutions acknowledged and upheld his rights but the police would have prevented his defending them, as likely to involve a breach of the peace. No alternative means which an illiterate native could possibly know how to use to advantage were provided. And, between Durmugam and the seat of law, Darwin, were petty officials disinclined to move, since there was no rule or principle, and content to fall back on private judgments: polygamy was wrong, anyway; the game was to the young; he had who could hold; one wife was enough for any man; the blacks had no morals; Durmugam had a criminal record.

The old man's appeals did reach Darwin, but when I passed through the settlement in the middle of the year, nothing had happened. Durmugam then acted on the only matter within reach, the sexual abuse of his wife. He called together all the men concerned, denounced them (in English, so that no one could misunderstand, and Europeans might hear), and soundly thrashed two with his fists. One was Waduwiri, the ring-leader, the other Pundjili. I had seen him striding downriver and, suspecting bad trouble, had vainly tried to intercept him, but he had eluded me. When I told him later that I had searched for him with the idea of holding him back he grinned and said, 'I knew what you were going to do'. He was feeling very good about the day. 'Those bloody Moiils,' he said, 'they are not men. All they think about is humbugging women.' He described where he had hit them, and what poor things they were for not fighting back. He said he would make them pay him £6 each.

After I left the river his wife and daughter were suddenly returned to him, and he was also told that the young men had been banished to Snake Bay. Then, out of the blue, the trouble started again. The youths reappeared in the locality, having tricked the officials in Darwin. They began to send impudent messages to Durmugam, and the young wife was again abducted. The second youth spread the word that he would come for the daughter whenever he felt like it; no one could stop them; the Government was on their side. The perplexed Durmugam asked me on my next visit a few months later if this was so, and I could only say that the Government did not seem to be on his side. I then interceded on his behalf with the authorities.

Among the Mulluk Mulluk, the consanguines of Durmugam's faithless wife, there was a strong feeling of shame. Other Nangiomeri were his defenders too, and the girl's co-wives gave her a thrashing when she returned for (as they told me) bringing shame on an old man. In other tribes, there were mixed feelings, perhaps mainly cynical amusement, but several polygynists were thoughtful and some of the young bloods delighted. They seemed to be drawing the inference that the Government did not mind how they got women.

The emotion of shame is perhaps the most powerful in Aboriginal life. But it is not only a restraint; it can be a goad as well. Like most of the emotions of negative valuation, it is stronger than those which are positive. Durmugam may have wept over Barij and Muti, he may have wanted to kill Waluk and Lamutji—he was also ashamed not to. As he himself put it, he was 'made' to kill the first two, and 'had' to kill the second two. He responded, at least in part, to entirely social pressure. The pressures on him since 1952 have been very great. He wants, he is expected, and, by some, he is dared to do something. The young men ridicule him, behind his back, and out of the reach of his arm. Those 'bastards of Moiils' send malicious messages that they will come for his women whenever they feel like doing so. He is not a man to live with expungible shame and, at our last meeting, I had the strong feeling that if his rights were not acknowledged and restored he would either turn his face to the wall and die, or there would be another affair of blood. I do not necessarily mean that Durmugam would himself go out and kill someone, but that several people would die—several, because there is a scale of human shame. A single killing will not expunge a great humiliation. The victims could be almost anyone—the youths, the woman, a man like Waduwiri, or even people without apparent connection though, in native eyes, guilty of agency.

A little later, at Port Keats, I picked up a few threads which made me thoughtful. A woman had been abducted from the Victoria River by a Murinbata man, and the secret sponsor of the affair was supposed to be Waduwiri, one of Durmugam's main enemies. Tjimari, the intriguer, was trying by subtle means to frighten the Murinbata into returning the woman on the ground that her abduction had angered the Victoria River Aborigines who would otherwise now be bringing bullroarers to Port Keats. He was spreading the story that the woman had slighted Karwadi—in short, was preparing the ground for her mass rape or, possibly, death. Some quiet visits were made to Durmugam by a brother and a classificatory father of the abductor, with a purpose I could not learn. The first outlines were there of the labyrinthine process of gaining support and sanction for two sides. I could not discern Tjimari's deeper intent, nor Durmugam's.

The tension increased when, in spite of the isolation of Port Keats, we heard that Waduwiri had ensnared and killed a certain Split-Lip Mick, a truly villainous man who had completed a gaol sentence for the murder of Tiger Dapan some years ago. Waduwiri had welcomed Split-Lip on his return to the Daly River and had camped with him in apparent amity for some months. A day came when Waduwiri deftly divided a hunting party in two so that he and Split-Lip were left alone. It was then the work of a moment to distract Split-Lip's attention and pierce him through with a shovel-spear. The wounded man showed a ferocious will to live. He shouted for help, ran into the timber, managed somehow to pull the spear through and out of his body, and only then collapsed. Waduwiri stood over him long enough to say, 'You forgot about Dapan; well, it is Dapan who is now killing you.' Then he too ran, to escape the other party now racing through the timber. He was arrested later but for reasons I am unable to explain was soon out of custody. Split-Lip clung to life for about eight days.

It was now clear that serious trouble was brewing. A number of hatreds were at an intense pitch. How would they align themselves and who would rally to the lines? I spent much time trying to predict what would happen, but there were too many unknowns. Then Alligator Ngundul, Durmugam's mother's sister's son, died at Port Keats for no apparent reason. One of his sons came angrily to me, held out an arm, struck it with his other hand as though to cut the arm in two, and thus showed by how much his father's life had been cut short. He swore then and there to find The Flesh of the Road, the Murinbata name for the warlock. Soon afterwards he set out for Victoria River with a lock of his father's hair to put the matter to a divination. My guess was that Durmugam's shame, the grief of his new loss, the release of Waduwiri, and the divination going on in secret hundreds of miles away were moving inevitably together. Waduwiri prudently kept away from the Daly River and began to put out feelers as to his reception at Port Keats if he were to come. But I did not see any place as now really safe for him. And there the matter rested when I wrote this article.

***

The unusual man in unusual circumstances—it is within such a frame that Durmugam's social personality is best seen. His outlook was positive, and his conduct hopeful and constructive, until his great troubles set in, but even then he held on tenaciously, trying to find a solution. Where many Aborigines were bewildered or even crushed by the complexity, weight and mysteriousness of Europeanism, or sought sullenly to isolate themselves from it, Durmugam tried to come to working terms with it while staying his own man. I never heard him speak harshly of a European, or heard of his being in conflict with one. If spoken to angrily or contemptuously, he would walk away, showing no outward sign of feeling.

He remains for me the most characterful Aboriginal I have known, but I could not confidently put him in any more specific category. I saw no neurotic or psychotic quality in him. His passions were by nature strong, and he was a man of determined will. He lacked the luminous intelligence of Melbyerk, but had a far stronger sentiment for Aboriginal ways. I am sure he was deeply moved to live by the rules of his tradition as he understood it. He wanted to live a blackfellow's life, having the rights of a man, and following up The Dreaming. He venerated his culture; when he grew older, he even found it intellectually interesting. 'It comes round again,' he would say of the system of subsections, 'it comes round!' The symmetry and precision of this organisational form fascinated him. His desire to see the Aboriginal norms of life realised, and his restraint in the ordinary circumstances of life, were perhaps the two most abiding impressions he left on me. His lifeobjects, his scale of values, the terms he would accept for their attainment, and the costs he would sustain, all made sense in relation to those qualities.

Aborigines like Durmugam can never be 'assimilated'. They will retreat from this latterday solicitude as they did from the ignorant neglect of former times. The only thing he liked about Europeanism was its goods. I do not believe he ever formed a deep attachment to any European, myself included. He knew that I was making use of him and, as a due for good service, he made use of me, always civilly, never unscrupulously or importunately, as with Tjimari. He was told, poor man, that I had great influence; he knew that I commanded a small force during the war, and he developed this fact into the idea that I was the 'boss' of all the soldiers he saw; Tjimari told him I was a lawyer who 'stood up for the blackfellows'. So when he was in trouble he turned to me. He was disappointed that I could not do much for him but, characteristically, he went away without reproaches to try to find a way to help himself. He was conscious, perhaps for the first time in his life, of a crippling weakness: his eyesight had almost failed. He said to me: 'I cannot see where to throw a spear. I cannot see if anyone is sneaking up on me.'

Durmugam, in my opinion, represented and embodied all the qualities which the blacks admire in a man, if he is one of their own. A good hunter, a good fighter, and a good brother; a man who kept his promises and paid his debts; a man who left other women alone (he was no philanderer) unless invited to enjoy them; and a man with a 'hot belly' for his rights. After his death, his stature will grow in Aboriginal eyes. He will be spoken of as 'a big man', as, indeed, he always seemed to me.

His fundamental attitude to life was productive. The only negativism appeared in his later years, and even that was, so to speak, positive—a rejection of the mere activism which captivated the young men and women after the trauma of war (a regiment of troops was stationed at The Crossing, and many Aborigines were swept into a labour corps), and the first true impact of a monetary economy in a condition of inflation. The secularisation was far-reaching and corrosive, psychically and socially. The young man's remark, 'If I live I live, if I die I die', had seemed to Durmugam monstrous. To him, *how* a man lived and what he lived *for* were of first importance. But he himself had in part succumbed. He now spent much time playing poker for money (there were five aces in one of his packs of cards); and, for the first time in his life, he accepted money from me. His material wants were more complex and at a higher level. He still went bootless, but wore a hat and well-kept shirt and trousers.

Aboriginal culture leaves a child virtually untrammelled for five or six years. In infancy, it lies in a smooth, well-rounded *coolamon* which is airy and unconstraining, and rocks if the child moves to any great extent. A cry brings immediate fondling. A child may still cry at three as a sign that it wants something—water, attention, carrying. Its dependence on and command of both parents is maximal, their indulgence extreme. To hit a young child is for them unthinkable. A shake, or a sharp word, both rare, are the most an exasperated parent will do. The behaviour patterns thus formed are rudely broken in males by the initiations (always pubertal, sometimes prepubertal as well) after a gradual softening from the fifth or sixth year, when little boys may be seen throwing stones at their mothers, or abusing them, while the women laugh. At initiation new psychic paths are made by isolation, terror, fatigue, pain, mystery, music, drama, grave instruction—means implicitly prescient and in overt use a memorable spectacle. One inward path is ruptured, another substituted, and life thereafter is one continuous re-integration. There are quite probably neural as well as psychic and social reasons why, after initiation, an Aboriginal youth responds but poorly to other possible worlds opened to him. Neural, since there has been a cortical integration of intense quality; psychic, since his responses have been deeply conditioned to limited stimuli; social, since only a limited range of objects of action have positive valence for him.

Durmugam was initiated, as he says, 'in the bush', at a time (about 1913) when a relatively large number of Aborigines could be assembled and the full panoply of ceremonial forms could be followed. He emerged a blackfellow for life. He did not simply reach manhood: he was *given* it, was *made* a man by men who stood for and taught him to stand for a tradition in part only revealed. Later, as I have narrated, he learned the full tradition, not of his own, but of neighbourly tribes. The conditioning was not only thus completed, but vivified, by the new presence of Kunabibi, and by the repetition and intensification of stimuli consistent with those of the trauma of initiation.

I came to believe, in the end, that the 'hot belly' and the calm face of this man were consistent. The initiations teach boys to be men: to know pain and ignore it; to feel fear and master it; to want, but to bear the necessary costs; to grasp that outside society they are nothing (in the isolation of initiation they are called 'wild dogs') and, inside it, the masters; that through them The Dreaming is 'followed up'; that the tradition is 'the road'. The vital impulses are not crushed, but steered; the social conscience forecloses these fields only to leave those open; the male ego is beckoned to a defined dominance. The 'hot belly' is not only allowable, but premial, in an Aboriginal man. The calmness, self-possession, and dignity are the marks of a well-socialised Aboriginal; and the Aboriginal following up The Dreaming is a man who has his feet on surety.

The emphasis on rules, forms, norms, and the like, which vexes so many anthropologists who have not encountered Aboriginal culture, and seems to be a bias of the analysts, is not an error of scholars. It is objectively there. It is simply a function of a need, or necessary condition, of Aboriginal life: an elaboration of means serving ends which have canonised values. The life of the mature, initiated male is the practice of the doctrine.

Durmugam's life, in broad, seems to me to vindicate this thesis. He came to good terms with Europeanism, but found it saltless all his days and, at the end, bitter too. It had some few goods—mundane things which were either substitutes for Aboriginal equivalents (axes, knives, houses) or additions in no way competing with anything in 'the way'—which he took and used, sensibly. But it never attracted him emotionally, it did not interest him intellectually, and it aroused only his material desires.

He might perhaps be looked on as a study in benign dissociation. At the conscious level he had found a way of living with duality, an oafish Europeanism and an Aboriginal idealism. I sometimes thought that his slowness, which was certainly not a retardation, might be the measure of the difficulties of transition, for two scales must always be consulted. His general orientation towards the hard facts of actuality was, however, excellent. He could always tell me the day of the week if I forgot it; his mind held a mass of concrete detail about European things, people and events; he would calculate quite impersonally and rationally about farmer X or Y; and in the same breath, so to speak, pass to the other, an Aboriginal, realm of equivalent detail and actuality. It was not that one was conscious and the other para-conscious: they were *co* conscious. Yet, paradoxical and contradictory as it may seem, he could dissociate and not merely separate the two. To be sure, a clinical study by someone competent, and I was not, might transform the picture, but I saw no signs of secondary personality; he was a unified person, who, somehow, could bridge two worlds and, while preferring one, live with two. A clinician might have found evidences of neurotic or psychotic habit because of the fears, hatreds, warlockry, and killing in which he was embroiled. I would argue, however, that these were situational, and not psychogenetic. The postulates of Aboriginal culture, and the conditions of Aboriginal social transactions in a bizarre context of life, suggest such an explanation. The reality Durmugam saw was defined by a tradition which he believed. If the test of belief is what a man will die for, and if a man is what he loves, I have said enough to enable others to form a judgment of this Aboriginal. For him, as I understood him, the hills stood, the rivers ran, the sky hung there timelessly, men went on being what they had to be because the All-Father did thus and so in the beginning, and a living man could do that and should do this until he died. Vexing, rather inexplicable things came from outside the tradition. He utilised what he could, endured what he had to, and for the rest did his best to follow up The Dreaming.

***

All this was written while the old man was still alive. He died in Port Darwin Hospital in August 1959, of an inoperable cancer of the stomach. Before then he had developed leprosy of one foot and had shown signs of a failing heart. He was cared for through a succession of illnesses at the new Mission of the Sacred Heart on the Daly River and made several trips to Darwin for medical attention.

A European of sensibility who knew him over his last years remarked on his dignity, patience, courtesy to Europeans and readiness to meet any request for help. A nun asked Durmugam if he would like to teach the young Aboriginal boys the wood-working in which he excelled, and he responded with delight. He showed the enchanted children how, with no tool but the stud of an old knife, to coax a flawless, complex shape out of wood so tough that it soon dulled axe and saw. The things he best knew how to make were spears, and he carved a great many hooked spears with perfect craftsmanship. All the work showed the love of form, balance, and symmetry which characterised him. In this setting he seemed anything but a man of blood. There was a gentleness about him with children which I had noted even when he was young.

The last illness developed rapidly and though for some time unwilling he consented at last to go to Darwin again. An operation showed that nothing could be done for him. He was not told of his condition and the doctors did what they could to keep him alive and in good spirits. Some of his distant kin told me that when they saw him in hospital he spoke of his sickness as but a little thing. Evidently he did not expect that he would die so soon. At the last he was given Catholic baptism and burial at Rapid Creek not far from where the

Jesuits had founded the mission which they transferred to the Daly River a decade before he was born. An unusually large number of Aborigines (including Waduwiri) went to the funeral. Many had not known him in life.

It was an unlikely end for such a man. While the old culture still had force Durmugam went long distances to take part in the funerary rites which were once a spectacle of the region. The last time he did so was perhaps twenty years ago. On that occasion he went to Malboiyin, on the border of his tribal country, to stamp into the ancestral earth—after the fashion of the rite—the ashes of a certain Belweni (not the man of the same name mentioned earlier). In other circumstances this would also have been done for Durmugam.

The body of Belweni had been put by affines on a platform of boughs and left there to moulder for years. His chattels, save for one thing, had long since been broken up and burned. One of the two rites of quittance had been held; the last possession had been destroyed in a fire on which close kin had prepared a meal. The preparations for the second rite were complete. The body, dried and shrunken by long exposure, had been broken into pieces, burned to a mixture of ash and charcoal, and then ground to powder. All that was left was a small container of paper-bark and a few handfuls of fine substance. The parcel had been taken from its place under the pillow of Belweni's mother and was now at Malboiyin. It was to help in the due interment of these remains that Durmugam went with many others—kith, kin, friends, and enemies—to Malboiyin, Belweni's ancestral clan-estate.

In the last rite the small parcel of dust was put in a hole within a cleared circle. Valuable things were laid on top as symbolic gifts. The grass around the clearing was then fired. The gift-givers soon withdrew the goods, and two clustered formations of clans ran forward through the smoke and smoulder. Each was daubed with pipeclay and came brandishing spears. The formations alternately encircled the grave, by this time covered with earth, and moved in line by measured and rhythmic steps so as to form an anticlockwise spiral with a point slowly nearing the grave. All the movements were in time to a chant in part melancholy and in part somehow triumphant. Each spiral halted as its leader's feet were on the grave. All the men in the formation then turned and rushed upon the centre. There, crowded together, each man stamped his right foot repeatedly, thrust his spear-point towards the grave, and added his voice to a chorus of chanted cries simulating the calls of wild things, the river currents, and the breaking surf.

Each formation vied with the other to vivify the rite. In the background were wailing women and, at a distance, a solitary singer wandering up and down as he sang in seeming detachment from all else. No one knew the meaning of the song. The singer had learned it by some mystical means he would not or could not disclose. The rite halted at sundown but at intervals throughout the night, while others slept, the singer would rise, go out beyond the glow of the fires, and then wander singing in the darkness.

With the sun the two formations performed the spiral rite once more. Then there was nothing more to do. The spirit of Belweni was now quit of material form and of worldly ties and things of the past. Until now it had had to watch over its own bones and haunt the locality of its bier. The rite had freed it to go somewhere—no one can be sure where—to find a new mode of entry to the visible world. No doubt all this too would have been done for Durmugam had things worked out differently.

According to Aboriginal belief at any time now each of his *pule* (friends), of whom I had the honour to be one, will suddenly miss some valuable thing and hunt for it in vain. It will never be found again. This will be the work of Durmugam's spirit making a sign from another plane of life. The belief is tenuous and hard to put into words. The sign is somehow also the mark of a secondary death. The ideas of absolute extinction and of indestructible soul or spirit may both be found in the belief system. Now one, now the other seems stressed. The same sort of thing is true of the social organisation and the associational life generally. It is as though the nature of things were a complementary duality, with human character as the integral.

Every now and then, when one is recording the genealogies of the Aborigines, a name is mentioned which brings a great show of animation and admiration. Men hold up their hands as if measuring the size of a huge tree. They say: *kadu pañgoi, kadu nãla, kadu mulak!* ('A tall man, large and fierce.') Quite often such men are known or reputed to have been warlocks, or ghostseers, or wise men, the three classes of spiritists. Durmugam was none of these. Possibly he was thus more free psychologically to come to terms with Europeanism. But by the same token, being no manipulator—and this suspicion always hangs around the three classes—he may have had a simpler and more passionate absorption in his own culture.

How much of the treachery, hatred, and bloodshed in which he was involved was due to the decay of a tradition, and how much was of its very nature, it is not possible to say. A case might be made for either or both. His times were so thoroughly out of joint that ideal and real could only drift farther apart. But the force and integrity he showed could readily be seen by anyone not blinded by the veils of race, culture, and interest.

1959

The Dreaming (1953)

The Australian Aborigines' outlook on the universe and man is shaped by a remarkable conception, which Spencer and Gillen immortalised as 'the dream time' or *alcheringa* of the Arunta or Aranda tribe. Comparable terms from other tribes are often almost untranslatable, or mean literally something like 'men of old'. Some anthropologists have called it the Eternal Dream Time. I prefer to call it what many Aborigines call it in English: The Dreaming, or just, Dreaming.

A central meaning of The Dreaming is that of a sacred, heroic time long ago when man and nature came to be as they are; but neither 'time' nor 'history' as we understand them is involved in this meaning. I have never been able to discover any Aboriginal word for *time* as an abstract concept. And the sense of 'history' is wholly alien here. We shall not understand The Dreaming fully except as a complex of meanings. A blackfellow may call his totem, or the place from which his spirit came, his Dreaming. He may also explain the existence of a custom, or law of life, as causally due to The Dreaming.

A concept so impalpable and subtle naturally suffers badly by translation into our dry and abstract language. The blacks sense this difficulty. I can recall one intelligent old man who said to me, with a cadence almost as though he had been speaking verse:

>White man got no dreaming,
>Him go 'nother way.
>White man, him go different.
>Him got road belong himself.

Although, as I have said, The Dreaming conjures up the notion of a sacred, heroic time of the indefinitely remote past, such a time is also, in a sense, still part of the present. One cannot 'fix' The Dreaming *in* time: it was, and is, everywhen. We should be very wrong to read into it the idea of a Golden Age, or a Garden of Eden, though it was an Age of Heroes, when the ancestors did marvellous things that men can no longer do. The blacks are not at all insensitive to Mary Webb's 'wistfulness that is the past', but they do not, in aversion from present or future, look back on it with yearning and nostalgia. Yet it has for them an unchallengeably sacred authority.

Clearly, The Dreaming is many things in one. Among them, a kind of narrative to things that once happened; a kind of charter of things that still happen; and a kind of *logos* or principle of order transcending everything significant for Aboriginal man. If I am correct in saying so, it is much more complex philosophically than we have so far realised. I greatly hope that artists and men of letters who (it seems increasingly) find inspiration in Aboriginal Australia will use all their gifts of empathy, but avoid banal projection and subjectivism, if they seek to honour the notion.

Why the blackfellow thinks of 'dreaming' as the nearest equivalent in English is a puzzle. It may be because it is by the act of dreaming, as reality and symbol, that the Aboriginal mind makes contact—thinks it makes contact—with whatever mystery it is that connects The Dreaming and the Here-and-Now.

***

How shall one deal with so subtle a conception? One has two options: educe its subjective logic and rationale from the 'elements' which the blackfellow stumblingly offers in trying to give an explanation; or relate the objective figure it traces on their social life to things familiar in our own intellectual history. There are dangers in both courses.

The first is a matter of learning to 'think black', not imposing Western categories of understanding, but seeking to conceive of things as the blackfellow himself does.

In our modern understanding, we tend to see 'mind' and 'body', 'body' and 'spirit', 'spirit' and 'personality', 'personality' and 'name' as in some sense separate, even opposed, entities though we manage to connect them up in some fashion into the unity or oneness of 'person' or 'individual'. The blackfellow does not seem to think this way. The distinctiveness we give to 'mind', 'spirit' and 'body', and our contrast of 'body' *versus* 'spirit' are not there, and the whole notion of 'the person' is enlarged. To a blackfellow, a man's name, spirit, and shadow are 'him' in a sense which to us may seem passing strange. One should not ask a blackfellow: 'What is your name?' To do so embarrasses and shames him. The name is like an intimate part of the body, with which another person does not take liberties. The blacks do not mind talking about a dead person in an oblique way; but, for a long time, they are extremely reluctant even to breathe his name. In the same way, to threaten a man's shadow is to threaten him. Nor may one threaten lightly the physical place from which his spirit came. By extension, his totem, which is also associated with that place, and with his spirit, should not be lightly treated.

In such a context one has not succeeded in 'thinking black' until one's mind can, without intellectual struggle, enfold into some kind of oneness the notions of body, spirit, ghost, shadow, name, spirit-site, and totem. To say so may seem a contradiction, or suggest a paradox, for the blackfellow can and does, on some occasions, conceptually isolate the 'elements' of the 'unity' most distinctly. But his abstractions do not put him at war with himself. The separable elements I have mentioned are all present in the metaphysical heart of the idea of 'person', but the overruling mood is one of belief, not of enquiry or dissent. So long as the belief in The Dreaming lasts, there can be no 'momentary flash of Athenian questioning' to grow into a great movement of sceptical unbelief which destroys the given unities.

There are many other such 'onenesses' which I believe I could substantiate. A blackfellow may 'see' as 'a unity' two persons, such as two siblings or a grandparent and grandchild; or a living man and something inanimate, as when he tells you that, say, the wollybutt tree, a totem, is his wife's brother. (This is not quite as strange as it may seem. Even modern psychologists tend to include part of 'environment' in a 'definition' of 'person' or 'personality'.) There is also some kind of unity between waking-life and dream-life: the means by which, in Aboriginal understanding, a man fathers a child, is not by sexual intercourse, but by the act of dreaming about a spirit-child. His own spirit, during a dream, 'finds' a child and directs it to his wife, who then conceives. Physical congress between a man and a woman is contingent, not a necessary prerequisite. Through the medium of dream-contact with a spirit an artist is inspired to produce a new song. It is by dreaming that a man divines the intention of someone to kill him by sorcery, or of relatives to visit him. And, as I have suggested, it is by the act of dreaming, in some way difficult for a European to grasp, because of the force of our analytical abstraction, that a blackfellow conceives himself to make touch with whatever it is that is continuous between The Dreaming and the Here-and-Now.

The truth of it seems to be that man, society and nature, and past, present and future, are at one together within a unitary system of such a kind that its ontology cannot illumine minds too much under the influence of humanism, rationalism and science. One cannot easily, in the mobility of modern life and thought, grasp the vast intuitions of stability and permanence, and of life and man, at the heart of Aboriginal ontology.

It is fatally easy for Europeans, encountering such things for the first time, to go on to suppose that 'mysticism' of this kind rules *all* Aboriginal thought. It is not so. 'Logical' thought and 'rational' conduct are about as widely present in Aboriginal life as they are on the simpler levels of European life. Once one understands three things—the primary intuitions which the blackfellow has formed about the nature of the universe and man, those things in both which he thinks interesting and significant, and the conceptual system from within which he reasons about them, then the suppositions about prelogicality, illogicality, and non-rationality can be seen to be merely absurd. And if one wishes to see a really brilliant demonstration of deductive thought, one has only to see a blackfellow tracking a wounded kangaroo, and persuade him to say why he interprets given signs in a certain way.

The second means of dealing with the notion of The Dreaming is, as I said, to try to relate it to things familiar in our own intellectual history. From this viewpoint, it is a cosmogony, an account of the begetting of the universe, a study about creation. It is also a cosmology, an account or theory of how what was created became an ordered system. To be more precise, how the universe became a moral system.

If one analyses the hundreds of tales about The Dreaming, one can see within them three elements. The first concerns the great *marvels*—how all the fire and water in the world were stolen and recaptured; how men made a mistake over sorcery and now have to die from it; how the hills, rivers, and waterholes were made; how the sun, moon, and stars were set upon their courses; and many other dramas of this kind. The second element tells how certain things were *instituted* for the first time—how animals and men diverged from a joint stock that was neither one nor the other; how the black-nosed kangaroo got his black nose and the porcupine his quills; how such social divisions as tribes, clans, and language groups were set up; how spirit-children were first placed in the waterholes, the winds, and leaves of trees. A third element, if I am not mistaken, allows one to suppose that many of the main institutions of present-day life were *already ruling* in The Dreaming, e.g. marriage, exogamy, sister-exchange, and initiation, as well as many of the well-known breaches of custom. The men of The Dreaming committed adultery, betrayed and killed each other, were greedy, stole and committed the very wrongs committed by those now alive.

Now, if one disregards the imagery in which the oral literature of The Dreaming is cast, one may perhaps come to three conclusions.

The tales are a kind of commentary, or statement, on what is thought to be permanent and ordained at the very basis of the world and life. They are a way of stating the principle which animates things. I would call them a poetic key to Reality. The Aboriginal does not ask himself the philosophical-type questions: What is 'real'? How many 'kinds' of 'reality' are there? What are the 'properties' of 'reality'? How are the properties 'interconnected'? This is the idiom of Western intellectual discourse and the fruit of a certain social history. His tales are, however, a kind of answer to such questions so far as they have been asked at all. They may not be a 'definition', but they are a 'key' to reality, a key to the singleness and the plurality of things set up once-for-all when, in The Dreaming, the universe becomes man's universe. The active philosophy of Aboriginal life transforms this 'key', which is expressed in the idiom of poetry, drama, and symbolism, into a principle that The Dreaming determines not only what life *is* but also *what it can be.* Life, so to speak, is a one-possibility thing, and what this is, is the 'meaning' of The Dreaming.

The tales are also a collation of *what is validly known* about such ordained permanencies. The blacks cite The Dreaming as a chapter of absolute validity in answer to all questions of *why* and *how.* In this sense, the tales can be regarded as being, perhaps not a definition, but a 'key' of Truth.

They also state, by their constant recitation of what was done rightly and wrongly in The Dreaming, the ways in which good men should, and bad men will, act now. In this sense, they are a 'key' or guide to the norms of conduct, and a prediction of how men will err.

One may thus say that, after a fashion—a cryptic, symbolic, and poetic fashion—the tales are 'a philosophy' in the garb of an oral literature. The European has a philosophic literature which expresses a largely deductive understanding of reality, truth, goodness, and beauty. The blackfellow has a mythology, a ritual, and an art which express an intuitive, visionary, and poetic understanding of the same ultimates. In following out The Dreaming, the blackfellow 'lives' this philosophy. It is an implicit philosophy, but nevertheless a real one. Whereas we hold (and may live) a philosophy of abstract propositions, attained by someone standing professionally outside 'life' and treating it as an object of contemplation and inquiry, the blackfellow holds his philosophy in mythology, attained as the social product of an indefinitely ancient past, and proceeds to live it out 'in' life, in part through a ritual and an expressive art, and in part through non-sacred social customs.

European minds are made uneasy by the facts that the stories are, quite plainly, preposterous; are often a mass of internal contradictions; are encrusted by superstitious fancies about magic, sorcery, hobgoblins, and superhuman heroes; and lack the kind of theme and structure—in other words, the 'story' element—for which we look. Many of us cannot help feeling that such things can only be the products of absurdly ignorant credulity and a lower order of mentality. This is to fall victim to a facile fallacy. Our own intellectual history is not an absolute standard by which to judge others. The worst imperialisms are those of preconceptions.

Custom is the reality, beliefs but the shadows which custom makes on the wall. Since the tales, in any case, are not really 'explanatory' in purpose or function, they naturally lack logic, system and completeness. It is simply pointless to look for such things within them. But we are not entitled to suppose that, because the tales are fantastical, the social life producting them is itself fantastical. The shape of reality is always distorted in the shadows it throws. One finds much logic, system and rationality in the blacks' actual scheme of life.

These tales are neither simply illustrative nor simply explanatory; they are fanciful and poetic in content because they are based on visionary and intuitive insights into mysteries; and, if we are ever to understand them, we must always take them in their complex content. If, then, they make more sense to the poet, the artist, and the philosopher than to the clinicians of human life, let us reflect on the withering effect on sensibility of our pervasive rationalism, rather than depreciate the gifts which produced the Aboriginal imaginings. And in no case should we expect the tales, *prima facie,* to be even interesting if studied out of context. Aboriginal mythology is quite unlike the Scandinavian, Indian, or Polynesian mythologies.

***

In my own understanding, The Dreaming is a proof that the blackfellow shares with us two abilities which have largely made human history what it is.

The first of these we might call 'the metaphysical gift'. I mean the ability to transcend oneself, to make acts of imagination so that one can stand 'outside' or 'away from' oneself, and turn the universe, oneself and one's fellows into objects of contemplation. The second ability is a 'drive' to try to 'make sense' out of human experience and to find some 'principle' in the whole human situation. This 'drive' is, in some way, built into the constitution of the human mind. No one who has real knowledge of Aboriginal life can have any doubt that they possess, and use, both abilities very much as we do. They differ from us only in the directions in which they turn their gifts, the idiom in which they express them, and the principles of intellectual control.

The Aborigines have no gods, just or unjust, to adjudicate the world. Not even by straining can one see in such culture-heroes as Baiame and Darumulum the true hint of a Yahveh, jealous, omniscient, and omnipotent. The ethical insights are dim and somewhat coarse in texture. One can find in them little trace, say, of the inverted pride, the self-scrutiny, and the consciousness of favour and destiny which characterised the early Jews. A glimpse, but no truly poignant sense, of moral dualism; no notion of grace or redemption; no whisper of inner peace and reconcilement; no problems of worldly life to be solved only by a consummation of history; no heaven of reward or hell of punishment. The blackfellow's after-life is but a shadowy replica of worldly-life, so none flee to inner sanctuary to escape the world. There are no prophets, saints, or *illuminati*. There is a concept of goodness, but it lacks true scruple. Men can become ritually unclean, but may be cleansed by a simple mechanism.

There is a moral law but, as in the beginning, men are both good and bad, and no one is racked by the knowledge. I imagine there could never have been an Aboriginal Ezekiel, any more than there could have been a Job. The two sets of insights cannot easily be compared, but it is plain that their underlying moods are wholly unlike, and their store of meaningfulness very uneven. In the one there seem an almost endless possibility of growth, and a mood of censoriousness and pessimism. In the other, a kind of standstill, and a mood which is neither tragic nor optimistic. The Aborigines are not shamed or inspired by a religious thesis of what men might become by faith and grace. Their metaphysic assents, without brooding or challenge, to what men evidently have to be because the terms of life are cast. Yet they have a kind of religiosity cryptically displayed in their magical awareness of nature, in their complex totemism, ritual and art, and perhaps too even in their intricately ordered life.

They are, of course, nomads—hunters and foragers who grow

nothing, build little, and stay nowhere long. They make almost no physical mark on the environment. Even in areas which are still inhabited, it takes a knowledgeable eye to detect their recent presence. Within a matter of weeks, the roughly cleared camp-sites may be erased by sun, rain and wind. After a year or two there may be nothing to suggest that the country was ever inhabited. Until one stumbles on a few old flint-tools, a stone quarry, a shell-midden, a rock painting, or something of the kind, one may think that the land had never known the touch of man.

They neither dominate their environment nor seek to change it. 'Children of nature' they are not, nor are they nature's 'masters'. One can only say they are 'at one' with nature. The whole ecological principle of their life might be summed up in the Baconian aphorism—*natura non vincitur nisi parendo:* 'nature is not to be conquered except by obeying'. Naturally, one finds metaphysical and social reflections of the fact.

They move about, carrying their scant possessions, in small bands of anything from ten to sixty persons. Each band belongs to a given locality. A number of bands—anything from three to four up to twelve or fifteen depending on the fertility of the area—make up a 'tribe'. A tribe is usually a language or dialect group which thinks of itself as having a certain unity of common speech and shared customs. The tribes range in size from a few hundred to a few thousand souls.

One rarely sees a tribe as a formed entity. It comes together and lives as a unit only for a great occasion—a feast, a corroboree, a hunt, an initiation, or a formal duel. After a few days—at the most weeks—it breaks up again into smaller bands or sections of bands: most commonly into a group of brothers, with their wives, children, and grandchildren, and perhaps a few close relatives. These parties rove about their family locality or, by agreement, the territories of immediate neighbours. They do not wander aimlessly, but to a purpose, and in tune with the seasonal food supply. One can almost plot a year of their life in terms of movement towards the places where honey, yams, grass-seeds, eggs, or some other food staple, is in bearing and ready for eating.

The uncomplex visible routine, and the simple segmentation, are very deceptive. It took well over half a century for Europeans to realise that, behind the outward show, was an inward structure of surprising complexity. It was a century before any real understanding of this structure developed.

In one tribe with which I am familiar, a very representative tribe, there are about 100 'invisible' divisions which have to be analysed before one can claim even a serviceable understanding of the tribe's organisation. The structure is much more complex than that of an Australian village of the same size. The complexity is in the most striking contrast with the comparative simplicity which rules in the two other departments of Aboriginal life—the material culture, on the one hand, and the ideational or metaphysical culture on the other. We have, I think, to try to account for this contrast in some way.

Their creative 'drive' to make sense and order out of things has concentrated on the social rather than on the metaphysical or the material side. Consequently, there has been an unusually rich development of what the anthropologist calls 'social structure', the network of enduring relations recognised between people. This very intricate system is an intellectual and social achievement of a high order. It is not, like an instinctual response, a phenomenon of 'nature'; it is not, like art or ritual, a complex type of behaviour passionately added to 'nature', in keeping with metaphysical insight but without rational and intelligible purposes which can be clearly stated; it has to be compared, I think, with such a secular achievement as, say, parliamentary government in a European society. It is truly positive knowledge.

One may see within it three things: given customs, 'of which the memory of man runneth not to the contrary'; a vast body of cumulative knowledge about the effects of these customs on a society in given circumstances; and the use of the power of abstract reason to rationalise the resultant relations into a system.

But it is something more; their social organisation has become *the source of the dominant mode of Aboriginal thinking.* The blacks use social organisation to give a bony structure to parts of the worldoutlook suggested by intuitive speculation. I mean by this that they have taken some of its fundamental principles and relations and have applied them to very much wider sets of phenomena. This tends to happen if any type of system of thought becomes truly dominant. It is, broadly, what Europeans did with 'religion' and 'science' as systems: extended their principles and categories to fields far beyond the contexts in which the systems grew.

Thus, the blacks have taken the male-female social principle and have extended it to the non-human world. In one tribe I have studied, all women, without exception, call particular birds or trees by the same kinship terms which they apply to actual relatives. In the same way, all men without exception use comparable terms for a different set of trees or birds. From this results what the anthropologist calls 'sex totemism'. The use of other principles results in other types of totemism. An understanding of this simple fact removes much of the social, if not the ritual, mystery of totemism. Again, the principle of relatedness itself, relatedness between known people by known descent through known marriages, is extended over the whole face of human society. The same terms of kinship which are used for close agnatic and affinal relatives are used for every other person an Aboriginal meets in the course of his life: strangers, friends, enemies, and known kin may all be called by the same terms as one uses for brother, father, mother's sister, father's mother's brother, and so on. This is what an anthropologist means when he says 'Aboriginal society is a society of kinship'.

It might even be argued that the blacks have done much the same thing with 'time'. Time as a continuum is a concept only hazily present in the Aboriginal mind. What might be called *social* time is, in a sense, 'bent' into cycles or circles. The most controlled understanding of it is by reckoning in terms of generation-classes, which are arranged into names and recurring cycles. As far as the blackfellow thinks about time at all, his interest lies in the cycles rather than in the continuum, and each cycle is in essence a principle for dealing with social interrelatedness.

***

Out of all this may come for some an understanding of the blackfellow very different from that which has passed into the ignorance and vulgarity of popular opinion.

One may see that, like all men, he is a metaphysician in being able to transcend himself. With the metaphysic goes a mood and spirit, which I can only call a mood and spirit of 'assent', neither despair nor resignation, optimism nor pessimism, quietism nor indifference. The mood, and the outlook beneath it, make him hopelessly out of place in a world in which the

Renaissance has triumphed only to be perverted, and in which the products of secular humanism, rationalism, and science challenge their own hopes, indeed, their beginnings.

Much association with the blackfellow makes me feel I may not be far wrong in saying that, unlike us, he seems to see 'life' as a one-possibility thing. This may be why he seems to have almost no sense of tragedy. If 'tragedy is looking at fate for a lesson in deportment on life's scaffold', the Aboriginal seems to me to have read the lesson and to have written it into the very conception of how men should live, or else to have stopped short of the insight that there are gods either just or unjust. Nor have I found in him much self-pity. These sentiments can develop only if life presents real alternatives, or if it denies an alternative that one feels should be there. A philosophy of assent fits only a life of unvarying constancy. I do not at all say that pain, sorrow, and sadness have no place in Aboriginal life, for I have seen them all too widely. All I mean is that the blacks seem to have gone beyond, or not quite attained, the human *quarrel* with such things. Their rituals of sorrow, their fortitude in pain, and their undemonstrative sadness seem to imply a reconciliation with the terms of life such that 'peace is the understanding of tragedy and at the same time its preservation', or else that they have not sensed life as baffled by either fate or wisdom.

Like all men, he is a philosopher in being able to use his power of abstract reason. His genius, his *métier,* and—in some sense—his fate, is that because of endowment and circumstance this power has channelled itself mainly into one activity, 'making sense' out of the social relations among men living together. His intricate social organisation is an impressive essay on the economy of conflict, tension, and experiment in a life situation at the absolute pole of our own.

Like all men, too, he pays the price of his insights and solutions. We look to a continuous unfolding of life, and to a blissful attainment of the better things for which, we say, man has an infinite capacity. For some time, nothing has seemed of less consequence to us than the maintenance of continuity. The cost, in instability and inequity, is proving very heavy. Aboriginal life has endured feeling that continuity, not man, is the measure of all. The cost in the world of power and change is extinction. What defeats the blackfellow in the modern world, fundamentally, is his transcendentalism. So much of his life and thought are concerned with The Dreaming that it stultifies his ability to develop. This is not a new thing in human history. A good analogy is with the process in Chinese poetry by which, according to Arthur Waley, its talent for classical allusion became a vice which finally destroyed it altogether.

A 'philosophy of life', that is, a system of mental attitudes towards the conduct of life, may or may not be consistent with an actual way of life. Whether it is or is not will depend on how big a gap there is, if any, between what life *is* and what men think life *ought to be.* If Ideal and Real drift too far away from one another (as they did at the end of the Middle Ages, and seem increasingly to do in this century) men face some difficult options. They have to change their way of life, or their philosophy, or both, or live unhappily somewhere in between. We are familiar enough with the 'war of the philosophies' and the tensions of modern life which express them. Problems of this kind had no place, I would say, in traditional Aboriginal life. It knew nothing, and could not, I think, have known anything of the Christian's straining for inner perfection; of 'moral man and immoral society'; of the dilemma of liberty and authority; of intellectual uncertainty, class warfare, and discontent with one's lot in life—all of which, in some sense, are problems of the gap between Ideal and Real.

The Aborigines may have been in Australia for as long as 10,000 years. No one at present can do more than guess whence or how they came, and there is little more than presumptive evidence on which to base a guess. The span of time, immense though it may have been, matters less than the fact that, so far as one can tell, they have been almost completely isolated. Since their arrival, no foreign stimulus has touched them, except on the fringes of the northern and north-western coasts. To these two facts we must add two others. The physical environment has, evidently, not undergone any marked general change, although there has been a slow desiccation of parts of the centre into desert, and some limited coastline changes. The fourth fact is that their tools and material crafts seem to have been very unprogressive.

If we put these four facts about the Aborigines together—1) an immensely long span of time, 2) spent in more or less complete isolation, 3) in a fairly constant environment, 4) with an unprogressive material culture—we may perhaps see why sameness, absence of change, fixed routine, regularity, call it what you will, is a main dimension of their thought and life. Let us sum up this aspect as leading to a metaphysical emphasis on abidingness. They place a very special value on things remaining unchangingly themselves, on keeping life to a routine which is known and trusted. Absence of change, which means certainty of expectation, seems to them a good thing in itself. One may say, their Ideal and Real come very close together. The value given to continuity is so high that they are not simply a people 'without a history': they are a people who have been able, in some sense, to 'defeat' history, to become a-historical in mood, outlook, and life. This is why, among them, the philosophy of assent, the glove, fits the hand of actual custom almost to perfection, and the forms of social life, the art, the ritual, and much else take on a wonderful symmetry.

Their tools and crafts, meagre—pitiably meagre—though they are, have nonetheless been good enough to let them win the battle for survival, and to win it comfortably at that. With no pottery, no knowledge of metals, no wheel, no domestication of animals, no agriculture, they have still been able, not only to live and people the entire continent, but even in a sense to prosper, to win a surplus of goods and develop leisure-time occupations. The evidences of the surplus of yield over animal need are to be seen in the spider-web of trade routes criss-crossing the continent, on which a large volume of non-utilitarian articles circulated, themselves largely the products of leisure. The true leisuretime activities—social entertaining, great ceremonial gatherings, even much of the ritual and artistic life—impressed observers even from the beginning. The notion of Aboriginal life as always preoccupied with the risk of starvation, as always a hair's breadth from disaster, is as great a caricature as Hobbes's notion of savage life as 'solitary, poor, nasty, brutish and short'. The best corrective of any such notion is to spend a few nights in an Aboriginal camp, and experience directly the unique joy in life which can be attained by a people of few wants, an other-worldly cast of mind and a simple scheme of life which so shapes a day that it ends with communal singing and dancing in the firelight.

The more one sees of Aboriginal life the stronger the impression that its mode, its ethos, and its principles are variations on a single theme—continuity, constancy, balance, symmetry, regularity, system, or some such quality as these words convey.

One of the most striking things is that there are no great conflicts over power, no great contests for place and office. This single fact explains much else, because it rules out so much that would be destructive of stability. The idea of a formal chief, or a leader with authority over the persons of others in a large number of fields of life—say, for example, as with a Polynesian or African chief—just does not seem to make sense to a blackfellow. Nor does even the modified Melanesian notion—that of a man becoming some sort of a leader because he accumulates a great deal of garden-wealth and so gains prestige. There are leaders in the sense of men of unusual skill, initiative, and force and they are given much respect; they may even attract something like a following; but one finds no trace of formal or institutionalised chieftainship. So there are no offices to stimulate ambition, intrigue, or the use of force; to be envied or fought over; or to be lost or won. Power—a real thing in every society—is diffused mainly through one sex, the men, but in such a way that it is not to be won, or lost, in concentrations, by craft, struggle, or coup. It is very much a male-dominated society. The older men dominate the younger; the men dominate the women. Not that the women are chattels—Dr Phyllis Kaberry in her interesting book *Aboriginal Woman* disposed of that Just-so story very effectively—but there is a great deal of discrimination against them. The mythology justifies this by tales telling how men had to take power from women by force in The Dreaming. The psychology (perhaps the truth) of it is as obvious as it is amusing. If women were not kept under, they would take over!

At all events, the struggle for power occurred once-for-all. Power, authority, influence, age, status, knowledge, all run together and, in some sense, are the same kind of thing. The men of power, authority and influence are old men—at least, mature men; the greater the secret knowledge and authority, the higher the status; and the initiations are so arranged (by the old men) that the young men do not acquire full knowledge, and so attain status and authority, until they too are well advanced in years. One can thus see why the great term of respect is 'old man'—*maluka,* as in *We of the Never-Never.* The system is self-protective and self-renewing. The real point of it all is that the checks and balances seem nearly perfect, and no one really seems to want the kind of satisfaction that might come from a position of domination. At the same time, there is a serpent in Eden. The narrow self-interest of men exploits The Dreaming.

Power over things? Every canon of good citizenship and common sense is against it, though there are, of course, clear property arrangements. But what could be more useless than a store of food that will not keep, or a heavy pile of spears that have to be carried everywhere? Especially in a society in which the primary virtues are generosity and fair dealing. Nearly every social affair involving goods—food in the family, payments in marriage, inter-tribal exchange—is heavily influenced by equalitarian notions; a notion of reciprocity as a moral obligation; a notion of generously equivalent return; and a surprisingly clear notion of fair dealing, or making things 'level' as the blackfellow calls it in English.

There is a tilt of the system towards the interests of the men, but given this tilt, everything else seems as if carefully calculated to keep it in place. The blacks do not fight over land. There are no wars or invasions to seize territory. They do not enslave each other. There is no master-servant relation. There is no class division. There is no property or income inequality. The result is a homeostasis, far-reaching and stable.

I do not wish to create an impression of a social life without egotism, without vitality, without cross-purposes, or without conflict. Indeed, there is plenty of all, as there is of malice, enmity, bad faith, and violence, running along the lines of sex-inequality and age-inequality. But this essential humanity exists, and runs its course, within a system whose first principle is the preservation of balance. And, arching over it all, is the *logos* of The Dreaming. How we shall state this when we fully understand it I do not know, but I should think we are more likely to ennoble it than not. Equilibrium ennobled is 'abidingness'. Piccarda's answer in the third canto of the *Paradiso* gives the implicit theme and logic of The Dreaming: *e la sua volontate è nostra pace,* 'His will is our peace'. But the gleam that lighted Judah did not reach the Australian wilderness, and the blacks follow The Dreaming only because their fathers did.

1953

Caliban Discovered (1962)

The history of the development of European knowledge of Aboriginal mentality, character and custom is a melancholy one. Australia, for some time neither a colony of exploitation nor one of settlement but a prison—for those guilty of 'inconveniency and hurt' in a land with 160 felonies punishable by death—was peopled by newcomers whose preconceptions of all they were to see can scarcely have been equalled. We could study what happened as the product of many things—the times, events, interests, conditions, personalities, policies—and of course they all had much to do with the painfully slow growth of understanding. But that would gild what must be said plain: what we are studying in the main is European bias expressing itself in hard, narrow and very nearly intractable prejudices which for a long time prevented the voice of objectivity from being heard. And we could as well dub it the history of misunderstanding as of understanding, for although bias has now gone, or all but gone, much misunderstanding remains.

In each of four centuries—from the 17th onward—over which the Aborigines have won European attention there were complicated warps of outlook towards them and, from those warps, the facts about them were given twists. We cannot set up single-sentence fictions about 'the 17th century mind' or the 18th, 19th or 20th century 'minds', or suppose that men thought differently in 1799 than in 1801. If such lines can be drawn—and let the historian of ideas do it—these are probably not the years on which to settle. Nevertheless, there were vast changes in mentality and atmosphere between 1644 (the time of Tasman and Hobbes), 1770 (the time of Sheridan, Johnson, Rousseau and Cook), and 1898 (the time of Trollope, Sir James Frazer, and Spencer and Gillen). We are thus dealing with several—at least four—distinguishable lineages of thought. The oldest can be linked with the first discoverers who barely—and grudgingly—accorded the

Aborigines the status of human beings. The second may be said, with a little courtesy, to have begun at about the same time: an attempt at objective observation of their racial style, material culture, languages, and forms of social life though, for a long time, only unconnected fragments of good knowledge resulted. The third was a rather brief phase of romantic idealism that stemmed in part from Rousseau's fiction of 'the noble savage' and in part from the whole 'trick and condemnation of civilisation'—with its vast changes of ideas, tastes and sentiments—in the 17th and 18th centuries. The fourth is difficult to categorise since it was a mixture of old and new things. In the early years of settlement insensibility towards the Aborigines' human status hardened into contempt, derision and indifference. The romantic idealism, unable to withstand the shock of experience, drifted through dismay into pessimism about the natives' capacity for civilisation. Objective observation went on, though in a sporadic way, and some of the best of all estimates of Aboriginal mentality, character and culture were made at that time by men who refused to be overborne by the prevailing indifference or gloom. To that medley evangelical Christianity and the new secular creed of progress added their power, but in an atmosphere far different from that of the first dismaying years.

    A new way of life had taken root. The western plains were open; the coasts were known; one exploration after another brought its excitements. Men dreamed of fortunes from virgin land and the golden fleece. The squatters toyed with the idea of political oligarchy; free men came in; the 'currency lads' to whom the colony was home as well as birth-place—Mr Commissioner Bigge noted how tall, awkward, quickminded and irascible they were—made radical demands on life; there was an obsession with money-making. New vistas, new ideas, new conditions, new problems. If in England 'the virtues of a Christian after the Evangelical model were easily exchangeable with the virtues of a successful merchant or a rising manufacturer' and 'a more than casual analogy could be established between Grace and Corruption and the Respectable and the Low' the transposition of the ethic in Australia was made easier by the presence of a now despised race. The pastoralists brushed them aside; here and there the Church ministered to them, even wept over them; and, among both, there was much talk of Providence's plan. But regret was 'hardly more reasonable than it would be to complain over the drainage of marshes or of the disappearance of wild animals'. A gleaning of the records of 1820–50 produces scores of sorrowful expressions of regard for 'the real welfare of that helpless and unfortunate race'; tenfold that number of condemnations of them as debased, worthless and beyond grace; and, one-hundredfold, acceptances of their inevitable extinction. To such mentalities, scientific study of the Aborigines could only be useless, worse, a waste. Study problems that would soon cease to exist?

We have spoken of 'lineages' of thought, not of formed traditions. Australia has few traditions—of its own, and as distinct from myths—by which living and thinking are disciplined. Its institutions have British forms but a coarsened content, and its ethos of life has an empty focus. No great issue in its history ever touched, let alone turned upon, Aboriginal affairs until the decade of the 1950s. For the rest of the time the three main mentalities—disdain, turning to dislike and contempt; romanticism, turning to despair and morbidity; and a bankruptcy of ideas, turning to indifference—in some fashion ran side by side, among different sets of men, until very recent times.

***

The first veritable primitives—Caribs, Eskimoes, Negroes—who were taken to western European capitals in the 16th century were objects of wonder but evidently not of disdain. The 'savages' of that time were rather the nearer barbarians, such as the wild Irish tribes. These were the 'vile caitiff wretches, ragged, rude, deformed' of which Edmund Spenser, self-exiled in Ireland, had written in the *Faerie Queene*, as were the 'savages' living 'as brute beasts' whom Captain Cuellar, a Spaniard from the wrecked Armada, saw when cast away on the west coast of Ireland. These were common 16th century views. At the very end of the 17th century John Dunton, an English traveller, could still write of the Irish beyond the Dublin pale with a more cruel contempt—'a nation of vermin' he called them—than was yet really characteristic of commentaries on the primitive peoples, though there had been an increasing denigration of them after the middle of the century, by which time the first reports of the Australian Aborigines had been made by the Dutch navigators. The transfer of sentiment from kith near at home to strangers at the world's edge was a concomitant of the upheaval of mind and life from which eventually would come the idea of a European civilisation. The idealisation of Europe's hopes for itself ran with the growing contempt for near and distant peoples untouched by the civilising process. The disdain for peoples who lacked 'civility', which, in the days before Europeans spoke of 'civilisation' in the abstract, meant broadly the dignities of social order and culture, was in some sense a measure of the pride taken in emancipation from the past, very much as, in the late 18th century, a romantic idealisation of natural society, in which there were no arts to fling garlands of flowers over men's chains, accompanied the disenchantment with Europe's own state of life. It was the fate of the Aborigines to be caught by the rising tide of disfavour and to be stranded by the ebb of romanticism.

The Dutch navigators and William Dampier, the Briton, who had brushed the coasts of the Australian continent, had formed the poorest opinion of the inhabitants. In 1606 Willem Jansz blundered along the western shore of what would later be called Cape York, under the delusion that it was part of New Guinea, and met 'savage, cruel, black barbarians who slew some of our crew'. Dirk Hartog in 1616 left a memorial of his visit in the west, and then for two decades a Dutch ship appeared every two or three years somewhere on the 5000 miles of coast between Cape York and Nuyts' Land. Nothing is known of their encounters, but it seems unlikely from later Dutch commentaries that they had anything favourable to say. In 1623 Jan Carstenz, trying to repeat Jansz' course, skirmished with the Cape York Aborigines at several places, kidnapping three and killing two in circumstances which warranted a higher opinion of their mettle than he recorded: 'the most miserable and unsightly creatures than any I have ever seen in my age or time'. Tasman, before his second voyage in 1644, was cautioned to beware of 'rude, wild, fierce barbarians' and, on his return from a long traverse of the northern and western coasts, reported that he had seen only 'naked, beachroving wretches' who seemed to him 'excessively poor, and in many places of a very malignant nature'.

There is little to choose between the Dutch viewpoint and that of Dampier. He was the first British navigator known to have landed on an Australian shore, and the first European to have described the Aborigines at any length. He made two visits (1688 and 1699) and his account of the inhabitants was such that he might have been lifting some of his phrases from the Dutch reports. In any study of the long and, on the whole, discreditable history of European outlooks on the Aborigines Dampier is a significant figure. How clear, candid and trustworthy his eye!—so long as one judges it by his descriptions or sketches of the flora and fauna of the unknown land. What delight to the new natural philosophers! In the flora, for example, every leaf was given its due shape, proportion and curl. But when he looked on the human inhabitants he could see only 'the miserablest people in the world', a 'poor, winking people' who seemed to him to 'differ but little from Brutes'. The new empiricism towards nature was one thing, towards man another. His descriptions were vivid, a little heartless, and in several respects simply wrong, as Sir Joseph Banks was to point out. Hair 'like that of the negroes'—wrong. Skins 'coal black, like that of the negroes of Guinea'—wrong. No food except weired fish (as Bradley also thought at first); no weapons suitable for catching birds or beasts (as Phillip also thought); no huts or shelters—all wrong, or but the accidents of place and occasion.

It was essentially this estimate that de Brosses, 'the ablest geographer of his time', kept alive by his mid-18th century description of them as 'thoroughly brutal, stupid, incapable of work, and insensible to the advantages of trade'. Many things to be said of the Aborigines at or soon after the foundation of settlement and to be repeated until the very end of the 19th century, were so reminiscent of Dampier's phrases that they might have been copied from him, as his from others. The simian imagery was a case in point. There the Aborigines stood, he has said, grinning at him and at one another 'like so many monkeys'. The simile persisted for an extraordinarily long time. One may dip into the commentaries almost at random and come up with an example. On 5 May 1788 Daniel Southwell, mate of H.M.S. *Sirius,* writing to his mother, said that Aboriginal antics were 'more like monkeys than warriors'; indeed, 'their chatt'ring, tho' something more sonorous, puts one in mind of these gents'. In 1827 the sardonic surgeon Cunningham referred to 'their abject animal state' and asked: were they not at 'the zero of civilization, constituting in a measure the connecting link between man and monkey tribe?' For, really, he said, 'some of the old women seem to require only tails to complete the identity'. M. Élie le Guillon, chief surgeon of the *Zelée,* identified them unhesitatingly in 1832 as 'Nature in its poorest and most imperfect stage, the link between ape and man'. The Reverend A. Polehampton, writing in 1862 of his experiences in Victoria during the gold rush, remembered them as 'little less ugly than the gorillas; which, indeed, to my mind, they much more nearly resemble than white men, or the higher type of blacks'. In the 1870s, when Anthony Trollope was likening the deportment of 'dignified' Aborigines to 'that of a sapient monkey imitating the gait and manners of a do-nothing white dandy', the Reverend J.G. Wood mentioned drawings—'widely circulated on account of their grotesqueness'—which gave an impression that 'the aboriginal is to the European what the spider monkey is to the baboon'. A member of the South Australian Parliament, Mr (later Sir) W.M. Sowden, described some of the (recently detribalised) Aborigines of Port Darwin in 1882 as 'less manlike than a grinning and chattering monkey', and in 1895 A.F. Calvert felt obliged to remonstrate with those who still thought of the western Australians as 'mere baboons'. Other racialist imageries may have had as long a history: few can have carried such an increasing load of obloquy.

The belief that the race had something less than human status was but the first of a series of European 'visions' of the Aborigines. Each the product of a cognitive structure of strong emotional tone, each subordinated experience to the narrowed understanding imposed by a mental framework, notice being taken only of those parts of experience which the mentality and sentiments could accommodate. It is a defect of the word 'vision' that it draws attention, not to the furniture of European minds, or to the ways in which the furniture was arranged by interests, but to the content of the resultant 'view'. However, it brings out usefully the different ways in which Europeans tended to 'see' the native Australians.

There have been perhaps seven or eight fairly distinct views which can be labelled, with little more distortion than is inevitable in putting a tag on any dominant tendency. They were visions of Caliban, of The Noble Savage, of The Comic Savage, of The Orphan or Relict of Progress. Of Primal or Protozoan Man, of The Last of His Tribe, of The Ward in Chancery, and of The Reluctant European. Broadly speaking, they followed one another in that order, but they also overlapped and even became mixed up, so that to assign or limit any one of them to a precise period is difficult. Innumerable men whose lives overlapped had views of the Aborigines with nothing in common. There were always odd men out, of independent mind, or behind or ahead of general tendency. The extent to which any vision was actually influential over any period, and amongst whom, is a task for an historian of ideas. So far the subject has scarcely been investigated.

A history of the views of individuals or the passing emphases of policy could do violence to broader, deeper realities. The notion of successive visions could thus be a wrongful image. We may find, as already suggested, that we are dealing with lineages of thought which have all been present from the beginning but braid their way through Australian history rather like the inland rivers that flow, disappear, and emerge again in what had seemed waterless country. To single out for unusual emphasis the visions of Caliban and of The Noble Savage, as we have so far done, is justified by the fact that they provided a stock of elements which a changing Australian social philosophy has rearranged or revalued in other visions.

If The Noble Savage is Caliban humanised and untruly romanticised, then The Comic Savage is The Noble Savage reversed and mocked in a Georgian mirror. It is perhaps at first less obvious that The Orphan of Progress is still in part Caliban, and in part The Comic Savage, now made ignoble too, for the axioms of Victorian progress denied him not only the capacity for civilisation but also the moral right to it. Primal Man, the creation of the anthropologists of the late 19th century, is one of the most curious visions, not quite of Caliban, but of a very close collateral, perfectly expressed by Sir James Frazer:

> in the secluded heart of the most secluded continent the scientific observer might reasonably expect to find the savage in his very lowest depths, to detect humanity in the chrysalis stage, to mark the first blind gropings of our race after freedom and light.

Primal or Protozoan Man, unable by nature long to survive ('their doom is to be exterminated; and the sooner their doom be accomplished—so that there be no cruelty—the better will it be for civilization', wrote Anthony Trollope) became The Last of His Tribe when Henry Kendall, 'the sweet singer' of the Australian bush, as a poet sometimes can, found words for the coming wisdom of his day. The vision of The Ward in Chancery is perhaps a break in the logical sequence. A generation ago demographic reality revealed The Last of His Tribe to be a figment. He was succeeded, though slowly, by a vision of The Ward in Chancery. One may still see in The Ward the faint outline of The Orphan or Relict, now become the foster-son of The Noble White Australian, prepared to make an *amende honorable* under a new social philosophy of conscience. The Aboriginal, having long been denied the privilege of being himself, is now to be given the greater privilege of becoming an Australian. It is from some such sequence that the modern Aboriginal emerges as The Reluctant European.

In a large sense, then, our study of the Aborigines is necessarily also a study of European preconceptions of them. This is as true of the development of scholarly knowledge as of the general affairs in which they and Europeans became intermixed.

***

To understand Aboriginal culture, the customary way of life, is to see that it had its own civility and that, in particular matters, it was touched by genius. Those facts are being recognised only now, after an intellectual, psychological and moral struggle of the utmost difficulty. It is essential to study the growth of knowledge concerning the Aborigines against the background of that struggle.

Some fascinating matters of ethnic and cultural history have to be left open for lack of knowledge. The Aborigines are involved indissolubly with the human history not only of New Guinea, Indonesia and south-east Asia but also of places beyond. At present we do not know exactly how. But only the short-sighted would set limits to the horizons that will open up when we understand more about the provenance of the Australoid skulls found as far away as Palestine and the valley of the Indus; or of the quite mysterious stone-culture that left pestles, mortars and clubs in New Guinea; or of the older lithic cultures, so reminiscent of many found within Australia, that are being studied throughout the vast archipelago and on the littoral of Asia.

There are other things too, 'faint as a figure seen at early dawn at the far end of an avenue': the trail of the sacred bullroarer—the 'magic wheel' of Simaetha's passion—that leads from the continent through New Guinea and thence to antiquity; the startling likeness between some Aboriginal art-motifs and others still extant in Asia and Africa; and the haunting resemblances that some have suggested between Hindu music and that of Arnhem Land.

We may have to rest content now with what we know about the first European adventurers. But all that is the nearer scene: we are divided from them by only one two-thousandth of the time that lies between the present and the first coming of the dark people to Australia. As our knowledge of what took place over those aeons is built up—by archaeology, and by studies in comparative genetics, linguistics and anthropology—we shall understand more readily the tragedy of the events that occurred after Europeans arrived. For it will make more clear two things—the immensity of the gulf between the two traditions, and the decay of the old sense of humankind in the European tradition that allowed Herodotus to write in a neighbourly way of strange peoples, and made him think Cambyses mad for scorning Persian and Egyptian religious rites.

The first meetings of black and white took place at a time when, given the ideas then ruling in Europe, tragedy had to follow, whether from plain insensibility or—worse—romantic sensibility, and—worse still—religious and scientific preconception. The newcomers at first were simply incapable of grasping that the Aborigines had any culture at all. When in the course of time ideas had changed sufficiently to let them see that Aboriginal life might have a virtue of its own they saw that virtue through a disenchantment with their own life and time. Then objectivity had a long encounter with religious, secular and scientific preconception. By the time a truly empirical anthropology emerged perhaps half the continent had been emptied of its native people.

***

From his brief stay ashore at Botany Bay and from observations made at other places in 1770 Sir Joseph Banks judged that the country was very thinly populated. Captain Cook was of the same opinion. So too were some of the original colonists in 1788 but there were others who, taking counsel of fears which were consonant with ignorance of the land and its inhabitants, thought uneasily about the unknown numbers of savages who might hem them in. One diarist felt that 'there is something odd in their never being seen but in small (numbers), except by accident, tho' there is every reason to suppose they are numerous'. In the next few months he and others saw groups large enough to appear to confirm that surmise. On one occasion he sighted 'a body of near a hundred drawn up with an unexpected degree of regularity, having something the (appearance) of discipline...' Later (from a boat, and at a safe distance) he was the mystified witness of some sort of demonstration by more than 200 Aborigines on the foreshore at Manly Cove. On the harbour itself trustworthy counts had been made of canoes in which there were between 133 and 147 people at different times. Two large assemblies, one of which numbered more than 300 and stayed in the same vicinity for about a week, disclosed themselves on the south shore between Port Jackson and Botany Bay. How to interpret such observations? What mode of life did they betoken? How could even small numbers survive in a land so 'destitute of natural resources' that in a whole month hunger-driven European hunters could obtain only three small kangaroos? Cook (according to Hawksworth) had been inclined to think that the Aborigines did not even 'live in societies, but like other animals were scattered about along the coasts, and in the woods'. Phillip himself never at any time comprehended how they could survive in the wilds. He could not fathom 'whether they live in the woods by choice, or are driven from the society of those who inhabit the coast, or whether they travel to a distant part of the country'. It seemed to him 'hardly possible that they could obtain any kind of food with their spears'. It took

Bradley four months to discover that they had any other kind of food than fish. Many of the colonists continued to think so for a long time.

Here was a mystery. One of its products was a strong undercurrent of anxiety that, somehow, somewhere in the unknown bush, large numbers of savages might hover and descend at any time. Nearly a year after the landing credence was given to a panicky report that 2000 Aborigines were mustering a mile from Sydney. A military party, hurriedly assembled, found that there had been but 50, all of whom had fled when some convict workers had pointed spades at them in the manner of guns. The apprehensiveness of course had many causes. The bush itself was a mysterious dimension, seeming to have a brooding, sinister quality. The enclosing scrub, the silence, the tracklessness, the strangeness had a disorienting effect, and made timorous even men of hardihood. 'The bare idea of being lost in one of the arms of Port Jackson' struck David Collins with horror: 'insanity would accelerate the miserable end that must ensue'. There was the sense too of being 'sequestered and cut off ... from the rest of civilized nature'. Added to it was the more or less continuous dread of want in 'a country so forbidding and hateful as only to merit execration and curses'. But the most productive cause was the inability to bring to perspective the numbers and modes of life of the native population.

***

The colonists without knowing it were looking on part of a marvel of adaptive culture. From coast to coast the continent was peopled by upwards of 500 congeries of nomadic bands which were spaced in such a way that in plan the effect was like that of an enormous spider-web. It was in that sense a marvel of nature too because it duplicated the territorial divisions exhibited by all natural species that colonise their environments. The exact number of congeries may never be known because the violence, disease, depopulation and drift which came with Europeans emptied large areas very quickly, often before the arrival of Europeans in or even near them, and long before scholarly study began. The territorial system collapsed before it was entirely understood but enough is known of it to allow the principles to be stated in firm outline.

The basic arrangements of life were most remarkably similar throughout Australia. The core of society was a localised band with a mean size probably between 20 and 50 persons depending on the richness of locale. Each band was in the main a cluster of closely related families which co-operated to exploit with minute care a particular tract of country known intimately because of the accumulated experience of many generations. For much of the year the Aborigines lived in the open, sheltering only from the most intense or persistent heat, cold, rain and wind. Against such conditions they might build small, low huts and shelters of bark, boughs and grass, or take passing refuge in caves or under rocky overhangs, but having by habituation developed a high tolerance of discomfort they were often content with the shade of trees by day and a wind-break or dew-shield by night. In a few regions which were exceptionally well-off for water and food, or so pest-ridden and water-logged that only restricted sites were habitable, the rough hutments sometimes served as semi-static camps. The bands utilised their home-tracts according to a seasonal time-table. From time to time they ranged farther afield into the territories of neighbours, or shared with them the use of common lands, but each group identified itself with a continuous locality which it and others regarded as peculiarly its own. The whole continent was divided between many thousands of such bands—there could well have been as many as 10,000—each of which systematically combed its locale. The activities, at least in the short term, did little to change the landscape except that the burning of grass to flush game produced bushfires that often ran for long distances. The vegetation suffered severely and, in consequence, plants and animal populations must have changed radically over millennia of occupation, enforcing new human adaptations, but there can have been few countries where more than 1000 generations left so few physical traces. After a place had been left for long unvisited only thinned-out timber around a pool, a grass-grown midden, or abandoned stone-tools might suggest human habitation. A quarry where domestic ochre, or stone for tools and weapons, had been mined; a manufactory where the stone had been knapped and ground; a rock fishing-weir in a water-course or on a coastal flat; a ritual site where stones had been lined or piled into geometric shapes; a cave or shelter where artists had painted, pecked, engraved or abraded real or imaginary creatures and strange symbols—only such handiworks, in or on stone, had much chance of long survival. Wood and bone, where exposed, soon crumbled. The softer possessions of a people who went naked except in the cold southern winter, when furred skins were sewn into rough coverings, survived for long only in freakish circumstances.

The composition of the bands, the life-relations between them, the use of home-tracts and range-surrounds, and the extent to which the ranges of different bands might interpenetrate, are matters for detailed discussion. It will suffice here to say that a local band, tied—though not rigidly restricted—to a given territory was the foundation-group of society, if for the present the individual extended domestic family may be overlooked. The sizes of each band's home-territory and farther range (it is crucial to distinguish the two) varied with climate, topography, vegetation and food-supply. The reliability rather than the amount of rain was a primary determinant. On the semi-arid steppes and sandy deserts of the centre, where on an average less than seven inches of rain fell annually, and none at all might fall for many consecutive years, an individual family needed several hundred square miles to sustain itself. To speak of the 'density' of population is unrealistic for other than sedentary peoples but, for what it is worth to say so, the regions most favourable to nomadic ecology could not support much more than two persons a square mile. In only a few restricted areas was anything like that density attained. The figure of perhaps one domestic family to every 50–100 square miles, over a region as large as the United States less the State of Maine, represents the reality of occupancy about as well as any fiction of averages can. But, however inhospitable, every part of Australia seems to have been within the domain of a proprietary band, or was shared between the ranges of several.

There were larger regional aggregations of bands, which may be called 'tribes', but with a warning that the label, though it tags a definite grouping, denotes at best a rather loose congeries of bands with a common tongue and common customs. The Aborigines gave primary loyalty to the band to which they belonged, not to the congeries to which the band belonged. The common tongue was often, perhaps usually, a dialect of a larger family, and many bands were at least bilingual; gifted persons could be trilingual or more. Substantially common custom could be shared over even larger regions. The fact that several bands spoke one, or much the same tongue or had identical or similar customs did not imply that they owed each other allegiance on those grounds, or should act with, for or against any other group. Quite often the members of a tribe had no name for themselves, though they usually did for other tribes and for each of its constituent bands. Some were content to refer to themselves simply as 'we who speak such-and-such a language'. It was a universe of assured identity such that no tribe had particular cause to flaunt a name as the badge of identity, since no other had an interest to challenge it on that score. On the other hand, each band, or at least a nucleus within it (the difference is again crucial), had and preserved jealously an unmistakable identity. The structure and composition of such groups are intricate matters which remain in marginal doubt in several respects, but the broad principles are clear. Each band, of which there might be from two to twenty-five or more in a tribe, distinguished itself or its nucleus from all others by a name, or by several names, which might be those of the people, the language, a characteristic custom, the territory, its topography, the type of vegetation, a natural species, or the like; something that would differentiate it from all others, and be the ground or symbol of its identity. Any such name, in couple with a known locus, gave a band or its nucleus co-ordinates which, being those of no other, established and perpetuated its absolute identity.

The distinction between a band and its core or nucleus would take up many pages. A sketch of the main points will suffice here. A group of persons of *both* sexes closely related by *male* lineage constituted the core or nucleus, and may therefore conveniently be termed a 'clan'. They regarded themselves, and were regarded by others, as the living members of an ancient stock credited with having lived together in that locality from the beginning of things. At any time there were always more males than females of the stock living within the band of which it formed the core.

In all but exceptional instances females living permanently with a band were unmarried girls or infants. The reason was that two rules were being observed. One was a rule of law which required a mature female to 'marry out' of her clan under the principle of exogamy. The other was a rule of practice which led to a woman's living with her husband's band, of which his clan was the core. Thus, the mature, married women of a particular clan were normally to be found in most cases living with bands based on other clans, sometimes in very distant places, but usually within a restricted region. Married women often visited their paternal clan-kin, and might flee to them from cruel or angry husbands, or return to them as unwanted old widows. But any mature women living permanently with a band were 'foreigners' to it—the wives of men belonging by lineage to its clan; the wives of men visiting it from other bands; or the wives of men who for one reason or another—there were many possible reasons—preferred life with a clan and band not their own. At any time a band's complement might include persons of any or all such categories. Its membership was thus inconstant, whether in the phases of clustering or those of dispersal. But the mixed membership and the inconstancy did not, could not, create problems of identity or jural right. Only those members of a band who were also by male lineage members of the appropriate clan had title to the clan's name and religious traditions, and primary rights in the territory in which it was corporate.

The clan tie with locality expressed an intimacy which can hardly be over-stated. Every natural species was identified and named through its varieties; all plants and animals of use to man were known and their properties and habits well understood; the whereabouts, constancy and inconstancy of all water-supplies were imprinted on the memory; the relative bearing of any physical feature to any other was so much a part of common knowledge that, in family territory, orientation by night was almost as absolute as by day. Contiguous bands came to know each other's territories almost as well as their own because of constant visitation. The domain of any group of families was latticed by paths taking the shortest or the most practical routes between important food and water sources. Their placement articulated an immense stock of practical knowledge of what could befall that particular domain in short and long term climatic conditions, and they served like a venous system by which the band nourished itself on the natural yield of the terrain. Life could thus proceed in high confidence, catastrophe apart. No Aboriginal questioned his ability to survive in the places, and by the methods, of his ancestors. He was at one with his environment, neither its slave nor its master. Nevertheless it was a hard environment. A band could not keep together as a continuous mode of association or stay continuously at one camp. It had to divide into smaller parties in times of shortage and, in extremity, even into individual families, but it would reaggregate when good times came and would then cluster as long as possible in a well-favoured place to which it might have the sole prerogative but which it sometimes shared in tense amity with others. At times and places hundreds of people, drawn from many bands and tribes, might thus assemble. Friendly bands, not necessarily from the same tribe, might then fuse camps, interchange members, or commingle freely in the festivities, fights and rites that often were made features of just such occasions. But eventually the assemblies would break up and disperse to their own domains. The bands could be called 'nomadic' but it was a nomadism of a limited kind, bounded and even land-locked rather than unbounded and freeranging, because of the bond between a band and its traditional territory. This was fundamentally a religious relation. The Aborigines conceived it as a union of earth, sky and water on the one hand with spirit, body and personality on the other. A band did not 'own' land in the European sense. It and territory were twain; the connection was inextinguishable, the territory inalienable.

Having been 'shut off for centuries from the co-operative intelligence by which nations who are neighbours have created their common civilization' they had had to adapt ancient or invent new methods of sustaining life. They had done both with remarkable efficiency. They had no idea that plants could be cultivated or animals domesticated but in any case there were no suitable plants, or animals except the wild dog, which they gentled into human service. Nor did they know anything of the manufacture of metals: their tools, utensils and weapons were made of stone, bone, shell and wood. Nevertheless, they lived everywhere confidently, even where food and water were exiguous and, in most regions and at most times, they not only lived well but sweetened existence by spirited pursuits of life in no way concerned with mere survival. The problem of ecology on the physical plane was to maintain an equilibrium of effort and return and, on the social plane, to satisfy a want-structure at as high, constant and complex a level as the equilibrium would allow.

One of the main employments of intelligence was to keep low the fixed and variable costs of material life. Traditional routines, which had proved their dependability—the proof being that a long line of known, and therefore trusted, men had used and taught them—were clung to conservatively. Why look for new solutions of problems already solved satisfactorily? The 'savage' or 'primitive' façade concealed a rational calculus of gain and loss in terms of return for allocations of time, energy and skill, and exemplified a least-cost solution of maintaining an acceptable plane of material and social welfare. The least-cost routines left free time, energy and enthusiasm to be expended—as they were, without stint—on all the things *for* which life could be lived when basic needs had been met: the joys of leisure, rest, song, dance, fellowship, trade, stylised fighting, and the performance of religious rituals. Under the ethos of Aboriginal life, ecology and economy were carried on with minimal regard for the long tomorrows, not from improvidence, but because futurity was not in itself a problem. At the same time, where the costs of futurity could be anticipated and lowered, that was done. Rivers and tidal shallows were permanently weired for fish; wells were dug and maintained; heavy grindingstones were placed conveniently for later visits; rafts and canoes were put at dangerous crossings.

Their material equipment might better be described as brilliantly simplified than 'simple' or 'primitive'. It was evaluated critically for, as it was adapted functionally to, a range of understood conditions brought to the reckoning of principle. For example, in the rigorous environment of central Australia, where aridity put the highest premium on mobility, excess weight and complexity of equipment would have raised needlessly high the effort-costs of life. A single implement—the spear-thrower—was developed, with great ingenuity, to serve multiple purposes. It could be used also as a container for liquids, as part of a fire-saw, as a scraper or adze or chisel, as a shield and even a musical instrument. A man could clasp in *one* hand his spears and a device which not only increased their force and range but also met a range of needs for which special implements otherwise would have had to be carried. A perfected invention thus economised weight, mechanical complexity and effort so as to increase a hunter's mobility, range and striking force. Some of the peoples along the northern coast had seen the Macassan use of sails and probably fire clay-pots but evidently had made no sustained attempt to copy them. The northern-most tribes of Cape York had been able to compare and reject the efficacy of bows and arrows against spears. The explanation in each case was probably the same: such innovations offered no rational advantage in the Aboriginal ecological scheme, and would probably have affected for the worse the stabilised economy of human effort.

***

The pattern of growing irritation and hostility which had so vexed Phillip after May 1788 becomes intelligible in such a background. It was the first of the endless collisions which were necessary to occur throughout Australia because of the modes of Aboriginal land-occupancy and social organisation. There were to be as many collisions as there were bands and, in the least-favoured areas, as many as there were last-ditch watering-places for which the new livestock would compete. The records suggest that it was not until after the 1820s that there was a sharp realisation that 'every tribe has its distinct ground; and they will, of course, rather adhere to it, dispute its possession, and take revenge on the intruders, than fall back on other tribes of their own countrymen, and fight their way inch by inch with them'; even longer before it was admitted that 'we are not able to drive them away so as to secure ourselves, without their extermination'. Until that time the necessary to and fro of Aboriginal life seems to have remained merely puzzling. There had been, as we have seen, a flush of true interest to begin with but by the mid-1790s a 'harsher, angrier note' began to sound. The Aborigines were depicted as people who delighted to exhibit themselves as 'monsters of the greatest cruelty, devoid of reason, and guided solely by the worst passions'. By the early 19th century,

> experience was driving more and more settlers as well as civil and military officers to explain the treachery, cruelty, revolting habits and inferiority of the aborigines, and the ineffectual efforts of all attempts to civilize them, by their innate characteristics as a race. Experience was also convincing more and more people that violence and reprisals were the only methods the aborigines could understand. No one contemplated the extinction of the aborigines with remorse, guilt or regret; nor did anyone testify to a common humanity, let alone any sense that they too were made in the divine image.

In such a setting there could be no real impulse to develop informed knowledge.

The colonists, entering what they imagined to be a howling wilderness, were as mistaken in the broad picture as in the narrow. An immense network of human connections stretched over the continent in every direction. Every local band was a knot in the network. Any band's horizon was at the farthest a few days'—in the arid centre, a few weeks'—walk away, but each band was in touch with neighbour bands, and they with their neighbours. Well-defined arterial routes of communication and trade linked the coasts of the Indian, Timor, Arafura and Carpentarian seas with the Pacific and Tasman coasts. The local bands had no comprehension of the continental aspect; they knew the routes only in regional stretches; but the fact of totality was there; and many bands enjoyed precious goods, songs, dances, tales and rituals which were known to have come from long distances. Inland tribes had not heard of the sea and only those on the northern coasts had a glimmering of lands and peoples beyond; within the continent, history had set up traditional enmities, particularly between groups of tribes which, once widely separated, had become neighbours with sharply contrasted tongues and customs; but the lattice of local paths and the network of continental routes were evidence that Australia had been humanised from end to end before European civilisation arrived.

'To a philosophic mind', wrote the Reverend Thomas Fyshe Palmer, who had been transported for political enthusiasm, 'this is a land of wonder and delight. To him, it is a new creation; the beasts, the fish, the birds, the reptiles, the plants, the trees, the flowers are all new—so beautiful and grotesque that no naturalist would believe the most faithful drawings and it requires uncommon skill to class them.' Of the native inhabitants, not a word. Yet, given wit and patience, there was not an important fact concerning the topography, water supplies, natural products, climate and transits of any part of the continent which might not have been learned from the Aborigines. The hardships the newcomers suffered in discovering what was already known were self-inflicted wounds. The extent to which they misread their own interests were illustrated in 1796 when some of them, having ignored Aboriginal warnings that the Hawkesbury river was about to flood, saw their dear possessions swept out to sea. And this at a time when the colonists' descriptions of Aborigines might have been the work of Trinculo or Gonzalo in their worst moods. Perhaps the only difference was that a wry, not ungenial contempt had replaced Prospero's envenomed censure.

1962

'The History of Indifference Thus Begins' (1963)

On this first inhabited spot, from that time tranquillity ceased, and the foundation of a new country usurped the seat of silence.

—George Barrington, *The History of New South Wales,* 1810

The Instructions given in 1787 to Captain Arthur Phillip, the Governor-Designate of the intended penal colony in New South Wales, required him 'by every possible means to open an intercourse' with the Aborigines. He was ordered to begin barter with them, to estimate their numbers, and to report how association could be turned to the colony's advantage, but these practical aims were to be attained in a humanitarian way. He must 'conciliate their affections', enjoin everyone to 'live in amity and kindness with them', and punish all who should 'wantonly destroy them, or give them any unnecessary interruption in the exercise of their several occupations'.

Phillip, before leaving England, thought the Instructions entirely possible of performance. He nagged the authorities about scores of matters, but took the racial problems in his stride.

> I shall think it a great point if I can proceed in this business without having any dispute with the natives, a few of which I shall endeavour to persuade to settle near us, and who I mean to furnish with everything that can tend to civilize them, and to give them a high opinion of their new guests.

He even nurtured the hope that he might 'cultivate an acquaintance with them, without their having an idea of our great superiority over them, that their confidence and friendship might be more firmly fixed'. Before as well as after the landing, he gave 'strict orders that the natives should not be offended, or molested on any account and advised that, wherever they were met with, they were to be treated with every mark of friendship'. He forbade anyone to fire at them with ball or shot, and made clear that he would regard the killing of an Aboriginal as seriously as the killing of a European. 'This', he wrote, 'appears to me not only just, but good policy'.

His appreciation of what he would encounter in New South Wales drew on the experience of Captain Cook and Joseph Banks, the only authorities. Cook had found it necessary to fire a gun at some Aborigines who sought to oppose his landing in Botany Bay in May 1770, and (according to Dr Hawkesworth) he subsequently found that

> after the first contest at our landing they would never come near enough to parley; nor did they touch a single article of all that we had left at their huts, and the places they frequented, on purpose for them to take away.

Banks, before a Committee of the Commons in 1779, had given his immense authority to an opinion that 'there would be little probability of opposition'. He described the Aborigines as 'naked, treacherous' but 'extremely cowardly' and said that they 'constantly retired from our people when they made the least appearance of resistance'. To that impressionistic picture Phillip added a romantic gloss. He developed a theory that 'the only means of warding off a conflict with the natives was to place confidence in them'. From the moment of landing, that was what he tried to do. The approach spoke volumes for the idealism, and also for the muddled theory of human nature and society, which characterised him.

The older Aborigines of Botany Bay in 1788 would have remembered Cook's visit in 1770 and the main events of the week that he spent there. But that experience may have made the nine days' wonder between 18 and 26 January 1788 seem more overwhelming. During that period thirteen ships, eleven British and two French, entered the bay. They arrived in four divisions—one ship on the first day, three on the second, seven on the third, and two (the French squadron commanded by M. de La Pérouse) on the ninth. Any impulse among the Aborigines to mass against the strangers must have been paralysed by the increasing size of the divisions over the first three days. The ships' companies—seamen, soldiers and civilians, numbering 290—would have been visible, and the Aborigines may well have caught a hint too of the convicts, 717 all told, crammed below the decks. Such numbers were beyond their powers of computation or clear expression. They could only have likened them, in their characteristic similes, to the leaves of a tree or to ants in a nest, and felt at a loss to act. After the arrival of the third division there were three clear days on which they may have taken some sort of measure of the prodigy before them. Then, on 24 January, Phillip's hurried preparations, at the first sight of the French approach, to move the First Fleet from Botany Bay to Port Jackson, could well have suggested to them that all the ships were about to go and, like *Endeavour,* be seen no more. But the substitution of the French for the British in Botany Bay, on 26 January, would have dashed their hopes, and then added a new mystification for, with their quick ear for language, they would soon have realised that they were in touch with two different peoples speaking unlike tongues. What they made of it all is of course unknown. One can but piece together the rough outline of their reaction from exiguous entries in the colonists' journals, diaries, despatches and letters.

The records make much of the Aborigines' apparent hostility at first sight. As the ships entered Botany Bay, Lieutenant Phillip Gidley King, on *Supply,* saw 'several of ye natives running along, brandishing their spears'. David Blackburn, master of the same ship, noted the same thing: 'The Natives as we saild in Came Down to the Edge of the Clifts Making a Noise & Lifting up their Spears'. When *Scarborough* arrived next day, Private John Easty remarked on the 'great many Indians' who, naked and black, 'came down to the shore and shroutted att us and held up there weapons over their heads and shaked them att us'. The same thing happened at Port Jackson. To Daniel Southwell, the mate of *Sirius,* it seemed that

There was a something frantick in the manner of these petty veterans, their menacing gestures being occasionally interrupted by long considerings and excessive fits of laughter, in which there seemed to be more of agitation than of those pleasing emotions that usually excite risibility.

But the shaken spears did not necessarily indicate outright hostility, and the cries of *war-re, war-re,* which were presumed by the early colonists to mean 'go away', or 'bad, you are doing wrong', may have been (as Harrington later suspected) no more than a conventional response to anything startlingly new. Universally, the Aborigines used such gestures at all meetings of great significance; there was always something of ritual in them; and curiosity must have been at least equal to fear or anger.

At the first landing some Aborigines, according to King:

immediately got up and called to us in a menacing tone, and at the same time brandishing their spears or lances. However, the

Governor showed them some beads, and order'd a man to fasten them to the stem of the canoe. We then made signs that we wanted water, when they pointed round the point on which they stood, and invited us to land there. On landing they directed us by pointing to a very fine stream of water. Governor Phillip then advanced towards them alone and unarmed, on which one of them advanced towards him, but would not come near enough to receive the beads which the Governor held out for him, but seemed very desirous of having them, and made signs for them to be laid on ye ground, which was done. He (ye native) came on with fear and trembling and took them up, and by degrees came so near as to receive looking-glasses &c and seemed quite astonished at ye figure we cut in being clothed. I think it is very easy to conceive of ye ridiculous frame we must appear to these poor creatures who were perfectly naked. We soon after took leave of them and returned on board.

The man's first intent, under Aboriginal convention, would have been to discover Phillip's identity, the purpose of the visit—to find drinking water—having already been disclosed. In advancing alone Phillip did the right thing. But he should then have named himself, and asked after the other's name, both of which he could have done without difficulty by using simple signs. To press goods on the man at once was also a mistake. Under Aboriginal custom they could not have been given or taken without consideration of return. Phillip's offer probably appeared at least two-edged. Later, the Aborigines must have concluded that Europeans were simply soft-headed because of their largesse with valuable things. The notions of forcing friendship, and of winning liking by prestations, were psychological and sociological nonsense. But at the time, to one officer, the report 'savoured much of fellow-feeling and humanity'.

Soon after daylight on the 19th, a fishing-party saw the same group of natives, who seemed 'much more confident than they were the night before'. But although three boats explored part of the bay no other natives were seen. On the 20th, there were two landings, one under Phillip, who was said to have found the natives 'very sociable and friendly', the other under Lieutenant King, who found them neither: they 'hollor'd and made signs for us to return to our boats'. One of Phillip's front teeth was missing and the fact gave him instant standing among the Aborigines, who practised tooth avulsion as an initiatory rite. The deference paid to him by the other colonists must also have impressed the watchers, who would have dined out on every detail of dress, deportment and conduct. King, with a notable lack of success, tried to emulate Phillip's calm unarmed advance, bearing gifts of beads and baize. The goods were taken, but then the Aborigines 'in a very vociferous manner desired us to be gone, and one of them threw a lance wide of us to show how far they could do execution'. King thought it wise to retreat. On the way to the boats, he again offered presents; this time the Aborigines refused them and, 'ten times more vociferous', threw spears directly at the party, which was in a minority of five to twelve. King now felt the risk too great; he had a gun—loaded with powder only—fired; and at the report the natives 'ran off with great precipitation'. When the party had re-embarked, Phillip joined them, and at once showed both the persistence which characterised him and a something in his bearing and address which impressed the Aborigines.

> We relanded ... and ye same body of natives appeared, brandishing their lances and defying us. However, we rowed close in shore, and ye Governor disembarked with some presents, which one of them came and received. Thus peace was re-established, much to the satisfaction of all parties.

That was the first true interaction. On both sides, it probably caused as much confusion as it removed.

The Aborigines were not sure for several days that the strange beings who came on shore were truly human. They were particularly astonished by the hats, clothes and weapons, probably thinking them, as in the case of other Aborigines in many parts of the continent, incredible extensions of the body. They were also puzzled, by the hairless faces, to decide the sex of the strangers. There was 'a great shout of admiration' when one of the sailors was ordered to 'undeceive them' on the question of sex, and another when the bashful King covered a woman's nakedness with a handkerchief. The Aborigines offered the Europeans women, which were declined; the Europeans offered the Aborigines wine, which they tasted and spat out. On the whole, the Aborigines won the honours for hospitality; they singled out the man who had flung the spear, and stood 'pointing all their lances at him and looking at us, intimating that they only waited our orders to kill him'; or so King deluded himself. He probably puzzled the natives by making a special point of giving the man a present! Had King given the order to throw, he would have seen a marvellous exhibition either of spear-dodging, at which the Aborigines were brilliantly adept, or of how not to hit a man by the narrowest of margins. The parting was amicable enough, and selective memories of the reports led to later impressions of an 'easy reception' and 'a kind of cautious friendship'.

But some stereotypes which the colonists had brought with them were also vivified. 'Those poor creatures', under whose gaze King had felt ridiculous, were to David Blackburn 'to all appearances the Lowest in Rank among the Human Race'; to Edward Home, 'I think, the most miserable of the human form under heaven'; to Southwell, 'more like monkies than warriors'; to Bowes, 'altogether a most stupid insensible set of beings'; and to the log-keeper of *Fishburn,* '...quite harmless, only inclinable to thieving'. The same writer recorded that 'it was with difficulty that the Captain kept his hatt on his head'. But two seamen, 'straggling into the woods without arms or anything to protect themselves, sailor like, met with some natives, men, women and children, who were *very*

very friendly...' And David Collins, Phillip's secretary and Judge Advocate, was storing up the impressions that enabled him to write: 'how tractable these people are, when no insult or injury is offered, and when proper means are employed to influence the simplicity of their minds'.

While the ships were at Botany Bay, there were warning signs that injury *was* being offered. The seine nets were cast:

> no sooner were the fish out of the water than they began to lay hold of them, as if they had a right to them, or that they were their own; upon which the officer of the boat, I think very properly, restrained them, giving, however, to each of them a part. They did not at first seem very well pleased with this mode of procedure, but on observing with what justice the fish were distributed they appeared content.

A work-party cleared a path to a supply of fresh water: 'the natives were well pleased with our people until they began clearing the ground, at which they were displeased and wanted them to be gone'. Saw-pits were about to be dug: 'they expressed a little anger at seeing us cut down the trees'. But the colonists attached little significance to such signs, and apparently did not connect them with a pattern of reaction that became noticeable within a few days of the transfer to Sydney Cove. The Aborigines now showed a progressive disinclination to come near the settlement, and their general behaviour became less predictable. That the colonists wondered why says much for their eyeless judgment of their own doings.

On his first visit to Sydney Cove on 21 January, Phillip had found the Aborigines more confident than those at Botany Bay. The fresh water in the cove, the best supply in Port Jackson, made it a natural gathering place, and one can scarcely doubt that members of the local band, having seen the transfer of the First Fleet on the 24th and 25th, would have watched from the bush, on the 26th, the landing, masting of colours, the firing of a *feu de joie,* and the preparations for encampment.

Others, increasingly drawn by the spectacle and uproar, must have been agog at the relentless, baffling activity: scores of men felling the forest, hundreds marking out squares, mounds of goods piling up, endless traffic between ships and shore, martial parades, and boats exploring the harbour arms. Not even the scale of the visitation could have been clear until the nineteenth day, when the last of the convicts were herded ashore. The Aborigines had had no experiences by which to judge such things, or to see in them shapes of permanence. The realisation that it *was* an invasion, and that the strangers meant to stay, could have come only slowly. When at last it came, the dismay must have been profound.

As the days went by, there would have been sharp eyes and ears on all that happened. It is quite clear from the records that, even at Botany Bay, the Aborigines had begun to categorise the strangers. Worgan's *Journal* noted on the third day that

> they did not like the soldiers and made signs for us to take them

away, before they would venture to come near us. One of them was bold enough to go up to a soldier and feel his gun, and felt the point of his bayonet, looked very serious and gave a significant 'HUM'!

White's *Journal,* two days later, remarked that 'from the first, they carefully avoided a soldier, or any person wearing a red coat, which they seemed to have marked as a fighting vesture'. Now, the four social groups—officers, soldiery, seamen and convicts—would have been plainly distinguishable, and such formations must have seemed bizarre and inexplicable. Darkness probably hid from the Aborigines the first orgiastic meeting of the male and female convicts on the night of 6 February 1788: Bowes' *Journal* reports that 'The men got to them very soon after they landed, and it is beyond my ability to give a just description of the scene of debauchery and riot that ensued during the night'. But they may well have seen, though perhaps from a distance, something of other events that disfigured the first weeks of transplanted civilisation—the drunkenness and fighting, the drumming of malefactors out of camp, the attempts by convicts to escape, the first flogging (29 January), and the first hanging (27 February). A place which ten convicts, including one woman, had tried to flee by 23 February can have had little attraction for those outside it. There is little mystery in the Aborigines' apparent aversion.

Some of the early writers give the impression that, once the British had left Botany Bay, encounters with the Aborigines fell away abruptly. That was not actually the case. During the first six weeks only two Aborigines visited the settlement, but between 29 January and 29 February seventeen meetings were thought sufficiently important to be mentioned in journals. In two cases the Aborigines fled; in thirteen their conduct ranged between wariness and boldness; in two, conflict occurred; on 4 February some of them pelted a European seine-party with stones and, on the 19th, a group making a daring theft of iron tools near the settlement had to be 'peppered with small shot'. At Botany Bay, the French also had troubles. From unknown causes, they were 'often obliged to fire on the natives, for that they are become most dearing and troublesome'. M. de La Pérouse seems to have been at least as idealistic as Phillip, and his orders as strict, but he did not share Phillip's theory and therefore probably acted differently. Experience in the South Seas had made him suspicious of 'the perfidious caresses' of all savages. He thought the Aborigines 'extremely mischievous', complained that 'they even threw darts at us immediately after receiving our presents and caresses', and felt compelled to build a protective stockade. Plainly, the policies of trust and mistrust were equally unsuccessful.

The Europeans' inability to understand why they were shunned or attacked was obviously, though only in part, an expression of their total ignorance of Aboriginal life. They had no idea, it seems, that they were crowding at every place on to a confined estate whose every feature and object entailed proprietary rights and religious significances. Nor did they suspect for some time that they were upsetting a delicate balance between population and food supplies. For example, it took Lieutenant Bradley four months to feel he had sufficient proof that the Aborigines 'seek other food besides fish'. Phillip never comprehended how they could support themselves in what seemed to him the sterile, foodless bush. The whole system of nomadic ecology was so woefully misunderstood that, even half a century after the landing, the explorer Grey could still find pleasure in describing it. The first colonists had no comprehension that Sydney Cove had vital importance for a whole band, which was necessarily driven to depend on other places for food and water, to the embarrassment of other groups. But the settlement itself was a sufficient cause for the Aborigines to keep at a distance. In February, one convict was publicly hanged; twelve were given a total of 1172 lashes; the numbers of sick increased; and from such spectacles they would have turned away with loathing or fear. There must also have been repellent external evidence of the tension, hatred, brawling and drunkenness that, in spite of ferocious discipline, were turning Sydney Cove into what Clark later described as a 'whore's camp'—'I would call it by the name of Sodom', he said, 'for there is more sin committed in it than in any other part of the world'.

For such uncomprehended reasons the colonists, in the course of February, usually saw only very small numbers of Aborigines, whose behaviour seemed unpredictable. At the sight of Europeans, individuals or small parties hid or ran away, especially in the less frequented parts of the harbour; even near the settlement they showed wariness; none would come near at all if the soldiers were present, or unless guns were laid down. There were nevertheless some confident, even bold, encounters. The recorded meetings must have been but a fraction of the actual total, but those that are known to have occurred were less complete and frontal than had been the case at Botany Bay. Relations worsened during March, but the same mixed pattern continued through fewer encounters. Some Aborigines raided a fishing party; two convicts were wounded and a number were threatened; someone threw a spear at an officer and did not flee when a gun, loaded with ball, was fired. Even Phillip had a tiff, and was warned by a raised spear, during a visit to Botany Bay, where he showed the mixture of calm, courage and wrong-headedness that was to characterise most of his dealings with them. Now too came the first complaint about European maltreatment: an Aboriginal man, pointing to marks or bruises, told Phillip as best he could of a beating he had received. There were nevertheless many meetings that were civil, friendly, or without incident.

In April and May the recorded meetings were fewer again and Hunter observed 'the natives to decrease in their numbers considerably', but did not realise that the winter-pattern of dispersal had begun by which the coastal clans spread out along the sea-board, though not inland. The differences between the 'tree' or 'forest tribes' inland from the coast and the 'brush' (i.e. heath) or 'coastal' peoples were not yet understood, nor was there any grasp of the contrasted marine-estuarine and woodland ecologies. It became evident, especially in May, that they were very short of food. When given it by the colonists, 'they eat with an eagerness that convinced us they must have been very hungry'. But civil meetings continued. Some small groups came close to the settlement and, at Botany Bay, a European party slept tranquilly near a large gathering of men, women and children. However, a new element appeared: several instances were noted of open fear amongst the women, and of their menfolk's refusing to let them go near the colonists. Three convicts were murdered and one injured; a calf was wounded by a spear; some clothes were stolen. It was apparent that there was 'a pattern of growing irritation and hostility'.

The prevailing tendency among the colonists was to attribute the less understandable aspects of Aboriginal conduct to 'the fickle, wavering disposition of all savages', a proposition which revealed all too clearly what was wrong with their view point. At the same time Aboriginal insouciance and indifference struck some as puzzling. 'This day two of the natives app'd in camp without testifying any mistrust or indeed curiosity ... the novelty of such a scene seem'd in a g't measure to pass unnoticed by them'. A few 'passed close to the Sirius, without seeming to express, by their countenance or actions, either fear, curiosity or surprise'. Such experiences allowed no single opinion of the Aborigines, either as persons or as social beings, to form. Where one colonist remarked '...a Quiet, Inoffensive People', and credited them with being 'total strangers to Personal Fear and have a Quick Sense of Injury', another would note but '...an appear(ance) of stifled apprehension, with now and then a forced laugh and a look of astonishment at all they saw'. No one could fathom their reluctance to become close friends. Even the thoughtful, observant Watkin Tench asked himself: was it possible that Captain Cook had done something in 1770 that now 'prevented the intercourse that would otherwise have taken place'? One fact seemed particularly baffling: 'there is something odd in their never being seen but in small (numbers) except by accident, tho' there is every reason to suppose they are numerous' (although the same writer had seen 'a body of near a hundred drawn up with an unexpected degree of regularity, having something the app'ce of discipline'). The 'something odd' eventually led to uneasiness. Major Robert Ross, the officer commanding the marine companies, was 'by no means of the opinion' that the Aborigines were 'that harmless, inoffensive race they have in general been represented to be'.

When, on 30 May, two convicts were killed, Phillip's perplexity was such that he determined to force a confrontation—not with punitive intent but, so he said, to try to make the Aborigines who had been concerned aware of how highly he disapproved of any injury to them. But it is a little doubtful if that was his sole intent; some of the dead convicts' possessions were missing and, according to White, 'the governor was resolved, on whomsoever he found any of the tools or clothing, to shew them his displeasure, and, by every means in his power, endeavour to convince them of his motives for such a procedure'. Many colonists suspected at the time, and later all accepted, that the Aborigines 'must have been provoked and injured by the convicts'. In an incident a week before, when some articles had been stolen and recovered, a convict had knifed one Aboriginal man ('the proof could not be got—they were dismissed without coming before a criminal court') and it was supposed that the killing of the convicts was a retaliation. One of the Governor's ideas had been to display drawings showing a European shooting an Aboriginal and then being hanged, and an Aboriginal spearing a European and then being hanged. As like as not, the Aborigines would have reasoned: shoot an Aboriginal and hang any European; spear a European and hang *some other* Aboriginal.

In two minds, and certainly with only a hazy notion of what he was going to do, Phillip put himself at the head of an armed party of eleven—nine redcoats and two convicts, in Aboriginal eyes the feared and the despised—and plunged into the bush. So clumsy an excursion was probably bound to fail, and fail it did. No one knew the country well; a large, arms-bearing party asked for evasion; and, without a word of the language, Phillip could not have made his meaning clear—anyway, not without risking worse misunderstanding. In the event, they all got lost; they met no natives at all on the first day, though they saw some fishing placidly on Botany Bay; and, on the second day, they blundered on two very large groups whose presence had been entirely unsuspected. It is not necessary to suppose that such large gatherings took place from hostile intent. The Aborigines were also affected by the 'rage for curiosity' which had all the colonists, including Phillip, in its grip, and there is much to suggest that they felt the fascination of the novel—and the horrible. The thunder of the ordnance on the King's birthday would in itself have been enough to bring all the Aborigines between Broken Bay and Port Hacking to the neighbourhood of Port Jackson.

The first group numbered about three hundred, and among them were some who 'at first seemed rather hostilely inclined, and made signs, with apparent tokens of anger, for us to return', though some individuals 'shewed little fear or distrust'. By coolness and restraint, Phillip was able to come to an amicable relation. But some of the credit also lay with the Aborigines; indeed, only the foresight of one of them saved the Governor from a surprise meeting with the second large group, not in view, but less than a mile away. His luck might not have held a second time. Had there been anything practicable in his plan, the meetings gave him a good opportunity to explain himself, but he seems to have made no attempt to do so, having seen nothing to connect either of the parties with the murders. He did not know that not far away was the head of another convict who had been killed some time earlier. But the Aborigines he encountered must have known, and they may well have concluded from the whole episode that to kill convicts was not only of no account but might even induce Phillip to reward them. The fact of this murder was revealed three weeks later by a runaway convict who had returned, half starved, only to be hanged for theft. According to his story, the Aborigines did not use him ill, and even on one occasion fed him. But they would not have him with them, and towards the end of his adventure 'would have burned him' had he not escaped.

A large group, again more than three hundred strong, was still between Port Jackson and Botany Bay a week later, but they 'walked out of the track our people were in, & let them pass without showing any mischeivous intention'. The knowledge of such gatherings disturbed the colonists, who began to take precautions. Parties of fewer than six armed men were forbidden to go into the bush and at least one ship kept its boats within the cove. Nevertheless, there were still several friendly encounters, and not until the end of the month did the undercurrent of anxiety show how strong it was. Towards midnight on 27 June, the voices of many Aborigines—some sentinels supposed from twenty to thirty—were heard from darkness near the women convicts' tents. The voices (a sure sign that no attack was intended) ceased abruptly when the sentinels cried out, no doubt quaveringly, the midnight's 'all's well'. Whether the report was true, or the product of nerves, was never settled. The continuing nervousness was exemplified by an incident six months later. A rumour that two thousand armed Aborigines were mustering a mile from Sydney town led to a momentary panic. A second report gave the number as four hundred. A military party, hurriedly organised, found that there had been but fifty, all of whom had fled when a working-party of convicts pointed spades in the manner of guns.

The hope of amity and trust between the races had obviously miscarried by the middle of 1788. Whether fewer meetings occurred as the year went on, whether writers bothered less to mention them, is perhaps not certain, but the number of recorded incidents grew and, with them, the Governor's perplexity. On 9 July the Aborigines attempted what he called the only 'unprovoked act of violence'—the forcible seizure of a catch of fish after some had been shared; on the 22nd, they chased a convict party for two miles; on the 27th, they speared a convict and next day stoned a sailor. In August, September and October the story was much the same. During those months, several men were killed, and others wounded or threatened; one (a marine) disappeared; there was a daring raid on the hospital's herd of goats, and a quarrel over a fish-catch; a spear was thrown at an officer taking a census, and one at Phillip's own party after returning from a walk to Broken Bay, where he had met nothing but friendliness and thoughtful kindness. It now seemed that the Aborigines near Sydney had ceased to discriminate between officers and men, soldiery and convicts, stragglers and formed parties, and had either lost some of their respect for firearms or would take advantage of any reluctance to use them.

A significant change took place in Phillip's outlook at this stage. It is smoothed over in his own account, but emerges through his secretary's.

> On the 24th (October) a party of natives, meeting a convict who had straggled from the settlement to a fence that some people were making for the purpose of inclosing stock, threw several spears at him; but, fortunately, without doing him any injury. The governor, on being made acquainted with the circumstances, immediately went to the spot with an armed party, where some of them being heard among the bushes, they were fired at; it having now become absolutely necessary to compel them to keep at a greater distance from the settlement.

No talk now of conciliating their affections; or of living with them in amity and kindness; of confident friendship without display of force; of giving them a high opinion of their new guests: the turnabout was complete. Yet, a week afterwards, Phillip could still admit that 'it is not possible to punish them without punishing the innocent with the guilty...' Two months later, at the end of 1788, he made another turnabout, and the way in which his mentality veered is a question of primary interest for the historian of racial relations.

As the winter of 1788 approached, conditions in the settlement deteriorated. Fresh provisions grew scarce; the catches of fish fell off; and the cutting of building-timber over a large tract frightened the game away so that few kangaroos, which were the colonists' only fresh meat, were caught. Sickness and scurvy increased, and deaths from all causes mounted to more than sixty. Every day ailing men foraged for foodstuffs and medicinal plants, and fishing parties went out almost every other day. The strain on food supplies provoked the Aborigines, and they must have been irritated too by the physical disturbances. Every week marines tramped to Botany Bay, and exploration parties went north and west. The local bands thus had both cause and occasion to keep at a distance, while making what retaliation they could. And, as if understandable causes of dismay were not enough, there were also events to play on their secular and superstitious fears. On 4 June, in celebration of the King's birthday, *Sirius* and *Supply* fired 21-gun salutes at sunrise, noon and sunset. On *Supply,* Blackburn noted in his journal that 'No cannon had ever been fired since our Arrival on the Coast', and wondered whether the Aborigines 'might take such a Terrible Noise as a Denunciation of War'. On 22 June, as the sun declined, the shock of an earthquake 'came from the South West like the wave of the sea Accompanyd by a Noise like a Distant Cannon. The Trees shook their Tops as if a Gale of Wind was Blowing'.

At about this time, Watkin Tench, that 'candid and liberal mind', with many others was puzzling over the fact that the intercourse with the Aborigines was 'neither frequent nor cordial'. He had at first suspected it to be due to their fear, jealousy or hatred. Then, as he wrote:

> I confess that, in common with many others, I was inclined to attribute this conduct to a spirit of malignant levity. But a farther acquaintance with them, founded

on several instances of their humanity and generosity ... has entirely reversed my opinion; and led me to conclude, that the unprovoked outrages committed upon them, by unprincipled individuals among us, caused the evils we had experienced.

Phillip's outlook developed in much the same way. In the midst of the troubles of May 1788 he assured Lord Sydney that 'nothing less than the most absolute necessity' would ever make him fire on the Aborigines, though he tacitly admitted that he had come close to it. But he could not yield his thesis that confidence was the key. He harped on that theme until early 1790, by which time he had destroyed all Aboriginal confidence and may have lost his own. In 1788, being still unable, evidently, to grasp that two communities so constituted could not imaginably live together without friction, and being deeply committed to what Tench, with some irony, would later call, 'those speculative and laborious compositions on the advantages and superiority of a state of nature', he had necessarily to find a scapegoat. The convicts were readymade for the role.

Perhaps *Blackwood's Magazine* went a little far (in 1827) in describing them as 'the most murderous, monstrous, debased, burglarious, brutified, larcenous, felonious and pickpocketous set of scoundrels that ever trod the earth', but they were a very hard lot, if not for being where they were, then for withstanding their fate with such desperate vitality. They were probably at the bottom of some, perhaps many, of the worst troubles; the records are not very explicit; understandably, because the marines declined to supervise the convicts and their supervisors had to be of their own kind. It seems certain, however, that they had much to do with the Aborigines openly, and the surreptitious traffic was probably constant. Illicit relations were easier by night than by day, and it was recorded that 'neither the fear of death or punishment prevents their going out at night'. The most condign reprisals—in one case, 150 lashes and fettering for twelve months for a party which had 'daringly and flagrantly broken through every order which had been given to prevent their interfering with the natives'—had little effect. The documents were curiously silent about sexual traffic between Europeans and the 'sooty sirens', as one appreciative officer called them. But in a society in which even some officers had convict concubines, and in which women were few (the sex ratio among the convicts in 1788 was three to one), the male convicts probably made persistent efforts to gratify their appetites through the native women. There was, as well, much purloining of Aboriginal fishing-gear, weapons and canoes by men desperate for food and without equipment of their own. But soldiery and seamen were probably also involved in such delicts. They certainly helped to irritate the natives by the 'rage for curiosity'—a mania for collecting artifacts. No amount of blame heaped on the convicts can sufficiently explain the general troubles. The Aborigines did not always attack them and, when they did, it could have been because such miserable wretches were as convenient a target as they were, for Phillip and his officers, a convenient scapegoat.

Racial relations had thus passed through three phases by the last months of 1788—the 'cautious friendship' of the first few days; the 'neither frequent nor cordial' intermezzo of the late summer and autumn; and the often open animosity of the winter and spring. In November, Phillip had to admit that the Aborigines 'now avoid us more than they did when we first landed'; rather oddly, in view of the October raid, he did not seem to connect that fact with his own conduct. A fourth phase now began. The Governor professed himself 'tired of this state of petty warfare and endless uncertainty', of 'inconsequent fraternization and inconsequent hostility', and of a stalemate in which 'not a native has come near the settlement for many months'. Having, in October, found it 'absolutely necessary' to force them away, he now saw it as 'absolutely necessary' to force them in. He decided to capture some by force. There were evidently two motives, one immediate, one more remote. Immediately, as Tench put it, kidnap

> would either inflame the rest to signal vengeance, in which case we should know the worst, and provide accordingly; or else it would induce an intercourse, by the report of which our prisoners would make of the mildness and indulgence with which we used them. And farther, it promised to unveil the cause of their mysterious conduct: by putting us in possession of their reasons for harassing and destroying our people.

Or, as Phillip phrased it somewhat later,

> it was absolutely necessary that we should attain their language or teach them ours, that the means of redress might be pointed out to them if they are injured, and to reconcile them by showing the many advantages they would enjoy by mixing with us.

More remotely (but perhaps nearer the bone), according to Tench again:

> intercourse with the natives, for the purpose of knowing whether or

not the country possessed any resources, by which life might be prolonged, as well as on other accounts, becoming more and more desirable, the Governor resolved to capture two more of them.

That observation was made some nine months after the first capture, but perhaps the lapse of time had only uncovered the thought.

Arabanoo, the first prisoner, was taken at Manly Cove on 31 December 1788. A second man escaped after a desperate struggle, and no doubt spread a tale of treachery. The captive (according to Tench's description, which may have idealised the man) was about thirty, not tall but robust, and with a face that suggested manliness, sensibility, and thoughtfulness rather than animation. His voice, at its best, was soft and musical. He behaved with cleanliness and decency, was quickly courteous to women, and gave an impression of gentleness and humanity. Children flocked to him. He showed gravity and steadiness, together with dignity and independence, brooking no insult but giving none. Although peaceable and easily led, he often turned the tables, with humour, against those who teased him. Strong liquor repelled him: he turned away from it with disgust and abhorrence, as he did also from the sight of a convict being flogged. He had, or showed, less intelligence than other Aborigines the colonists came to know, but he endeared himself more: 'perhaps the only native who ever attached himself to us from choice; and who did not prefer a precarious subsistence among wilds and precipices, to the comforts of a civilized system'. The 'choice' came about when Phillip unfettered him, leaving him almost free of restraint, out of gratitude for help to native victims of a smallpox epidemic which, in the second quarter of 1789, brought about the deaths of perhaps half the Port Jackson Aborigines and unknown numbers elsewhere. For a while there were three natives in the settlement—Arabanoo, and a boy (Nanbaree) and girl (Abaroo) who had been found bereft. Arabanoo might then have escaped but did not try to do so. On 18 May 1789 he died from the disease. Phillip thought his plan 'utterly defeated'. Arabanoo had had no real opportunity to talk with other Aborigines, so his capture and death can have taught them nothing, unless it was that friendly overtures could not be trusted. If it taught Phillip anything then it was not visible in his subsequent conduct.

At that time, Aborigines at any distance from Sydney, seeing the Europeans possibly for the first time, still 'showed every sign of welcome and friendship to the strangers'. But around the settlement 'the same suspicious dread of our approach, and the same scenes of vengeance on unfortunate stragglers, continued to prevail'. Even a Negro convict, who twice tried to thrust himself on the Aborigines, was repulsed. Within the settlement, conditions were worse and morale had slumped. Faction, jealousy and spite were at work. There had been a falling off in loyalty to Phillip. Many colonists now felt like John White, the sick, over-worked Surgeon-General, that they were in a country 'so forbidding and so hateful as only to merit execration and curses'. Phillip, moved now by the second rather than the first motive, ordered two more Aborigines to be made captive. That was done, much against the grain of the officer who had the duty, on 25 November 1789.

One of the men, Colby, escaped after a week; the other, Benelong, five months afterwards. He was to become something of a personage in the colony, but that was later. According to Tench's account (which certainly did not idealise Benelong, or Baneelong as his name was first spelled) he showed himself, during his captivity and immediately afterwards, to be about as unlike Arabanoo in personality and character as well could be. He appeared a volatile egotist, mainly interested in love and war; a tease, a flirt and very soon a wine-bibber; a trickster and eventually a bit of a turncoat. His captors cared for him as well as they could in what were now 'desperate circumstances' because of food shortage. Phillip at this time seems to have been divided between a rising fear of the Aborigines and a falling confidence in them. In February 1790 he wrote that there was now little to be feared; that the Aborigines had never betrayed a confidence placed on them; and, on what evidence is not clear, that they had continuing confidence in 'some of us'. He and his officers tried to hide from Benelong the facts of the famine in case, somehow, the knowledge leaked out to the surrounding Aborigines and led to an attack. Benelong nevertheless felt the pinch and it often made him 'furious and melancholy' although, on the whole, the enforced association seemed to please him. But he escaped by a trick on 3 May 1790. Of stronger personality than Arabanoo, and quicker to learn, he had had excellent relations with many of the Europeans, including Phillip. He seems to have taken away with him a smattering of English, a love of liquor (possibly he invented the name 'tumbledown' by which the Aborigines knew it in the early years), an assortment of scrambled facts about Europeanism, and doubtless a fund of stories—including, probably, one about a white woman he had kissed. After the escape, Phillip still had thoughts of an attack in one corner of his mind: in

June, he wrote that there was little risk of an attack on any building; 'not that I think they want innate bravery—they certainly do not—but they are sensible of the great superiority of our arms'. Significant relations then apparently ceased for four months. Apart from the fear of other captures, want must have driven the Aborigines towards the outer fringes of their domains. Both garrison and convicts were starving: 'the dread of perishing by famine stares us in the face'. A fifth phase of relations started in September and October 1790, by which time, incidentally, many of Phillip's domestic difficulties were easing. A chance encounter at Manly Cove between some of his officers and perhaps two hundred Aborigines—among them Benelong, emaciated and at first difficult to recognise—brought the Governor hurrying to restore friendship. On that occasion his courage and magnanimity never showed to better advantage, and his ignorance of Aboriginal mentality and tendency to worse. He was speared in an incident, the accounts of which differ in important details, but there seems little doubt that the fault was mainly his. He ignored signs of equivocation before the attack took place; he indulged his 'rage for curiosity' at what was clearly the wrong time; he ignored a minatory gesture; he used precisely the wrong word to calm either an affronted or frightened native; and he reached for a weapon even though only with the intent of discarding it. In all these respects he was more his own victim than that of his assailant.

The deeper motive of the attack remains a mystery. Historians tend to regard the assault simply as the act of a frightened man. That seems probable. There were at least six major grievances which could have been expressed in the attack. They would have been held (1) by the man who struggled free when Arabanoo was captured; (2) by relatives and friends of Arabanoo, grieving over his death; (3) by Colby, his relatives and friends; (4) by Benelong, his relatives and friends; (5) by men with a marriage claim on Abaroo, the nubile girl held in the settlement; and (6) by relatives and friends of Nanbaree, the young boy held in the settlement. Any one or all would have been a sufficient motive for a public remonstrance against Phillip. The actions of his attacker, one Wileemarin, up to the time the spear was thrown, were consistent with a remonstrance that need not necessarily have led to a direct assault. Perhaps Phillip's worst mistake was to shout words intended to mean 'bad! bad!', which was more an accusation than an appeal or warning. And had he stood still, instead of advancing, Wileemarin might not have thrown. To his credit, he allowed no retaliation, and harboured no resentment.

The wound, from which he recovered slowly, was the penultimate irony of his policy. Perhaps the ultimate irony was that when, mainly through Benelong, in early October 1790, numbers of Aborigines began to come freely to the settlement and, at long last, it could be said that 'from this time our intercourse with the natives, though partially interrupted, was never broken off', other Aborigines from Rose Hill, farther west, now came to Sydney to express 'great dissatisfaction at the number of white men who had settled in their former territories'. The western bands, seeing the treasures being lavished on the now-mendicant Benelong and his friends as part of the price of peace, no doubt drew conclusions which, had Phillip known of them, must have surprised and disappointed him. That was the start of a chain-reaction which, as settlement expanded, and even ahead of it, drew one tribe after another into parasitism on Europeans.

At the end of 1790 Phillip's policy came to its sixth phase. His huntsman, a convict named M'Entire, was speared at Botany Bay and died slowly and miserably. The man was widely known to be detested by the Aborigines, having long 'been suspected by us of having in his excursions shot or injured them'. The murder put Phillip in a great passion: 'I am fully persuaded that they were unprovoked and the barbarity of their conduct admits of no extenuation'. He ordered out a punitive party. At first he determined that he would have ten Aborigines shot and their lopped heads brought back, together with two captives. The attack was to be made by surprise and force: no duplicity, no signs of amity, no response to friendly advances, 'for such conduct would not only present treachery but give them reason to distrust every future mark of peace and friendship on our part'. Women and children were not to be harmed, nor any huts burned. The two men taken were to be hanged 'in the presence of as many of their countrymen as can be collected after having explained the cause of such a punishment'. Here indeed was a change from the man who, earlier, had said that he could not bear the thought of 'punishing the innocent with the guilty'. But he asked for suggestions from the officer ordered to command the force, and instantly fell in with part of a proposed modification: to capture six, execute some, and later send back the others to spread the lesson. Phillip then gave his final order:

>...if six cannot be taken, let this number be shot. Should you however find it practicable to take so many, I will hang two and send the rest to Norfolk Island for a period, which will cause their

countrymen to believe that we have despatched them secretly.

The dutiful men went out, carrying axes and bags for the heads. On a first occasion, fifty-two strong, they failed to take any Aborigines, though they saw some. Much to their embarrassment they met Colby, whom Phillip had tried to bribe—and, in desperation, incapacitate by stuffing him with food!—to stay away from Botany Bay so that he could not warn the Aborigines of the impending raid. A second sortie, ten days later, collapsed in tragi-comic circumstances, and the whole idea was called off.

Had the punitive expedition succeeded, it must have greatly damaged Phillip's reputation. Possibly it might have led to his indictment or recall: there were men in the colony who, from various motives, might have capitalised it as others were to try to do in a somewhat similar case in South Australia in 1840. In the upshot it cost him the respect of at least one officer, who was revolted by the affair and kept it on his conscience. A modern historian has wondered why, since 'it was such a very abstract sin'. Doubtless Lieutenant Dawes had no taste for murder. Phillip could not have made it appear even judicial murder. He did not intend to hold a trial; he wanted to hang some natives, and any would do. There were other curious aspects of the incident. The Governor brushed aside the known character of M'Entire, a tremendous villain who, knowing he was dying, was heard to 'accuse himself of the commission of crimes of the deepest dye, accompanied with such expressions of despair as are too terrible to repeat'; although he denied any particular wicked offences against the Aborigines, no one believed him. Moreover, Phillip nagged Benelong, who was known to have a particular loathing of M'Entire, to go with Colby in search of the murderers; and at one stage he expected Colby—'Botany Bay' Colby, as he was called—to act against his own kin, the Botany Bay band.

After this revealing affair, Phillip's stay as Governor lasted a further two years. Over that time, according to an historian, 'the native question sank into unimportance', which means that no one bothered any more about it. The Aborigines commingled freely with the colonists, and it was recorded that 'a great many have taken up their abode entirely among us', so that 'every gentleman's house was now become a resting or sleeping place for some every night; whenever they were pressed for hunger, they had recourse immediately to our quarters'. Whether the Governor imagined that his policy had now succeeded remains uncertain, for he did not say, but there is evidence that the status of Aborigines was already in transition, and one may trace to this period the beginnings of the scorn and dislike of them, and the indifference to their fate, which were to become so strongly characteristic of Australian mentality. Thomas Watling, an artist-convict who arrived at Port Jackson just as Phillip was preparing to leave it, compared the prisoners' lot with the indulgence shown to the Aborigines, and commented bitterly: 'this may be philosophy, according to the calculation of our rigid dictators; but I think it is the falsest species of it that I have ever known or heard of', and of course he was right.

The Governor had brought the harbour clans into close continuous touch with all classes of the European populace, in accordance with his idea that 'every means shall be used to reconcile them to live amongst us' but, as far as the record allows one to judge, saw nothing wrong with the outcome and, to all appearances, washed his hands of it. To the officers the Aborigines were

> an amusement and an alleviation of the post's tedium. To the convicts they were people inferior even to themselves. They tried to take their own wrongs out on the black man or to make what profit they could out of him.

The well-intentioned hope of preventing contact with the convicts lest 'the women be abused and the natives disgusted' thus perished. Few of the other good things that Phillip had hoped would come from close association really eventuated, except that many Aborigines picked up enough English to make themselves understood; indeed, their linguistic facility began to be noticed in the first few days at Botany Bay. In 1792 George Thompson recorded in his *Journal:*

> they are very quick in learning to speak English, and will repeat any sentence after you immediately, particularly any tune. When in their canoes, they keep constantly singing while they paddle along. They have the French tune of Malbrook very perfect; I have heard a dozen or twenty singing it together.

A few colonists learned a little of the Port Jackson dialects, but the officers who seem to have had the gift of tongues, or a lasting interest in Aboriginal culture, did not stay in the colony, so that their knowledge had little effect; so little, indeed, that thirty years later a missionary complained that 'no one has yet attempted to study the language'. That was at a time when it was still official policy to 'ease the natives into a civilized community' and, west of the Blue Mountains, at Bathurst, where the calamity of Port Jackson was being repeated, the first Christian service ended with 'a very excellent, appropriate sermon, strongly impressing the justice, good policy and expediency of civilizing the aborigines or black natives of the country, and settling them in townships'. For many years after the 1790s no significant use was made of Aboriginal knowledge of the best routes through the country, of tracts suitable for settlement, or of useful natural products. The disrupted bands certainly learned nothing of 'the advantages they will reap from cultivating the land', and racial violence became more or less constant.

At Phillip's departure there were already present both the elements, and the conditions for the persistence, of two realities which continued without material change, except for the worse, over the next 150 years. One was a pattern of racial relations, the other a structure of racial equities. They were the products of a process—meeting, sporadic violence, a general struggle, and the imposition of terms by the stronger—which always appeared wherever settlement went. After a true economy formed, in the second decade of the nineteenth century, the pattern contracted: one side or the other plunged straight into the general struggle. The colonists' 'mania'—the word is their own—for stock and land soon disclosed as axiomatic that 'a hunting and pastoral economy cannot co-exist within the same bounds'. Consequently, Aboriginal society survived only outside the pastoral bounds. Within them, the racial pattern—dominance and subjugation—became a rule of practice, and the structure of equities—the Europeans' maximal, the Aborigines' minimal—became if not an open rule of law, then its tacit convention.

During the five years under study there were two societies interacting in a single field. An ethnocentric approach, either in anthropology or historiography, to the facts of a two-sided racial struggle, must be regarded as insufficient. One cannot accept as *intellectually* adequate the judgments that dismiss the Aborigines as 'a melancholy footnote to Australian history' or are content, after some remarks on the sadness of it all, to say that history made of them 'a codicil to the Australian story'. To point out too that 'the aboriginal race has always possessed enthusiastic friends, but the friends have never agreed upon a consistent and practical policy for the black man's preservation' transfers, a little too blandly, an onus to where it does not belong. The primary axiom of settlement, or at least of development—that Aboriginal and European society could not or must not be allowed to co-exist—allowed little, if any, room for such a policy, even had it been practicable, which may well be doubted. It seems to follow that one cannot make full human sense of the development of European life in Australia without reference to the structure of racial relations and the persistent indifference to the fate of the Aborigines; in short, without an analysis of the Australian conscience. Part of such a study would be the apologetic element in the writing of Australian history, an element that sticks out like a foot from a shallow grave.

One cannot dismiss the fact that three realities co-existed with the unfolding of 'the Australian story'. Racial conflict persisted wherever any

Aborigines survived; many Aborigines made continuous efforts to adapt themselves to new conditions of life; and, among a few Europeans, an interest in the subjugated race never wholly died. The relevance of those facts may have been unappreciated or denied; they may have been passed over in the writing of history; but, without them, there could have been no ground or spring for the renascent humanitarianism of the 1930s. In other words, there was more than an accidental correspondence between the ruin of Aboriginal, and the making of European, life in Australia. There was, in fact, a functional concomitance. The interdependence was more clear at some times than at others.

It was particularly clear in the decades of the nineteenth century in which material development and the spoliation of the native life were most intense. The vilification of the Aborigines reached its pitch precisely over that period. Few national histories can have afforded a more blazing and odious rationalisation of ugly deeds. The social historian does not have to depend on an art of discovering obscure correlations to document the facts. In the 1870s, Anthony Trollope probably spoke for a majority of Australians. 'Their doom', he said of the Aborigines, 'is to be exterminated; and the sooner that their doom be accomplished—so that there be no cruelty—the better will it be for civilization'. In the next decade, Percy Russell wrote:

> Her shield unsullied by a single crime,
> Her wealth of gold and still more golden fleece,
> Forth stands Australia in her birth sublime,
> The only nation from the womb of Peace.

Phillip's period is interesting because it produced the materials whose decay-products made the ground fertile for such rank growths. The vision of primitive man was already trifocal—romantic, realistic and sardonic. As might perhaps have been expected, the collapsed romanticism turned into violence, the realism into indifference, and the sardonicism into contempt. The ensemble of violence, indifference and contempt suited the mood and needs of a transplanted people. What makes the case for a relational history, within a field containing two peoples, is the continuous working of a single influence with two victims—a sightlessness towards Aboriginal life, and an eyelessness towards the moral foundation of Australian development. Let us call it simply the fact of indifference. It denotes a whole syndrome of psychosocial qualities, which were as much an enabling cause or condition of Aboriginal ruin as they were of the shaping of European mentality and life in Australia. One cannot readily call to mind any important issue or problem, as the outcome of which Australian life became what it became, in which there was more than a derisory regard for Aboriginal concerns. That fact, if true, supports the thesis that the destruction of Aboriginal society was not the consequence of European development, but its price, which is a very different thing. The intuition of that fact was the maggot in Trollope's justification of the worst, and the demon in Russell's mythologising of the best, in Australian history. The year 1791 is a natural starting-point for a study of the consequences, among a people of British moral traditions, and among their victims, of a moral indifference which expressed socially, and inter-racially, the main postulate of settlement. The disposal of land, the development of law and order, the distribution of political power, the recognition of human rights, and the administration of justice must all have taken a different course, had it not been for the suffocation of conscience. And a number of chickens would not now be coming home to roost.

Phillip has been eulogised, in many ways no doubt rightly, as 'an ideal founder for any new colony', but only in respect of his management of European affairs in New South Wales, not in his dealings with the Aborigines. In that field, and by the test, not of what he said or may have wished, but of what he did and what it led to, Phillip emerges badly. One is hard put at times even to recognise the man said to have been 'endowed with common sense, kindliness, breadth of vision, firmness and sincerity'. He was undoubtedly courageous, kindly and of good intent. But many of his transactions with the Aborigines lacked common sense; his vision of them was so warped by presupposition that he misunderstood their character as persons and social being about as badly as he did the two-sided racial situation; and his 'sincerity' was all too soon overborne by considerations of 'good policy'—indeed, he appeared to forget all about them during the last two years of his stay. Apparently at no time did he see himself as a possible architect of their ruin, which in fact he was. But he seems to have been as impercipient towards the European society taking shape at Sydney. On his departure in 1792, he believed the colony to be 'approaching that state in which I have so long and anxiously wished to see it' whereas, within a month, it began to disintegrate under tensions he had helped to construct. By that time also he had induced the Aborigines in large numbers to become mendicants on the settlement. At the very doorstep of Government House there was 'a rendezvous for the blacks, where the soldiers joined them, singing and dancing in the evening', and no doubt sharing stronger pleasures as well. Nothing survives in the records to suggest that he saw anything amiss. Historians seem disposed to attribute all that was good in early Australian foundations to his courage, determination and prudence, and all that was bad to the conditions, including the human material, that limited him, but 'no historian would dare to speculate whether the pioneer's high reputation would have survived had he been forced to remain and face the problems of the next five years'. Among these problems were the degradation of many, and the alienation of most of the Aborigines within several days' march of Sydney. Given the fact and the constitution of the settlement, the upshot for the Aborigines of course would have been much the same, probably worse, under another Governor. Little as it is, that is perhaps all that can be said. One of his naval captains thought that 'God

Almighty made Phillip on purpose for the place, for never did man know better what do to, or with more determination see it done'. On the other hand Lord Howe, the Commander-in-Chief of the Channel Fleet, had hinted to Lord Sydney at the time of Phillip's appointment that he was scarcely the man 'for a service of this complicated nature'. In any study of Australian history in which Aboriginal affairs are put in the forefront, Lord Howe's judgment has much to recommend it.

Much has been said, and said rightly, in Phillip's defence. There was no hint of general principle in his Instructions concerning the Aborigines. At the most, he could find a *modus vivendi*. He experimented with the two notions—assimilation and expulsion—which have always polarised Australian thought. But, while making proper allowance for the ideas and standards of his time, including his notions of the human and social nature of Aboriginal man, one must observe that his methods were very untactical, on occasions slightly crazy. Most of his troubles had been with the bands south of the harbour; to raid the bands north of the harbour was an odd thing to do. It is hard to understand his reasoning that force *and* trickery would 'take away that fear and prejudice which they have continued to show ever since our first misunderstanding with them'. One naturally wonders why it never occurred to him to use go-betweens: he had several suitable officers of high intellectual capacity who had shown much interest in Aboriginal life. It would be charitable to assume that accumulating burdens and failing health proved too much for a man who has been described by a modern historian as two men in one: a man who 'with grace, dignity, industry and great self-control had won the battle for survival' and the man who 'had once wanted to hand over murderers and sodomites to be eaten by cannibals'. In New South Wales he had to be the arbiter of a more terrible external duality, which no one has yet found a way to bridge.

1963

The Aborigines (1938)

A tragedy underlies the rise of Australia from convict colony to dominion status. Often shamefully, and always miserably, the black tribes have died out wherever the whites have overrun the continent. The process of extinction still goes on in the remoter parts of the outback, out of sight of the white urban populations, and out of mind.

Year by year since 1788 the tribes have gone downhill. When the colony was founded the Aborigines probably numbered at least 300,000 but have now dwindled to about 50,000. Their decline was most rapid in the nineteenth century, in the years when the upward surge of the white Australian population widened the inner frontiers of the settlement at great cost of body and spirit, no less to the invaders than to the dispossessed tribes whose lands they seized. Officially, there are supposed to be 60,000 natives still alive, but this guess (it is little more) is almost certainly wrong. No proper Aboriginal census has ever been undertaken. A national headcount would probably show that 50,000 is a generous estimate. In any case it is a fact that about five-sixths of the original black population have been wiped out in 150 years, a rate equivalent to the death every year since 1788 of two large tribes totalling 1700 souls.

The position today is that if every person of any degree of native blood now alive in Australia (including the wretched half-caste remnant in the eastern States) were brought together in the Northern Territory, there would be only one person to every ten square miles. The rest of the Commonwealth—six States, including Tasmania—would be completely empty of the former native population. About the only traces of them which would remain would be a few not-too-well preserved rock carvings and paintings, a midden or two, some scanty records and collections in universities and museums, and a handful of inferior books. As it is, the old tribesmen of

New South Wales and Victoria might as well have been shadows moving in the trees of the eighteenth century for all the imprint they have left behind. Will history be content to record their disappearance, and leave it at that?

The Australian point of view about it is shapeless. There are a few vestigial regrets appearing here and there in a mass of solid indifference. Implicitly, perhaps, this may mean that the loss of the primitive tribes is held, after all, to be heavily outweighed by the gain of the wealthy democracy which has replaced them; and it is true that there are now nearly 7,000,000 white Australians and a materially rich civilisation where formerly there were 300,000 Stone Age Aborigines and a wilderness. The material and social achievements of the 150 years since 1788 have indeed been unparalleled. It is also true that we embrace futility by piously wishing that the liberal regrets of today had been operative yesterday. Then, acquisitiveness and eagerness for progress drunk or sober were the driving incentives to colonial effort, and *laissez-faire* was still the golden rule on frontiers as well as in cities. Most of the conquest of Australia, and thus most of the obliteration of the tribes, took place between 1830 and 1890, the period in which economic expansionism, land hunger and pioneering were at their strongest. In such a period nothing which was then politically practicable could have been done to isolate the simple Australian tribes. They went down like ninepins, and made no mark on the ground.

There are few signs that the life and death of the tribes have made any mark at all on Australia; the thought, culture, even the literature of the dominion, have scarcely been affected. The native tragedy does not yet serve as the motif of dramatic, literary, or artistic work of any consequence. There are no epics on the last of the tribes. There are no national monuments to a vanishing people, yet there is a monument to a mythical Dog on a Tucker-Box nine miles from Gundagai. There are not even a great many writers commercialising the disappearance of a quaint and at least tourist-worthy race. Spurious boomerangs are still made for tourists, and others only slightly less spurious for innocents who visit the encampment at La Perouse, but most of these artifacts are so inferior that even tourists pass them by. Each year in the golden winter of north Australia motor-tourist parties are visiting some of the more accessible Aboriginal camps, but they see little and take away less. The Aboriginal languages have enriched the Australian vocabulary with such words as boomerang, kangaroo, billabong, woomerah, warrigal, wallaby, and some hundreds of others. Some of the Australian slang has its roots in the east-coast native dialects. A few hundred towns are known by more or less corrupted versions of improperly preserved native names, spelt in barbarous phonetics which cannot wholly corrupt the original and underlying euphony of the words. Yet for every Woolloomooloo and Dee Why there is a second-hand Kensington and an imitation Kew.

If the future poets and dramatists of Australia ever learned what a wealth of mythology, rich in its imaginative feeling and with a true ring of human drama about it, has been allowed to die unrecorded with unkempt old men in their squalid camps on the fringe of so many Australian towns, they may well write down Australia's nineteenth century with a narrower halo than it now wears. It may be felt one day that such native stories as that of Dingiri, the tired hunter, who in the beginning of the world sat down on a stone late one afternoon when he had wearied himself in pursuit of a kangaroo, and composed a song which is sung today over a thousand miles of Aboriginal country, are worth their place in an Australian anthology. There are hundreds like the story of Dingiri still taught and sung in the native areas of Australia. In all probability they will never be recorded as that of Dingiri has been.[2]

---

[2] The stone on which Dingiri sat may still be seen in north Australia. The native myth goes on to say that Dingiri grew colder and colder as night came on, and as the shadows came over him, blacker and blacker until he was the colour of the stone. He kept on singing to himself and at last, growing stiff, made an attempt to rise, but

What other mark have the tribes made on Australia? A minor poet or two, an artist here and there in a century, a scientist allowing his feelings to outweigh his detachment, a few missionaries, and very few others, have been fired (apparently out of their time) by what has seemed to them to be the needless sadness of the tribal extinction. The few things which have been painted or written in this spirit are now barely remembered. The reform movements thus initiated have in most cases tailed away ineffectually. Thought, literature, and culture have in general remained almost innocent of any touch which is of Aboriginal origin or derivation. And meanwhile the blacks have kept on dying in a context of general unawareness and indifference.

They have left behind them a social debris in hundreds of encampments of

---

found that he had turned to stone. Another blackfellow who had crept up heard Dingiri singing and weeping, and ran away, taking the memory of the song with him. He taught it to others, and it is still sung today at initiation ceremonies over an immense area of the Northern Territory.

full-blood and mixed-blood descendants who are enmeshed by appallingly difficult economic and social problems, to the solution of which a negligible proportion of Australia's intellectual activity is directed.

It would be remarkable if, given the background of Australian thought and culture as they are in 1938, the treatment of Aborigines or public interest in them were far in advance of present levels. Policy cannot move far ahead of conviction, or of the level of knowledge on which policy must necessarily be based. Nor can the actual *working* of policy, the way in which in operation it bites down upon the problems with which it is supposed to deal, have greater strength than the strength of the conviction, the interest, and the knowledge behind it.

The 'Aboriginal problem' is, indeed, very far away and unreal to the urban and near-urban populations of Australia, and to their leaders. Few of them have ever seen a blackfellow. The disappearance of the tribes is not commonly regarded as a present and continuing tragedy, but (for some curious reason) rather as something which took place a long time ago, in the very early days, and so is no longer a real complication. Nor is it accepted, save by a few people, as a matter for self-reproach. On the contrary. The 150th anniversary of Australia's foundation was celebrated with only the bleakest and most unimaginable reference to the stricken native people for whom it was also, in its way, an anniversary.

The blacks have never been able to make a formal protest, except by an occasional spear. They have never been able to stir and hold any lasting interest in their plight. They themselves have no notion of tribal tragedy on a national scale, nor perhaps would it interest them if they had. Most of their interests and loyalties are narrowly tribal. The petition sent to the King by eighteen hundred civilised natives in 1937, asking to be saved from extinction and given political representation in Parliament, was the only articulate national plea they have yet made on their own behalf, and they were almost certainly prompted to it. The interest taken in their welfare by a few missionaries, protection societies, and secular organisations is very much a luxury in which only a thin selvedge of urban interest concerns itself. It draws no support from the mass of the people.

Doubtless most of this apathy is due to the fact that the tribes never stood and fought the invaders in the resolute and able way of the Zulus and Maori. The Aborigines were never politically minded enough to speak of their 'rights', or to demand minimum conditions for the cooperation they undoubtedly did give, and still give, in the work of settlement. They never set up any real competition for the land of which they have been dispossessed without compensation. Not having any established villages or hamlets they could, and did, bend their frontal line whenever the whites came, and after flinging a few spears, cooperated in their own destruction by accepting a parasitic role which enabled them to live peaceably near the intruding whites.

Today the blacks are without legal or constitutional rights as such. They were shabbily treated in the Australian

Constitution. They cannot vote, they are not represented in Parliament, they may not own land, they command no political power either indirectly or directly. They are not eligible for pensions, even if they are civilised. The scattered camps in the east are pushed as far away from the white towns as possible, and even their presence is deprecated. Most of the larger groups live in areas so remote from the centres of Australian life and thought that they cross the periphery of daily interest only when they are felt to be worth space in the headlines. This has usually meant that they are in the headlines only in the context of atrocity charges, murder and witchcraft trials, prospectors' tales of rich strikes, occasional reports of scientists, or in association with highly emotional movements of the reform of native policy and administration. Headline notoriety has been as fickle and ephemeral for them as it has been for others so honoured. Tomorrow there have been new headlines and new interests, and the tribes have quickly ceased to be of public (newspaper) interest. No forceful public personality has ever taken up their case, and they suffer from a number of unattractive ones who have. Not even the Australian proletariat has felt any apparent sympathy for the Aboriginal under-dog. The trade unions ignore them. In other words there seems to have been nothing in Aboriginal history, in their present plight, or in the general public understanding of what is happening to them, that has really captured the Australian imagination.

It may be that such a sequence of general charges is unfair in the sense that it hints at the possibility of simple solution by change of heart. Unfortunately, the problem of the bewildered, undernourished, neglected, badly 'protected' blackfellow is not so simple. It is not 'a' problem but a series of extraordinarily intricate and difficult problems. The solution of not one of them is simple.

It may be unfair, too, not to have mentioned that a number of extensive reforms are apparently under way in Australia. But if one is fair, and mentions them, one might also point out that their very extensiveness is a measure of past inadequacy, and the reforms themselves are less significant than the long struggle with reaction which has been necessary to bring them about.

For many years no one interested in the blacks can have felt that everything possible was being done for the disappearing tribes. It has been evident that the policies and administrations of the six authorities (five States* and the Commonwealth) have not been cutting to the bone of the central problem—halting the tribes' downward slide. A number of organisations have pressed the Government for specific (but too partial) reforms. Other reforms have been maturing in the minds of the administrations themselves. In 1936 and 1937 many of these reform movements seemed to be bringing results at last. A special *Native Act* was passed in Western Australia. The Federal Government committed itself to some general promises. An interstate conference of Protectors of Aborigines was held at Canberra (the first such conference in Australian history). A select committee commenced an inquiry in New South Wales. In 1938 it seems possible that an extensive overhaul of existing policies and administrative methods may soon come.

As it stands, Australian native policy and administration is a curious mixture of high intentions and laudable objectives, loosely formulated in vague principles; almost unbelievably mean finances; an extremely bad *local* administration and an obstinate concentration on lines of policy which 150 years of experience have made suspect. At various points in its history, and even in its application today, it has been stronger or weaker at one or other of these points. Queensland is rather better in every way than north Australia or central Australia. Western Australia has ambitions to be better still. Victoria and New South Wales and Tasmania have no large-scale native problems. The settlers arranged that last century.

The explicit intentions of Australian native policy have invariably been phrased on a high ethical plane. As the Prime Minister, for instance, stated them in 1931, they are representative of the general objectives which have been set in all the States (except Tasmania). The tribes generally are to be 'protected', and sheltered from moral abuse and economic exploitation; those who need it are to be placed in inviolable reserves, and the rest adequately fed and housed and cared for; as many as possible are to be educated and trained to take a place in the life of the Australian nation.

Not infrequently when challenged with negligence, or perhaps the facts of an unpleasant atrocity, a leader of the Australian people publicly states his belief that it is nearly impossible 'for such things to happen here', and recites this policy as proof, with the implication that it is also a fair description of actual conditions. The intention is innocent, no doubt, but the brutal reality of conditions in many areas rushes up to show that in fact there is a plane of wishful policy and a plane of actuality, and that only a myth closes the gap between them. Strangely enough, it is not always an easy matter to see the gap. The under-nourishment of natives does not always show on the surface.

Harmful working conditions are often at their worst where patrol officers and protectors are too busy to go and so are not publicised. The constant violation of native reserves which are half as large as England is difficult both to prevent and to detect. Employers and protectors who are born in a countryside which has inherited and still works on the notions of last century ('natives don't understand kindness', 'never trust a blackfellow', 'the only good blackfellow is a dead blackfellow', 'treat them hard but be fair') can scarcely be expected to see the unkempt, apparently lazy, shiftless Aborigines in the same way as a reformer with different notions of justice and practicability, and with a different racial and moral ethic. Often enough the economic conditions of the outback have the battling white settlers with their own backs against the wall, so that they are able to hold on only by underfeeding and under-paying (when they pay at all) their black employees. Moreover, the blacks are so scattered, the outback so vast, the stations and farms so isolated, and the local protectors so untrained for their work, that accurate and detailed information about the natives seldom seems to reach the central administration. It is not hard, then, to see why there is a genuine inability on the part of many officials, administrators, and politicians to understand that what the terms of policy say should be so is not also true in fact.

The gulf between the requirements of policy and conditions as they actually are, and threaten to continue to be, will take years to bridge. A great leap of imagination will be necessary for many officials, local protectors, employers, and political leaders if the gap is to be bridged at all. If they make the leap without a proper grip of the facts it may be worse than if they do nothing more than they do now. They must also cease to believe their own myths.

If a corps of impartial and internationally accredited experts were to make a tour of Australia, inspecting every native camp, every station where blackfellows work, every town where there is an encampment of detribalised remnants, the facts which would come to light would make disturbing reading.

Most of the detribalised and semi-civilised natives would be shown to be badly under-nourished, and to be living precariously from hand to mouth on what in many cases is a wretchedly inferior diet. Many of them are short of essential proteins, fats, mineral salts, and vitamins. The number of Aborigines just over the threshold of scurvy, beri-beri, and other deficiency diseases must be very great. For instance, out of fifty-one children born on a station in central Australia from 1925 to 1929, only ten survived. Why? The others died from the effects of an unbalanced diet, principally from lack of vitamin C. This was in time of drought, and over a great area of native Australia drought conditions recur time and again. In the summerrain belt the winter dry season often becomes an annual drought in the areas where the last of the tribes now live, so that the food problem of even the nomadic and uncivilised natives may well be almost as serious as it is for the semi-civilised camps dotted throughout the settled areas. Official rations are issued in some of these areas to aged and infirm blacks, but the food received in this way is a mockery of an adequate level of diet. The rations were originally intended only to supplement the food gathered by natives in their traditional hunting way. But, unfortunately, in so many outback areas these official rations, which are inferior in quality and insufficient in quantity, have become almost the only food some natives receive. The rations thus given consist of a little white flour, and small quantities of polished rice, tea, sugar and tobacco. There is no official meat ration. The quantity is often just sufficient to encourage the native to stay around the ration depot, but not sufficient to give them all one square meal a day. In most cases the old, tired natives are obliged by tribal custom to share the food out with other members of the tribe. Thus, what in itself is insufficient to feed the old people themselves becomes part of the tribal foodstuffs as a whole. On this meagre standard of living, supplementing the poor and inferior official rations as best they can, many a tribe lives from ration day to ration day. A generous and sensible official gesture has thus been perverted in the course of a few years into a thoroughly ruinous principle.

Nor can it be said that the rations given by many private employers are much better. The fresh meat ration is invariably too small, the use of white flour and polished rice too common, and the physiological inadequacy of the diet in other respects far too obvious. A great many white men in the same areas are living on food which is very little better, because of the poverty of the pastoral and farming properties over so much of native Australia. But can it really be held that this white poverty is a sufficient reason for the ruinous under-nourishment of native employees and dependants, or that the restricted budgets of the native administrations are a sufficient reason for the under-feeding of detribalised Aborigines who are otherwise left unprovided for?

The tribes are admittedly very debilitated. Their fertility is low and their death-rate high. They have very little resistance to the spread of disease.

The relation of their present inferior diet to these conditions may be of supreme importance for their future. At the moment no one in Australia appears to be concerned or empowered to discover to what extent food-deficiency is actually to blame for their low condition. Policy proceeds with (apparently) almost complete indifference. The root of this absence of interest lies, of course, in the widespread ignorance of what conditions are actually like among the tribes.

The health of the Aborigines and the medical supervision over them in many areas are in much the same plight. Here, however, the factors involved are rather different from those responsible for the poverty of native nutrition. The blacks themselves make the control and treatment of disease doubly difficult by their fear, ignorance, and misunderstanding of attempts made to help them. They live in unhygienic camps, they actively help to spread disease among themselves, and often refuse treatment. But among nomadic tribes, native employees on cattle stations and farms, and in detribalised camps around white settlements it may be taken as a fact that provision for their health could be much better. In most camps there are still many cases of untreated venereal disease, yaws, fevers, colds, influenza, eye infections (many leading to eventual blindness), and tuberculosis.

Nowhere do the highly centralised nature of the native administrations, and their restricted finances, operate more disastrously than here. The blacks who have to be cared for are scattered over immense administrative areas. In the event of grave illness they have to be taken hundreds of miles to hospital in country which is for them strange and sometimes full of superstitious terrors. There are no funds for regular medical patrols of the bush areas. Natives on the outer fringes are thus not able to build up confident and familiar relations with medical men whom they could know as friends, whom they could rely upon and approach without fear. The authorities have tried to cope with these conditions by distributing medical stores, drugs, and simple equipment throughout the bush districts. Some malarial control is attempted and prophylactic measures sometimes taken. Lepers are put away in isolation and venereal cases treated whenever they become known. Local protectors are expected to watch for and take elementary precautions to stop the spread of epidemics, and to supervise the health conditions of both bush tribes and working natives.

The local protectors are usually men without medical knowledge, and without any training in the difficult problems of disease detection. In most cases they are untrained bush policemen, postal officials, or civilians with other interests to occupy the greater part of their attention. Through lack of knowledge and special training, or because of the indifference which so often comes to the isolated official, these men may not be able to detect the first signs of disease or of epidemics, or to see infections spreading, or to appreciate the evidence (which may be before their eyes) of, e.g., malnutrition, gonorrhoeal infections, or tuberculosis. Various forms of unrest and instability under the outward surface of tribal life may also escape detection for the same reasons. Many employers are indifferent or incompetent in comparable ways. They are often victimised by malingering employees, who thus make things harder for ailing natives. When natives are genuinely ill it may be physically impossible to get assistance in time, for distances are often so great and the isolation is often so complete, especially in the wet season. As a further complication, the shadow of native fear and superstition lies heavily on the whole situation. A tradition of sorcery makes them terrified of surgical attention. The removal of lepers to isolation camps from which there is no return makes other natives hesitate to go to distant centres for treatment for other simpler complaints. Their tendency to blame the death of tribesfellows upon the white person who administers treatment leads to other difficulties. Between their own ignorance, poor local supervision, and administrations handicapped by inadequate finances, it may be said as a statement of fact that native health throughout Australia is suffering badly.

The poverty of native nutrition may be attributed to a blind spot in the official version of the native needs, whereas the partial failure of the supervision of native health is due principally to poor finances, and to the local breakdown of highly centralised medical and administrative services. A fourth source of failure lies in the wrong *emphasis* of much of native policy.

Nowhere is this so clearly shown as in the problem of the native reserves. The provision of so-called 'inviolable' reserves has long been a cardinal principle in Australia. A close scrutiny of the history of reserves would probably show that not one has gone unviolated. Goldminers, cattlemen, prospectors and others have entered them almost at will. The 'sanctity' of the reserves, though still a catch-phrase of official apologetics, is well known to be one of the most bitter fictions in the history of the Commonwealth, but this is perhaps no longer the most important point. The principle of reserves is being steadily persisted with officially, although evidence has been accumulating for years to suggest that the reserves may be failing to do what they were intended to do—'protect' the still uncivilised tribes and preserve them from the effects of civilisation. What is the actual position? The areas of relatively dense native populations (where most of the reserves are) include Arnhem Land, the Fitzmaurice and Daly rivers (north Australia), the desert areas of South, central, and Western Australia, and the Kimberley district of north-west Australia. In most if not all of these areas the nomadic tribes are being very heavily influenced by white civilisation, although the nearest whites may be hundreds of miles away. The blacks are ceasing, or have ceased, to make their ancient stone tools. They smoke tobacco. Some of them wear whites' clothes. They are eager for tea and sugar and white flour, and do everything they can (except in a few isolated regions) to obtain manufactured European articles. Moreover, scientists have noted for years a serious undercurrent of unrest among these tribes. They are tending to drift away from their traditional tribal lands to live near white settlements where they can secure more readily the tobacco, tea, sugar, new foods, clothing and manufactured articles they have learned to value and to crave. This tribal drift is threatening to dissolve such so-called uncivilised tribes into small floating segments, each of which is likely to leave the main tribe and attach itself in parasitic fashion to a cattle station, mission, farm, or settlement. Once this stage has been reached the tribes will never return to the old nomadic life in the bush. Once a tribe is parasitic it is in the half-way house to extinction. This can actually be seen taking place over a large area. Sections of tribes like the Warramulla, Maringar, and a number in central Australia are already deeply (and perhaps irreversibly) affected.

At the moment it is no one's business to detect, track down or stop these population movements, although they seem to be eating silently into the last of the nomadic tribes. The appearance at Wave Hill of a band of drought-stricken blacks may mean little on the surface to the casual observer. Nor perhaps is there much to be concerned at in the fact that desert tribesmen come into Alice Springs and pretend to be local blacks. But such movements can in a very few years quietly drain away from huge areas the native populations they are officially supposed to hold. There is a distinct possibility that this has actually happened, and that official estimates of the nomadic populations in several areas are now largely fictitious. Ought we not to know with absolute certainty what is the precise position?

A great part of Australia's scanty enthusiasm is going into the drive for maintenance of these supposedly inviolable reserves, in the belief that, after all, here is one really useful thing that can be done. There is, unfortunately, a possibility of deep disillusion about them in the near future, and with disillusion may well come an exhaustion of most of the interest in further effort.

There is nothing to lose and much to gain, by learning with as much precision as possible exactly what is taking place on the reserves: what state the tribes are in, to what extent 'drift' has taken place, how big the actual populations are, how they are breeding, what nutritive assistance they need, what health measures need to be taken, and to what extent further breakup can be prevented. So long as these facts are not known a large part of native policy will be proceeding upon a false estimate of a situation which is now quite unwarrantably taken for granted.

***

Meanwhile, the tribes are indisputably dying. It is extraordinary, and puzzling, to note how many of the reforms which are being widely advocated at this moment in Australia do not bite squarely on such matters. Almost anything seems to be preferred to setting to work to deal vigorously with what is wrong in finance, nutrition, health, local administration, population control, administrative personnel, and certain manifestly outmoded lines of policy. Old notions are dying very hard. One receives the strongest impression that the kind of vision taken of native affairs in the nineteenth century, and many of the beliefs then built up, are still dominant. The development of policy is still in the stage of wordy challenge and wordy reply; of competition between high-toned general principles enunciated on the one hand by officials and Ministers, and on the other by missionaries, church organisations, and protection societies. Much of the debate is beside the point. The basic, driving, urgent needs of a shrinking, underfed, badlydoctored native population do not seem to be consistently and clearly stated anywhere in these discussions. There is constant official pleading to be told what remedies to apply, but a persistent refusal to see that some remedies are only possible if the above conditions are first satisfactorily altered, and the more urgent Aboriginal needs appropriately met. These courses of action are, in fact, themselves remedies.

The kind of question being asked is too often 'do missions spoil natives?' instead of 'will better feeding pull this tribe together?' The relative urgency of measures, locality by locality, to counter the destructive forces which are at work, does not seem to be on the agenda of any conference or on the programme of any body of reformers. The whole problem is vague in outline and confused in detail for lack of vigorous, systematic, competent analysis. Nor are the facts on which firm and generally acceptable decisions might be made possessed by any authority. The facts presented by missionaries are denied or qualified by the facts presented by officials. Neither missionaries nor officials are actually in full possession of all the facts. The need for more authoritative information on specific questions is itself by no means generally admitted. The position is that no one really knows where to go, least of all where to go first, which is perhaps the most important matter of all. Yet there are scores of plausible reformers, each armed with his own solutions, and a wandering grip on a few of the facts, ready to sail in among the tribes and save them.

The 1937 Conference of Protectors at Canberra, after a long and patient discussion of some of the issues, passed a series of resolutions which may be presumed to represent the ideas of the authorities whether traditional policies are still sound, which methods or principles need reform, and which changes are more urgent than others.

One resolution urges the need of a declaration about the 'destiny' of 'the race', but mentions only the mixed bloods. Another resolution urges the need for uniformity of legislation, but would leave administration to six different authorities. Another establishes a legal test of who may properly be considered a native. Another would remove the financial burden from the States and place it largely upon the Commonwealth, and the Conference as a whole naïvely hopes that Aboriginal welfare will not become a political question. Another stresses the need to obtain information from other parts of the world about racial problems, but the Conference rejected a proposal to investigate further the half-caste problem. Another advises against corporal punishment, the appointment of female protectors, and the admission of the public to future Conferences of Protectors. Other resolutions refer to the chaining of native prisoners, to procedure in Courts of Native Affairs, to the control of the use of opium and alcohol, to the supervision of missions and the payment of mission subsidies.

No one reading such a list would feel himself to be in the presence of urgency, even of complexity. No one would be aware, for example, of the possibility that unsettled tribes may be on the brink of passing over a line which means they are irreversibly on the way to break-up. One might reasonably infer that the Conference felt that no particular urgencies were involved, that 'the problem' could with equal utility be tacked at any point, without a clearly prearranged plan, without agreement on practical techniques to meet the everyday problems certain to be encountered. It is significant, too, that the Conference concerned itself almost entirely with highly general questions of policy, and postponed for a year consideration of such matters as control and prevention of disease, diet, working conditions, the fixation of a minimum Aboriginal working wage, and several other matters of primary importance.

In the matters actually dealt with, the objectives which were decided upon and the views expressed were often wholly admirable. It may be remarked, however, that some of the resolutions embodying those views and principles are not notable for their clarity. Yet they may become 'policy' and actually be implemented.

One resolution of great importance shows that the Conference felt the need of a clear understanding of the biological and social destiny of the mixed-bloods. According to this resolution, these mixed-bloods should be 'absorbed' by the white people of the Commonwealth. What 'absorption' implies was not dealt with, yet the Conference recommended that efforts be made to secure that objective, the assumption being apparently that it was a matter of fairly simple political decision. Is it really so?

If the present mentality of north Australia, to take only one native area, has any relevance to this new principle, as it must have, it seems probable that 'absorption' there can only mean a grudging acceptance on a basis of social inequality and inferiority, with the right of free economic competition by mixed-bloods strictly limited in practice, however equal in theory they may be. The present use of cheap full-blood and mixed-blood labour as a subsidy to keep the head of north Australian industries just above a bare survival level must inevitably bequeath very strong attitudes to future local generations. Is this 'absorption' in the meaning of the Conference? How is it to be prevented from becoming the actual meaning? It thus seems to be something like wish-fulfilment for the Conference to pass another resolution recommending that the full-blood children of civilised tribes near white settlements should be educated to 'white standard' (whatever that may mean) and then employed in 'lucrative' occupations which 'will not bring them into economic or social conflict with the white community'. The report of the Conference points out with unconscious but destructive relevance to this objective that in the Northern Territory the natural increase of the white population is minus 0.3 per 1000, while the natural increase of the mixed-bloods is at the astonishing rate of 18 per 1000. Nearly all the local mixedbloods are young, vigorous and potentially fertile.

The future is thus full of interest for the racial situation in the Northern Territory and for the working out of 'policy'. If left to itself the white population will shrink, while the mixed-bloods will increase rapidly. To the extend to which an attempt is actually made to 'absorb' them competition for a strictly limited number of jobs will probably be intensified, for, economically speaking, the north has been dying on its feet for twenty years, the unemployment rate has been high, and the effects of depressions have been felt with great intensity. These conditions seem likely to continue. The chance, therefore, that fullblood children of the future will be able to find 'lucrative' work without coming into conflict with whites and mixed-bloods (themselves probably in intense competition for jobs) seems at the best to be slender.

In this situation are involved most of the elements which for 100 years have made so much of Australian native policy a tragi-comedy. Here are high official aspirations, unimpeachable liberal social principles, an ambitious paper plan, an objective dimly conceived and pleasantly worded. Here, apparently, is belief that prejudiced men, case-hardened viewpoints, vested interests, a bureaucracy with a long tenure of office yet to run, and a proven difficult environment will belie their history and become conveniently malleable. Here is a partial and faulty grasp of the facts and forces which have to be reckoned with. Here, in fact, in the sphere of native relations, is the old vulgar error of socio-political 'policy'—a vague, wordy, pretentious statement of principle which whips up the support of generous, unthinking people, and omits to state (perhaps even does not envisage) that the principle can become literal fact only at the cost of sacrifices by entrenched groups and individuals who are unwilling to make sacrifices. Perhaps such disabilities inhere in the nature of high 'policy', but perhaps, also, that is not the point. What matters is that attempts are made to implement such 'policies', even though they are deeply rooted in confusion. Policy is put into operation with its head in a whirl, accompanied by the hope that things will sort themselves out. Success is always obscure and relative, and failure, in the nature of things, does not become visible for a long time. The real underlying issues have a good chance of becoming obscured, argument usually deals in distortions, and by the time failure is apparent and an attempt made to fit 'policy' to what are now thought to be the facts, the conceptual gulf between 'policy' and what may be the basic underlying needs at any moment may be disastrously wide. This is where defensive official myths start, and this is also why it is so hard for both officials and public to see where the truth lies in the deep well of bush Australia.

Take north Australia again as an example. The actual situation which is deeply relevant, say, to any principle of 'absorption' starts with the fact that a great many of the north Australian tribes are dead, and few people there regret it. The prevailing attitudes of white people towards Aborigines and mixed-bloods are also relevant. It is a fact that white parents in one of the largest north Australian towns recently protested violently at their children being taught (and, thus, they felt, contaminated) in the same class rooms as loosely trained mixed-blood children. There is a general local contempt (sometimes faintly kindly, but still contempt) for the full-blood Aborigines. Too many white men who marry half-caste women tend to be inferiors, and the *combo* (a white man who habitually keeps a native mistress) is thought to have degenerated. Moreover, it is relevant to note that sexual association between white men and full-blood or mixed-blood women is still heavily punishable by law. Despite this, half-caste children are being born at a disturbing rate, and not only from the union of mixed-bloods with other mixed-bloods. As a social phenomenon this means that mixedblood children are being conceived illicitly, are being born 'in sin', and are growing up regarded as 'a problem'. They are being given a crude education, and are not in any sense yet allowed to take a position in the life of north Australia which does not bring them at least some contempt and some social isolation. There is at the same time a strong undercurrent of objection to mission activities, and a feeling among perhaps the majority of whites that missions 'spoil' the natives. Side by side with this at least incipient racial conflict, there is, or has been recently, a degree of intra-white tension. As further factors in the general climate of opinion and social feeling, the recent social history of north Australia has been associated with industrial depression. There are still today a number of pioneers who are barely making a living, and are able to keep going only with the help of badly fed and often unpaid black labour. Here, then, is the bedrock on which a policy of local 'absorption' would have to build.

The general terms of this situation have been paralleled many times in Australian history. One could build up much the same background for each separate problem dealt with in this chapter. They are highly relevant because they have set, and will continue to set, the social context in which native 'policy' has to operate. They have already imposed iron limitations on what it could do and how it could express itself, with the result that it has been forced into distortions not contemplated originally. When such background forces have been sufficiently powerful they have made disreputable sail-trimming and blind-eye methods almost inevitable. In some notorious instances they have reduced aspects of the official native policy to a series of empty words. That is still true today of some native reserves, payment of native labour in some areas, and the 'moral protection' of some native women.

So far as the principle of 'absorption' is concerned, and for all other principles, the acid test for all the native areas of Australia is whether the leopard can actually change its spots. Can the pioneer fringes of Australia blot out such bitter complications as those sketched above, suspend all the convictions and attitudes which would be an embarrassment to the new 'policy', and on any given morning in

1938 set out, say, to 'absorb' their mixed-blood populations?

The argument of this chapter is not that policy-makers should abandon their hope of fusing the mixed-bloods with white stock, if they really want to attain that end. Nor is it urged that they should give up the notion of educating black children for useful and gainful occupations, or of 'protecting' or 'elevating' the Aborigines in any way they may decide. These are vague, very general, and highly controversial principles for the future of the Aborigines, but no criticism of policy *as such* is offered here. It is recognised that policy-making is the prerogative of Government, and of Government only, and may be whatever Government decides it shall be.

***

What is put forward, and with as much vigour as possible, is this:

We know that the Aborigines are dying out. The small increases noted here and there are beside the point. Elsewhere, only decreases are reported. Evidently, we do not wish them to die out, for preservation of the Aborigines is made so much of in every statement of policy. But if we find when a proper census is taken that 50,000 Aborigines are alive, we may consider ourselves to be fortunate. We know that five-sixths of the Aborigines have in fact died out in conditions not unlike those which the remaining tribes are now encountering. Yet we do not know what actually is happening to those tribes which are still alive. We do not know, for instance, with sufficient certainty, what is taking place on the tribal reserves. But we have direct evidence that the reserves are insufficiently protected and are constantly violated, and we have indirect evidence that the reserve tribes are probably being broken up by various forms of unrest and disturbance. As for the tribes not on the reserves, we know that in most cases they are living under wretched conditions, that many of them are suffering from diseases which could be treated, from malnutrition which could be relieved, from land-hunger and loss of interest in life, and we know that at least some of them are economically exploited. We know that there may be twenty or thirty different factors at work producing these conditions in each locality. But, taking the tribes one by one, we do not know (except in a few cases) the local incidence of any of these factors with the certainty we need if we are to be able to say with confidence: 'This tribe needs assistance of these kinds if it is to be preserved.' Even if we did know, we are aware that it would not be of much use, because the responsible administrations are crippled for lack of funds and are making shift with hopelessly small allowances. We know that many of the officials in closest contact with the Aborigines are not properly trained to be efficient protectors, and that there is a great need of men who know more about their job, are better paid, and will compare favourably with similar officials in other British native administrations. We know that the Aborigines are deeply aggravating their own plight by fear, ignorance, and lack of understanding of where their real interests now lie, thus making the task of the administrations doubly hard. Where the Aborigines and mixed-bloods are too few to be of economic importance, we know it to be true that there is a general contempt for them and prejudice against them, and that there may well be strong resistance to any attempt to raise their status nearer equality with whites. And we know that where the Aborigines live in greater numbers the 'problem' must be seen in true perspective against its background of rural and frontier white society, which is in many areas hard-pressed economically, often dependent upon black labour, and thus deeply involved in the future of native policy. Nothing is to be gained by understating the potential conflict which is likely to arise between white economic interests and reformers who would, perhaps not deliberately, but inevitably, place greater burdens upon them. We know that governments are being badgered by groups of reformers, some without any other qualification than an emotional obsession to do good, some better qualified but unaware of their own limitations, some well qualified by knowledge, and all of them bursting with solutions. We know that in this confusion of counsel there is no one authoritative and internationally-accredited person able to say 'It is probably better to do this than that.' We know there are State jealousies at work, and that while there is willingness to make native welfare a national financial responsibility there is no willingness to accept national direction. We know that an entrenched bureaucracy is also involved and will not be silent. We know that many phases of an adequate new policy are likely to encounter resistance or sabotage. We know that we are up against both natural as well as social forces which 'policy' does not seem ordinarily to allow for or to envisage. We know that the financial cost of any satisfactory reform will be heavy, and that to spend only a few thousand pounds where tens of thousands are needed will mock the sincerity of the official statement that Australia wishes to preserve the Aborigines.

But knowing these things is not enough. Many thousands of Australians know them in a vague way. There has been a failure to appreciate what such facts imply. Have they brought us any understanding of the changing needs of the Aborigines? Have they clarified the vision of those who are out for reforms? Have they been understood as making certain phases of policy more imperative than others? Have they made us see how astonishingly inconsistent we are to make economic sacrifices for Abyssinia but stonily to refuse to see the situation of our own black tribes for what it is? Have they enabled us to see that in many phases of native policy we stand almost nude?

There is need for some quality of statesmanship in Australian native affairs. There is need for an imaginative leap of administrative methods. There is need for continuity of effort over a number of years, for better men to do the work, for capable planning to meet and overcome opposition and defeatism, and for a strong directive personality who has also a deep insight into the meaning of the changes which have taken place in Australian native affairs. Perhaps the greatest need is for political sincerity. This can be tested by the question: 'How much will you spend?'

***

What steps are immediately necessary? One can answer by taking another question: 'Is it really Australia's wish to preserve the Aborigines?' If it is, and the wish is backed by money, the immediate steps are fairly clear. The Aborigines cannot preserve themselves, or be preserved, if they are not properly nourished, and their health safeguarded with real efficiency. These must be seen to immediately. They will prove to be immensely difficult, and will arouse criticism and opposition, but they are the *sine qua non* of native reform. If natives' bodies fail them, what use are other reforms?

Then, when we are sure that we can keep them vigorously alive and breeding, we can start to think what we really mean by *preserving* them. Preserving them for what? Under what social conditions? With what political and economic opportunities? With what liberties, what privileges, what restrictions? Do we really believe we are conferring a benefit upon them by preserving them? If so, will we really ensure that they do benefit?

There is no end to such questioning. These are the issues which plunge us instantly into the thick of controversy. At this stage there is no clarity, and much humbug, in the way the problems are being posed. We might let first things for once come first. We might start with an allotment of ample funds. A large vote is essential. Then we should remedy native malnutrition, control all disease among them, make an exact tribal census, stop population drift, provide the administrations with an expert diagnosis of the state of each tribe and its special needs, and raise the tribal standard of living. Until we offset or stop the conditions which are giving the tribes no chance of survival we can do very little for them. When we have done these things, if it is not already too late, we can launch them on the strange and unpredictable path of a primitive people preserved to some end which at the moment is clear to very few of us.

The extinction of the Aborigines is only inevitable if we allow it to be so.

We have not yet at any time in our history in any part of the continent made a resolute and intelligent attempt to do what we say is our intention.

1938

Continuity and Change among the Aborigines (1958)

Some time ago I thought that a suitable topic for my Presidential Address would be 'The Future and the Aborigines'. A great many people seem to have had the same idea for other addresses about the same time. I did not know this because I was still in a remote corner of the continent studying the Aborigines' past. I then learned that their future was to be discussed by a special symposium of this Section. The title of my address thus had to become 'Continuity and Change in Aboriginal Life'. The topic remains much the same. This is a good illustration of continuity and change.

It is not my wish to cross the wind or steal the thunder of others who are to speak later. I shall therefore limit myself to some very general observations on things which, being continuous from the past of Aboriginal life, and still of influence in the present, are likely to have force in the future, until the Aborigines cease to be themselves, which seems to be what we are about to insist upon their doing.

The abiding sameness and variations of Aboriginal life were much in my mind over the last year. While I was excavating a rock-shelter, which contained horizons of culture going back a long way in time, I found many human artifacts which my Aboriginal friends could not believe had been made by man. They insisted that some must have been made by Blue Tongue, the Lizard Man of The Dream Time. Judging by the depth at which I had found the implements some must have been made less than a century ago. Here a technical continuity had not only been broken but, so to speak, had been 'thought away'.

At places where The Rainbow Serpent had worked certain marvels which by tradition give life its continuity, the Aborigines looked quite unemotionally on The Serpent's marks, though they would not once have done so. They knew what many of the marks and paintings signified, but no longer cared. Modern life in certain ways has become actually discontinuous with tradition. Part of the universe of discourse in which The Rainbow Serpent was the chief symbol has receded. The rocks of this region are still bright with a mural art which has about it something timeless and tranquil. Only the old Aborigines know its significance. The younger ones have different interests and are bent on other things. But their activities and interests are in many ways still recognisably Aboriginal. How does one deal with what changes and yet stays itself?

There is a vast area of Australia where Aboriginal life is not what it was and never will be again. Many anthropologists have wrestled with what Malinowski would have called a *tertium quid,* something with its own character. Wherever any considerable body of Aborigines are left, and live together, they are living a life of their own. I cannot claim to know the whole of the continent and would like to be understood as speaking only of places and peoples I know well. None of the many hundreds of Aborigines I have studied at first hand impress me as already or as likely to be 'incorporated', or 'absorbed', or 'assimilated' into the surrounding system of Europeanism. The very contrary is true. Various European things—our authority, our customs, our ideas and goods—are data, facts of life, which the Aborigines take into account in working out their altered system. But I have seen little sign of its going much beyond that. Those Aborigines I know seem to me to be still fundamentally in struggle with us. The struggle is for a different set of things, differently arranged, from those which most European interests want them to receive. Neither side has clearly grasped what the other seeks. All this issues in a dusty encounter in which nothing is yet particularly clear.

    I desire to bring the fact of struggle to the fore because it seems to me the primary reality. Not that the struggle is now one of violence. This at least we can say of the Australian scene. One does not move in an atmosphere of stern repression and angry resistance. It is rather an encounter of two peoples who in general have failed to comprehend the ethos and structure of each other's lives. The atmosphere is one of anarchy and purposes obscurely crossed. We picture ourselves as trying to bridge the gap by goodwill, material help and general solicitude, and as rather baffled by the fact that there seems no firm place for the other pylon of the bridge, only ground which is shifting and uncertain.

This self-image is wrong, not in the sense that it misrepresents our best wishes, but in that our wishes are unreasonably based on a poor half of the facts. Let me try to show why this is so.

There are some thousands of Aborigines in one area I know living in varying conditions of life but now all lumped together into the category of 'wards of State'. They will not cease to be wards until they can prove to authority that they do not need 'special care and assistance'. They are listed in a census which I have compared with places and persons I know well. This document seems to give the Administration some pride, but it seems to me an inadequate piece of work. I condemn it on a number of grounds, not the least of which is its barbarous spelling of Aboriginal names in a kind of pidgin-phonetic. But, more importantly, it shows no understanding of the Aboriginal namesystems, of the facts of local organisation, of the structural division of groups, and of the language differences. These things would be taken as matters of vital consequence by any modern administration. They are of course of primary importance to the Aborigines themselves.

The reason why they seem to be dismissed as of no consequence is not known to me. It may have to do with the insistent official view that henceforth the Aborigines must be treated as 'individuals' and not as 'groups'. I am afraid this shows that authority does not know what it is doing. No policy or law can transform the Aboriginal from what he is in this region—a social person, tied to others by a dozen ties which are his life—into an abstract 'individual' in order to make the facts fit a policy. It is the policy which is wrong. An official view of this kind, arbitrarily imposed, shows only too plainly that we still have a long way to go to gain an understanding of how policy should be made and applied.

We keep on confounding our perceptual routines of mind with some sort of absolute social reality. We keep on with a presupposition that our styles of life have a natural virtue; and with the folly that an exact knowledge of the facts is a luxury and not a necessity of policy and administration. We add to these delusive slogans—such as the policy of 'assimilation through individualism'—and then wonder why we get into increased administrative difficulty.

I have said that Aboriginal life is not what it was. That is true, but in several senses. We are widely told that the Aboriginal tradition is 'collapsing' or already 'collapsed'. It is a picturesque way of putting things, but it is misleading. It suggests that what follows is a void or a fortuitous jumble. This is not the case. In a number of groups I know the tradition has 'collapsed' into something of a very different kind, a restless activism and opportunism. We should not think this strange. We are very familiar with this process in our own life. An idealism turns—'collapses'—into romanticism, a realism into cynicism, a liberty into licence. The activism and opportunism are very visible among the younger Aborigines. There are many growing points here. They are all indicative of much racial unrest to come. Very little inquiry—competent scientific inquiry—is being made into the states of mind, the grievances and aspirations of these young men and women. I have not made them my special province, but I know enough of the facts to make me feel sure that any official or public assumption that such people can be effortlessly 'assimilated', on other than their own terms, is not well based.

We have almost no experience so far of how Aborigines respond to present conditions, which are very novel. There is ample work, a high inflation coming from large expenditures, a softening of restraints and disciplines, a marked desire to go to the towns, a pressure for amenities and comforts, and a great deal more gambling and drinking. Anthropologists have seen this kind of syndrome very widely, in many countries, and know how it comes about and develops into more acute forms. Their fact-finding methods and reasoned counsel have often been of use to authorities elsewhere. Our own authorities do not seem persuaded that fact-finding is really necessary, or, at all events, that the established techniques of modern anthropology have any relevance. At times I wonder if there may not be a large file marked 'facts we would rather not know about.'

Some of the conditions among the modern Aborigines impel me also to wonder if anthropology itself should not reconsider some of its favourite ideas. Have we truly understood the process by which the modern Aborigines are, to some extent at least, transforming themselves as well as being transformed by things beyond their control?

***

I have come not long since from a part of Australia, the Fitzmaurice River in the Northern Territory, which is entirely empty of its former inhabitants. To the best of my belief, the Aborigines began to drift away from it as recently as the turn of the century, perhaps a little earlier. Some went east, south and south-west to cattle stations or to Wyndham, others north and east to stations, settlements or towns on the north-south road, even as far afield as Darwin itself. The original population must have been very substantial. The life-supporting power of the country is high by Aboriginal standards, although I found it somewhat inhospitable, and topographically too broken to have much attraction from a European's point of view. There is no evidence of any kind that the exodus was other than entirely voluntary. Expropriation or foreclosure of land did not occur. There was no forced labour. Conflict with settlers and police took place some distance away, but did not directly concern the riverine clans. The whole tract was—and still is—beyond the margin of European settlement and development. Now and then, one or two restricted localities on the southern bank may be visited by stock parties for the few days needed to round up wandering cattle. More rarely still, a prospector, dingo-scalper or crocodile hunter may go there briefly. At longer intervals again a police party may pass through one of the few routes by which the river may be forded. Otherwise it is quite deserted. Had it not been for the shelters I found, each with many splendid paintings testifying to the fact that men had been there who lived a life of high imagination, I should have no physical proof that it had ever been anything but the wilderness it is now.

The evidence, and discussions with natives who had lived there as children, satisfied me that the Aboriginal explanation is correct. They say that their appetites for tobacco and, to a lesser extent, for tea became so intense that neither man nor woman could bear to be without. Jealousy, ill will and violence arose over the division of the small amounts which came by gift and trade. The stimulants, if I may call them such, were of course not the only, or the first, European goods to reach them: probably iron goods were the first, but it was the stimulants that precipitated the exodus. Individuals, families and parties of friends simply went away to places where the avidly desired things could be obtained. The movement had phases and fluctuations, but it was always a one-way movement.

Now I think voluntary movements of this kind occurred widely in Australia. I will not say universally, but I have seen the process in several regions. There is a task here for historical anthropology. But even if our information is imperfect we must look all over again at what we *suppose* to have been the conditions of collapse of Aboriginal life. If we make a full allowance for what Andrew Lang called 'the ferocity and almost equally fatal goodwill' of Europeans, and for the spread of disease, the range and rapidity of collapse seems far too great for the known causes. We have been prone to argue, too directly, and probably far too simply, from half-known cases to unknown cases. Our models of explanation have been based either on the dramatic secondary causes—violence, disease, neglect, prejudice—or on the structure of Aboriginal society, or both.

The structure has been depicted as so rigid and delicate, with everything so interdependent, that to interfere with any part of it—say by fencing off the hunting territories, or by prohibiting ceremonies—is to topple the whole, in rationale, design and structure. But there is at least some evidence which allows one to say that here were a people exploring a potential of their structure, a people taking advantage of its flexibility. For one of the enabling causes of the exodus I have described was a circumstance which certainly existed over all Australia. The so-called tribes were not self-sufficing entities but were interdependent in many important ways. Interconnexions by marriage, economy, trade, friendship, ceremonial intercourse and patterned conflict were fundamental features of life. It has often been convenient, when dealing with a particular set of problems, or a particular group of people, to reduce the emphasis on the interconnexions, as a matter of convenience. But there are problems of study in which we must increase the emphasis. We then have to use the idea of an external social structure as well as an internal social structure. By 'external social structure' I mean the necessary relations of association with other collectivities.

The arrival of Europeans here and there in the region of which I speak—a vast region, never fully explored or occupied by the newcomers—was sufficient to unsettle Aborigines still long distances away. The repercussions spread, evidently with great rapidity, along the network of structural interconnexions. Eventually, for every Aboriginal who, so to speak, had Europeans thrust upon him, at least one other had sought them out. More would have gone to European centres sooner had it not been that their way was often barred by hostile Aborigines. As late as the early 1930s I was able to see for myself the battles between the encroaching myalls and weakening, now-sedentary groups who had monopolised European sources of supply and work.

The encroachers used every claim of right they had—kinship, affinity, friendship, namesake-relationship, trade partnership—to get and keep a toehold.

I will say something later of how this compares with the present time but, fundamentally, little has changed. The drive and vitality are still there. So is the external structure of the somewhat different groups into which the Aborigines have re-sorted themselves. And so, too, are many of the internal structures of thought and activity, or others derived from them.

A disintegration following on a voluntary and banded migration is a very different kind of problem from the kind we usually picture—that of the ruin of a helpless people, overwhelmed by circumstance, and by something like the mechanical collapse of their social structure. Whatever the secondary causes of the subsequent disintegration in this region, it was a voluntary movement which began it.

The primacy of that fact is important. It continues in the self-will and vitality of the Aborigines. These things are still very visible to those observers who are not blinded either by interest or preconception. They underlie what I represent as the modern struggle in parts where any considerable numbers remain.

The search for stimulants by these particular people must have been to them something like the spice-trade to the medievals. The new things gave a tang and zest to life which their own dietary lacked. In becoming their own voyagers, the Aborigines claimed, coaxed and fought an opening into an incomprehensible new world. Many died, and many others were ruined; those who survived found they could not go back; and it does not seem that many even wanted to. Nowhere, as far as I am aware, does one encounter Aborigines who want to return to the bush, even if their new circumstances are very miserable. They went because they wanted to, and stay because they want to.

The pathetic fallacy has much corrupted our understanding of this process. Our thinking is far too affected by the cases where violent secondary causes—gross neglect, epidemic disease, extreme malnutrition, punitive expeditions, and the like—in some mixture, wiped out whole peoples or left wretched groups of survivors. So strong are these paradigms of sentiment that we project them even onto large surviving groups of Aborigines not now meeting those extremes. We fail to grasp the zest for life which animates them because we did not see it in those who died so miserably.

Some of our general ideas may thus need drastic revision. A view which has had considerable influence in the past is that to part an Aboriginal from his clan country is to wrest his soul from his body. There is a real, and an intense, bond between an Aboriginal and the ancestral estate he shares with other clansmen. I have seen a man, revisiting his homeland after an absence, fall on the ground, dig his fingers in the soil, and say: 'O, my country'. But he *had* been away, voluntarily; and he was soon to go away *again* voluntarily. Country is a high interest with a high value; rich sentiments cluster around it; but there are other interests; all are relative, and any can be displaced. If the bond between person and clan-estate were always in all circumstances of the all-absorbing kind it has sometimes been represented to be, then migrations of the kind I have described simply could not have occurred.

***

Over recent years there have been many signs of heightened interest in the Aborigines. I think there has been some growth of public sensibility. We now celebrate an Aboriginal Sunday. An optimistic philosophy of racial relations is expressed in Commonwealth policy. Legislation has become more imaginative. Some administrative organisations and services have been set up at a cost which would have been beyond our wilder thoughts in the 1930s. But the movement is wider still. One does not have to make a special search to discover the increased extent to which serious publications deal with all things Aboriginal. Some quality of Aboriginal art, or at least what is being put forward as Aboriginal art, has caught the public's imagination. There is even a strong market for all kinds of works dealing with the Aborigines. Perhaps we have crossed a kind of watershed, almost without noticing the fact, as one often does on slowly rising country.

Less than a generation ago it did not seem at all likely that anything like this would happen. But wherever we put the crest of the watershed, we would certainly be ungenerous, and probably wrong, to put its rise in the post-war period. In the middle and late 1930s there was a stir of reform in several States. In 1937 a conference was convened at Canberra of Protectors of Aborigines from all the States, except, of course, Tasmania. As far as I am aware, there had never been any other such meeting in our history. I do not know to what extent the recommendations of this conference helped to shape what was to come, but they may well have done so. One recommendation called for a declaration about what it termed 'the destiny of the race', and another recommended the 'absorption' of the mixed-bloods. It was a limited vision, but the protectors were criticised by some for going too far and by others for not going far enough. How far we have all now outrun that vision! We have not settled much about the 'destiny' of the race—and how could we?—but we have determined their 'future', and by law at that.

One could wish that the authors of the policy of assimilation had found for it a happier name. The crunch with which the lion begins to assimilate the lamb and what follows are images best dismissed from the mind. Yet the physiological metaphor brings us uncomfortably near the truth. Assimilation means that the Aborigines must lose their identity, cease to be themselves, become as we are. Let us leave aside the question that they may not want to, and the possibility—I would myself put it far higher than a possibility—that very determined forces of opposition will appear. Suppose they do not know how to cease to be themselves?

People who brush such a question aside can know very little about what it is to be an Aboriginal. Not that we have ever been a people remarkable for an intelligent appraisal of other races and cultures.

At the end of the eighteenth and for some time into the nineteenth century, when very little of a factual kind was known of the Aborigines, they were widely seen as 'children of nature' or as 'noble savages'. The extent to which this stereotype influenced early observations is now coming under study. Mr Bernard Smith, an historian of art, and Mr Mulvaney, an archaeologist, have done much to advance our knowledge of the matter. Some of the least amiable stereotypes were induced by evangelical Christianity and social Darwinism in and over the course of the nineteenth century. They brought paganism into religious and philosophical contempt. The currency of their criticism cheapened as it became popularised. As late as 1894, Calvert still found it necessary to protest against the idea of Aborigines as 'mere baboons, possessing an innate and incurable deficiency of intellect rendering them incapable of instruction or civilisation'. It was probably to such sources that we owe as well the gloom and despondency which hung like a murk over all discussions and writings about

Aboriginal affairs for a long time. At the turn of the century we find Andrew Lang and a great many others still intellectually convinced that they must die out. Others kept on to this day confounding an insolvency of imagination with the laws of nature.

I shall leave to others the study of the succession of such ideas, the kind of ignorance and philosophical prejudice in which they were grounded, how they overlapped, what influence they had, over whom, for how long, and the ways in which they issued in the actual treatment of the Aborigines. Some of the younger historians, such as Russel Ward and the late Margaret Kiddle, whose death broke a partnership I had hoped to make with her in this field, have shown how much might be done. There are some large tasks of scholarship awaiting attention in this field. Few historians have found our relations with the Aborigines of interest, and historical anthropology has not developed here to any extent. As I have already said, we deal with the present and future on the basis of what we believe the past to have been. And from the first days of settlement, right down to the present time, our understanding of the Aborigines has been blinkered as well as spectacled. The blinkers have been emotional general ideas formed by some kind of social philosophy. The spectacles have been the facts we had in our possession and the interpretations we placed on them.

The blinkers and the spectacles often fitted together uncomfortably. There often were odd men out in their day, men whom something had made aware of a lack of fit between what the Aborigines seemed to be and the way they were made to seem by styles of vision then in vogue. Phillip and Macquarie were men of this kind; Grey the explorer was another; so, too, was Sir Baldwin Spencer. The visions they rebelled against were different, and the facts they could draw upon unequal, but they were singularly free, for Australians, from either sentiment or prejudice on matters of race, society and culture.

Are things in this respect any better than they were? I have just been studying a document, a Commonwealth document, which explains and defends the modern policy of assimilation. I cannot quote it in full, but I shall try to give a fair rendering of what it says, using its own words and phrases where possible.

The document sets out to persuade by building up some powerful general images of a kind which affect both the mind and the feelings. The first is one which I shall call the image of The Noble Friend of Aborigines. He is every good Australian. He is a man of sympathy, readily moved by Aboriginal sufferings. He seeks to keep a steadfast alliance between a warm heart, a cool head and steady hands. He is a man who always asks: 'What are the facts?' When the facts inevitably prove complex, he always says: 'Let us understand this question, wisely, clearly, exactly.' Then, having strained understanding, he settles down to do what is needed. The task is slow and painful, but he never allows the goal to fade. Difficulties keep on arising. He notes, with an unfailing intelligence, exactly what is happening, so that the warm heart, cool head and steady hands can do again exactly what is needed. The image is one of modern Everyman. Idealist, yet practical; rational, but warm-hearted; with an ear to the ground but with an inner vision able to see three generations ahead. And what is the vision? The former Aborigines distinguishable from us only by skin colour, if that.

The second image is that of The Flesh Creeper. This is not my choice of name. It is the way the document describes its own creation. The Flesh Creeper is explicitly likened to The Fat Boy in Pickwick. He is a type of man who seeks out the unusual and distressful to find something to which he may give an unnatural emphasis. He wishes to prick the conscience, to arouse feelings of horror which, the document says, are his reward. What does he desire? To make people hold out the open hands of help and friendship? No: to shut their fists in enmity.

A third image is then created. The name presents me with a difficulty. The document treats as a class all those who professionally, so to speak, 'deal in' Aborigines. The journalist, the cartoonist, the promoter of tourist attractions, and the anthropologist are mentioned. On the principle that men who deal in iron are ironmongers, or in fish fishmongers, I can see no objection to naming this image that of the Monger of Aborigines. This image is carefully drawn so as to include the anthropologist. Words like 'anthropology' and 'science' and phrases like 'looking through a microscope' are placed against other words and phrases, such as 'pet animal', 'oddity', 'tourist attraction' and, *per contra,* 'human being', so as to convey an impression that 'anthropology' and 'human being' are somehow contradictory or incompatible.

I have time only to mention a fourth image, which I may call that of The Wistful Aboriginal. This is splendidly drawn to suggest a human being set against the idea of 'a social problem' or 'a political puppet'. It is done by the use and placement of such words as 'hope', 'fear', 'ambition', 'despair' and so on. One thus learns that in the heart of The Wistful Aboriginal is a hope that he may 'live his life to the full as a full member of the Aboriginal community'. It turns out that The Noble Friend of Aborigines is offering The Wistful Aboriginal exactly what The Wistful Aboriginal is yearning after—assimilation. It follows, logically enough, that any Aborigines who are conscious of their race and separateness, and stress such facts, are acting unworthily. And, if there are others, not Aborigines, who promote such racial consciousness and separateness, they, too, probably have unworthy motive, and wish to keep controversy going for their own ends. The only people who want to advance the welfare of the individual Aborigines are therefore those who favour assimilation.

I do not particularly want to spend much time on this document. Its heart is in the right place if its head is not. In many ways it is *argumentum ad populum* (an appeal to public opinion) at its worst. It excites feeling and trades on ignorance. Few people in Australia know anything of the Aborigines at first hand. They therefore cannot judge arguments which seem to rest on good knowledge. Its stereotypes are about as sensible and as true as their nineteenth-century counterparts. The one that I find particularly interesting is that of the Aboriginal knocking at a door which selfish interests are trying to close against him. It does not agree with the facts as I understand them. There is a door, if you like, and the Aborigines are knocking at it: but in the regions of which I speak it is not the door of Australianism. It would be more accurate, using this image, to say that there are a number of doors through none of which the Aborigines seem to want to go, but through which different European interests are trying to pull them. And each door is marked: 'This way to our version of a full life.'

I do not know every Aboriginal in Australia, but those I do know show plainly that they want to combine Aboriginal and European things in a manner of their own choice. It is this strong preference which underlies the struggle I have referred to. Out of many hundreds, apart from those in areas where settlement is now a century or more old, I have met four Aborigines who wanted, as far as I could tell, to be fully Europeanised. Each was a woman and each went into a religious order. I have known several men who, having a good opportunity to live in a European fashion, preferred not to. I have never known any who seemed, as far as I could tell, to envy Europeans for much more than their skills and possessions. I have known many who, intuiting something of the pressures behind the mask over our way of life, were repelled, especially by the disciplines of regular work and fixed hours, and by the social costs we bear. I doubt very much if my experience differs greatly from that of others who spend much time with Aborigines.

There is no reason to believe that many Aborigines want the kind of future which is predetermined by assimilation. If there is evidence that many do not and if, further, we meet the position by making their decision for them, the issue takes itself to a plane where expediency has to look for ethical justifications. That there are immense pressures of expediency we all understand. But they do not answer the ethical questions. The principles are clear. Is this use of power arbitrary? Is the decision just? And is it goodneighbourly? Rigorously asked, and candidly answered, they will leave many people feeling uncomfortable. The policy does not envisage the Aborigines as having any right of option. To do so would challenge the assumption that assimilation is what they need and want. There are positive requirements which compel an Aboriginal to give up his own choice of life in order to gain things otherwise conceded to be his of right. The ethics of this policy thus seem very dubious.

The trouble is that our motives are mixed. We are concerned with our own reputation as much as, if not a little more than, the Aborigines' position. Such a policy makes us stand rather better with ourselves than we once stood, but it comforts us rather more than we have any reason to suppose it will comfort the Aborigines. It helps to expiate the past by a moral gesture to the future. The trouble with mixed motives is that they lead to crossed purposes. I think that much of the difficulty centres in the fact that we have persuaded ourselves we have only two options—the methods of the past and assimilation. The either-or approach scarcely seems necessary. There is a third possibility. And that is to found a policy on a real knowledge of what is taking place among the modern Aborigines, not on a *mystique* about their imaginary future. This leads me to a most difficult set of problems. Part of what the Aborigines are becoming is made up of obscure effects of what they were. Some of these effects are in radical conflict with the European *mystique* about the future.

***

In a certain region of north Australia a myth which is still told tells of events at a remote time in human history, The Dream Time. A great man, Angamunggi, was treacherously killed by his son, who had committed incest with his two sisters, Angamunggi's daughters. The girls were trusting and, we may presume, innocent. The son, Tjinimin, was filled with guile, malice and lust.

Having seduced his sisters, he next speared his father, while Angamunggi sat unsuspectingly, surrounded by his many children, at song and music during a festive gathering of all the clans. The father, in agony and about to die, lingered on to perform a series of marvels. He moved from place to place, and in doing so formed a track or path which is now sacred. At each resting place he tried unavailingly to staunch the flow of blood from the spear wound in his side. In some mysterious way his blood produced perennial pools and springs of water, which remain as his marks or signs. After a long wandering he took all the fire then in the world, tied it on his head with his own hair, and waded into the sea. Another man daringly snatched a brand just as Angamunggi was about to disappear under the waves. In this way fire was saved for men, who would otherwise have had to eat raw food, like animals. And, in his death agonies, Angamunggi gave men perennial waters. They were life-giving waters, for it was in them that, somehow, he also placed the spirits of all children who have been born since then.

A book could be written—indeed, I cannot promise not to write it—about the symbolisms of the myth. All I wish to do now is to resolve what is secondary and incidental into what is primary, and then rearrange the primary elements another way. What emerges is a story which suddenly becomes strangely familiar to us. A benign father is killed by his evil son. The son goes off among men. The father, by his death, gives men the fire and water which are the means of perennial life. Let us put this alongside another story: that of a benign father who sends his well-beloved son to redeem men by dying for them. By his death the son gives men a prospect of eternal life with the father. Here are two remarkably parallel intuitions about man and his whole situation. There is of course no historical connexion whatever.

Now, Angamunggi was not any kind of god. He made no covenant with men; he gave no moral instructions; he did not demand righteousness or supplication. Nor was he saint or sage.

He is conceived of as man, an immense man of great powers, including the power to work marvels. His name is revered, after a fashion, but not in any way worshipped, though he 'looked after' people. One patrilineal moiety called him 'father's father', the other moiety called him 'mother's father'. Sometimes he was called by both moieties *Yila Neki,* the Father of Us All. He was a benign image, personifying the good. His lot somehow typifies for the Aborigines the lot of men, which is both good and bad. His 'death' at Tjinimin's hands was metaphorical, or at least inconclusive, in that he is still somehow able to manifest himself: in the fertilising power of water; in the sacramental power of blood; in the manifold powers of fire; and in the vital principle which is in seasons, rain, tides, and the begetting of children by spiritual agency. All these, so to speak, are continuous functions of his powers in 'life' and 'death'. He is also manifested objectively: physically, as an immense snake supposed to inhabit deep waters; and by signs: the rainbow, which is taken to be his tongue or spit; by marks or paintings on rocks; or through things which men make, e.g. bullroarers, on which they incise or paint signs which are his marks and, being his marks, somehow have his efficacy.

This myth reveals a very characteristic structure of Aboriginal outlook, half implicit, half explicit. In the language of an older time, it is a 'type'. The word 'type' here means an original form or figure or model after which later things are made. What is modelled on or after the type is its 'antitype'. The Angamunggi-Tjinimin story is a collective representation, a 'type' of something about the whole human situation, an ultimate social reality, as the blacks understand it. Both the Old and the New Testaments make use of the idea of a type. The scriptural types are foreshadowing or prophetic models or figures of what is to come. St Paul tells us that Adam was 'a figure of him that was to come'. The prophetic element is not present in Aboriginal thought. Consequently, the actual or supposedly 'antitypical' life of men is not conceived of as moving to any kind of consummation. But the prefigurative element is there, with an eschatological quality. End and beginning are here at one, or supposed to be at one. This is the reason why the more reflective Aborigines, to a question 'why do you do this?' will often say: 'We follow up The Dreaming.' I have elsewhere said that they see life as a one-possibility thing with a once-for-all character. It is thus perfectly consistent that in actual life they should lack what we recognise as moral zeal or earnestness. And it is just as consistent that they should show a disinterest in 'development' as we understand it, and thus be thoroughly at cross-purposes with much that we want them to do.

A proper understanding of the structure of life and thought which produces such a myth helps to explain much that is otherwise baffling. So long as the image with that structure has force, it makes the Aborigines genuinely unable to comprehend many things. One of them is the central theme of Christian teaching, let alone its mystery. That is, the theme and mystery of sacrifice. It should be obvious why.

God's sacrifice of his son is almost, though perhaps not quite, the *contra S3* of Angamunggi's murder by his son. The one was an unmerited grace coming from perfect goodness, the other a gratuitous crime coming from unmitigated evil. In the Aboriginal myth we are dealing with the explicit, that is, the verbal expression of an intuition which is only in part conscious. Externally, so to speak, it issues in a story; the story states a mystery; the mystery seems to summate an intuition of the essential nature of social life; the intuition is framed on the model of the human family; and the mythological drama of the family is almost the reverse of the idea of sacrifice. No true juncture of the Christian and the Aboriginal mind can thus be possible. They face each other at a frontier of the mind and, as far as my experience runs, they go on without a true meeting. This is but one of several divisions of Aboriginal life in which, in my understanding, the same thing occurs. The contrasts are not absolute, but very radical. If they were absolute, not even a dusty encounter would be possible. When we finally isolate and study these fundamental structures we may find that we have much of the explanation of the quite marked disinterest the Aborigines have shown and still show in so many kinds of European activity.

Consider a few of the contrasts. We are deeply interested in futurity. We try to foresee, forestall and control it by every means from astrology and saving to investment and insurance: the Aborigines are scarcely concerned with it at all; it is not a problem for them. Their 'future' differentiates itself only as a kind of extended present, whose principle is to be continuously at one with the past. This is the essence of the set of doctrines I have called The Dreaming. Our society is organised by specialised functions which cut across groups; theirs on a basis of segmentary groups, often arranged with a geometric symmetry into twos, fours and eights, each having comparable sets of functions. Theirs is a self-regulating society, knowing nothing of our vast apparatus of state instrumentalities for authority, leadership or justice. Ours is a market-civilisation, theirs not. Indeed, there is a sense in which The Dreaming and The Market are mutually exclusive. What is The Market? In its most general sense it is a variable locus in space and time at which values—the values of anything—are redetermined as human needs make themselves felt from time to time. The Dreaming is a set of doctrines about values—the value of everything—which were determined once-for-all in the past. The things of The Market—money, prices, exchange values, saving, the maintenance and building of capital—which so sharply characterise our civilisation, are precisely those which the Aborigines are least able to grasp and handle. They remain incomprehensible for a long time. And they are among the foremost means of social disintegration and personal demoralisation.

Some of the differences which come from all this are best shown negatively, some positively. As a positive example, take the segmentary principle, which among us is so buried by functional specialisations that we almost forget its existence. A segmentary society is one built up from unit-parts or series of parts having a like structure. Aboriginal society is built up from types of clans, moieties and the like, which must remain separate but only in such a way that their separateness does not lessen the unity of the whole system or organisation. The separateness becomes an interdependent separateness. A man in one segment, wishing to take part in a religious ceremony, necessarily depends upon a man from another segment to put the proper signs on his body. Or, wishing to have his son initiated, must look to men from other segments to perform the crucial parts of the rite. The fact of other segments is a condition of his own fullness of life, not a competitor with its fullness. The fact of other functions is a condition of fullness of life with us too: but it is also the death of a certain kind of fullness.

The kind of fundamental differences I have mentioned—the attitude to futurity, the segmentary principle, the self-regulating system, the disbursive sumptuary plan of economy—and many others issue in a general design or plan of life at the opposite pole of our own.

Indeed if one tried to invent two styles of life, as unlike each other as could be, while still following the rules which are necessary if people are to live together at all, one might well end up with something like the Aboriginal and the European traditions.

Where we have gone most seriously wrong is in two things. We imagine that when these Aboriginal traditions break down, as they widely have, only scraps survive and survive fortuitously. The other mistake is to imagine that the way to change this kind of continuity is by the rational demonstrations.

It would be helpful to stop thinking of the Aborigines as a 'primitive' people. They are a highly specialised people and a contemporary people. Their modes of life and thought have been elaborated over at least as long a period of time as we ordinarily think of as composing European 'history'. Unless we see both their contemporaneity and their specialisation, we set up a false model, a kind of 'genetic' model in which they are depicted as 'simple' or 'earlier' or 'more primitive' than ourselves. The image is of people lying somewhere along a uniform linear serial sequence with us. According to this model, we thus have only to 'teach' or 'show' Aborigines where they made their mistakes and they will quickly become Europeans in outlook, organisation and custom. All we have to do is instruct them in the manifest virtues of our style of life and, without undue strain, they will follow. This is a fantasy. It perishes on a single fact of life. They have to 'unlearn' being Aborigines, in mind, body and estate. The problems of 'unlearning' are visible in a thousand miserable encampments around the continent. These camps in part mirror our self-centredness. In part they mirror also the Aborigines' inability to work miracles. Consider the outcome if we were to try to convert the modern price economy to the medieval principle of the 'just price'. Yet this principle is closer to modern principle than any of our cultural principles are to those of the Aborigines. Their rapid assimilation to European culture will be possible only by a kind of brain-washing.

Yet I am not arguing that their life and thought have never changed, or cannot change. It would be unwise to make such statements even if there were no evidence to turn to. Actually, there is a good deal of evidence. For example, the kinship structures show much evidence that in the past there were changes of the kind one calls 'development'. When the morphological study of kinship is complete, we may be able to deduce a lot of things about the speciation and variegation of these, their most resistant and continuous modes of organising social life. Then there are all the evidences of mural art. Compare the extreme realism of the so-called X-ray art and the extreme abstraction through which a vital human image is depicted by three lines. Here is another kind of change, not development, but 'alteration'. We cannot really suppose these styles altered autonomously. There must have been many psychic and social concomitants. There is, of course, abundant evidence of change in contemporary times. Anthropologists have studied scores of instances in which the Aborigines, by compulsion or choice, have abandoned places, things, customs, even language and possibly ideas (though of this it is naturally hard to be sure). They have also resisted many attempts to make them accept developments, alterations and substitutions, or have turned away from many opportunities open to them to do so. I cannot describe even in summary how it has worked out. My 'dusty encounter' must do for the moment. I think it is more important to consider the bearing on my two main statements: that the Aborigines are widely in an obscure struggle with us, and that the essence of the struggle is their wish to go their own way.

For what fundamental reasons do they resist? Is there a perceptual block of such a kind that capital-building and other such type-conceptions of our culture just do not make sense, since the form-ideas either do not exist or, if they do, are hooked up with contrary conceptions? Or shall we accept the easier hypothesis: that it is because they resent our denial to them of decent opportunities of education and participation in our life? I do not believe we shall get anywhere with questions of this kind until we revalue a good deal of our knowledge of both past and present.

***

I have shown how a search for stimulants, and for new kinds of wealth, led certain natives to their ruin. Voluntarily, by compulsion, or simply because a particular rationale vanished, they abandoned or modified one kind of activity after another. Eventually they came to things they would not, or did not know how to, abandon or modify. They reached a kind of residuum: the conventional practices of life, the due forms of marriage, the initiations of youths, the machinery of grievance settlement, and mundane institutions of this order. What was left was a sort of Low Culture as distinct from the High Culture of tradition. When this truncated life came under pressure—from failing numbers and the ageing of leaders—and when the objective circumstances of life were at about their worst (during the post-World War I period)—an effort was made to reconstitute the High Culture. In one place, after fifty years of Europeanism, another religious cult started. I think I was perhaps the first to see this cult in operation since it had been reported by Sir Baldwin Spencer. It replaced The All-Father by The All-Mother, Karwadi, who is The Old Woman of the Kunapipi cult studied by Dr Berndt. This was probably as close as the Aborigines could come to the type of religious cult familiar from Melanesian, Polynesian and other regions. Here it used a complementary idea which was beautifully appropriate, logically and psychologically—the idea of The All-Mother—to continue where The All-Father had failed. The theme was reconstitutive, not revolutionary or millenarian. Still no prophetic element! Still the guiding conception of continuity with The Dream Time! The bullroarer was swung to summon a new life-principle to a dwindling and needy people. And then The All-Mother in turn began to fail.

All this was twenty-five years ago. I was in the same place not long ago. The rites of The All-Mother had not been held for some time. The old were in conflict with the young, the men with the women. It would be only a little fanciful to say that the spirit of Tjinimin was abroad. An old man, once the most feared and influential in the region, was being derided. His wife had run away, taking his son—not her own child—as her lover, and his son had helped in the abduction of a sister. And all, old, young, and women, were in a conflict with Europeanism as marked as it had ever been. The war, with its upsets, and the post-war inflation, had drawn a boundary and had stretched to breaking-point what was left of a tradition. One could find without difficulty what the situation was. It can be put simply. The Aborigines were still not interested in anything but the externals and material possessions of Europeanism. They were as far as ever from grasping its rationale, its forms, or its values. They still wanted to go their own way. I could not but notice the extent to which opportunism, activism, fecklessness and light-headedness existed among the younger people. There was something like a mania for gambling. Theft and general dishonesty were more common than I had ever known before. There was also rather more antagonism towards Europeans, and a trickier, less naïve manipulation. Here is one of the worst difficulties. An Aboriginal who is 'unlearning' his traditional code does not end the process as a *tabula rasa:* he has been learning something else at the same time.

I had this kind of thing in mind when I spoke of the 'dusty encounter'. It is as good a phrase as any, though I might well have said, in Tönnies's words, that European and Aboriginal were 'associated in spite of separation' and 'separated in spite of association'. That is what it means. It is what one expects when *Gemeinschaft* meets *Gesellschaft,* when segment meets function, in such conditions of collision.

In my studies of this region the facts of struggle have kept on filling my eye. I doubt if it is a bias of observation. The region and the people are not so unlike others. The one thing that seems to continue is the effort of the restless, if baffled, Aborigines to work out terms of life they know how to handle. This is why they develop rather than alter, substitute rather than forgo, and give in only to try to outwit. Plainly visible through the process is the fact that it has a system, as every process must. It is as plain as daylight that this system is still fundamentally Aboriginal in type.

Here the former territories have been given up long since, but each adult knows his clan country and that of his mother. They are still indispensable names for use as pointers and reckoners. Each man can give at least part of his patriline. Not one but can say which is his moiety, those timeless divisions which existed even before Angamunggi. Very many have married wrongly, but few fail to express regret at the fact. The old trading system still runs on the same principles, though with many more breaches. The corporate clan estate is only a memory, but some of its signs—totemic markings—are still jealously guarded rights.

My professional audience may wonder why I have not given more time to such matters which, after all, are the hard stuff of anthropological study. I would simply reply that I prefer on this occasion to try to make a sketch of another kind of reality. There is a wholesome fear in modern anthropology of overloading abstractions with reality. We thus sometimes beg the question whether we have consulted the right reality in the first place. Behind the forms we abstract are men with ideas. The things I have concentrated on are persistent ideas about how life should be. The continuity of social forms rests on idea-continuity, and this in turn on the continuity with which interests are valued. Here there is an implicit as well as an explicit tradition. One of our problems is just the implicitness or wordlessness of some of the conceptions still powerfully affecting the Aborigines. Often one is not too sure even of the questions to ask, or of the right ways to ask them.

Both implicit and explicit traditions are functions of rational intellects. People who suppose the Aborigines to be without intellects of course will not readily credit them with rationality. That mistake is at the bottom of some of our most misguided actions. There is no necessary contradiction in speaking of a tradition which is both 'implicit' and yet 'rational'. The same visual sign, a circle or a set of concentric circles, may be a symbol of, i.e. stand for or 'mean', a waterhole, a camp, a woman's breast, or her womb, according to the context in which the sign is used. What is it about these which has struck a spark from Aboriginal imagination? The idiom of the European mind would allow—though nowadays a little grudgingly—a poet, or an artist, or a religious thinker to find a meaning to unify things so disparate. One of the timeless functions of poetry and art is to reveal, and of religion to sacralise, the gulfs which a mundane life opens between things the 'practical' and 'scientific' minds treat as disparate. Hence the 'divorce' of which we speak between 'life' on the one hand and art, poetry and religion on the other. The Aboriginal mind is free of these tensions. At least it was. Its most fundamental cast seems to be analogical and *a fortiori* metaphorical. The difference between analogy and other kinds of thought is really in the purposes of the thinkers. The Aboriginal analogy-finder sees likeness and similarity in order to construct symbolic unities. We see them in order to construct functional and systemic classifications for wholly different purposes. Reality is cut up, put into different compartments, and related to life in a very idiosyncratic fashion. What makes the Aboriginal idiosyncrasy difficult for us to grasp, or grasp easily, is the force of our Hebraic-Grecian-Roman tradition of intellectual and spiritual culture, and the modern mutations. But a waterhole, a camp, a breast and a womb really do have something in common: something to do with 'life' or the sustenance of life. This 'something' can be expressed by a sign, and whenever the sign is used it can point beyond itself to the things unified by its meaning. The sign can by use and wont become so much a part of men's concern with 'life' that the arbitrariness of the association, and the first insight by analogy, can fall below the level of the conscious and become part of the presuppositions with which one faces living. Much of Australian anthropology could well be re-examined on its dimension of symbolism. Miss Nancy Munn has recently studied complexes of visual signs among the Walbiri. We await the completion of her work with great interest.[3] Perhaps anthropology, like history, needs rewriting with each generation.

I am suggesting that the association of European and Aboriginal has been a struggle of partial blindness, often darkened to sightlessness on our part by the continuity of the Aborigines' implicit tradition. Implicitness does not imply lack of power. We are all subtly dominated by tacit presuppositions. What life is, how it should be lived, what it can and cannot become, what things in it are significant, what is their relative place, what their value: all these may be so well known, so unproblematic, that they do not have to be formulated in any clear way. A single idea and word—*God* or *moira*—may summate such ultimate meanings. The Aboriginal concept of The

---

[3] Published as Walbiri Iconography (Cornell University Press, 1973).

Dreaming is such a summation. The traditional pattern or design of Aboriginal life is grounded in this conception.

When the blacks speak of The Dreaming they offer something between a justification and a rationalisation of their life. It is not 'history' or 'explanation'. It is too mixed up with analogical devices of symbolic imagery to be a true exegesis, too unreflective to be an apologetic. It is part of a moving system, accompanying it like a shadow, in continuous correspondence with it, being modified as life modifies. Its naïveté is touched here and there by more profound reflections: the myth of Angamunggi and Tjinimin shows what a potential was there for inspirational thought. One cannot help but wonder what those elements might have turned into under the touch of an Amos, an Ezekiel or Isaiah, or someone like Jeremiah, who said of himself that he had 'a burning fire shut up in his bones'. The Aborigines 'made' The Dreaming as they went along, making it from such ingredients as were there. It was the kind of stuff on which prophets might have thrived, but no prophets arose, or none of whom we have heard. Yet they did in comparable conditions in Melanesia and Polynesia. Is there an explanation?

I recall having seen somewhere in the Australian literature, though I cannot remember where, a reference to an old Aboriginal woman who prophesied a time when the whites would be black and the blacks white. This is very reminiscent of things we know of from Melanesia and elsewhere. A search might yield something interesting. But the best results will come from an inquiry guided by theory. The facts we want to know may have to be built up. If I may quote Myrdal: 'Scientific facts do not exist *per se,* waiting for scientists to discover them.' Each such fact is 'a construction abstracted out of a complex and interwoven reality by means of arbitrary definitions and classifications'. The theoretical reworking of a great deal of our knowledge of the past is now very necessary. Incidentally, it does not greatly matter from this viewpoint if the traditional way of life has vanished. If my argument is correct, the fundamental plan will have the strongest continuity of anything in that life, and we shall readily recognise its persistence through all but catastrophic change. Thereafter we shall continue to meet with it in concealed and cryptic forms.

The works of men like Sir Baldwin Spencer and Dr Roth were written broadly to the model of natural history. The role they gave to the anthropologist was to record and describe the facts. This they did with great ability in a period when scholarship was still suffused by 'philosophical prejudices and an aura of sociological mysticism'. Because of their restraint one does not look to them for imaginative interpretations of what they saw. They are a sharp contrast with a scholar of equal distinction, Professor Radcliffe-Brown, who wrote his indispensable studies most deliberately from a theory of human science in general. His model was that of experimental natural science rather than natural history. A third contrast, and one at least as sharp, is with the work of Dr Roheim, who sought to interpret

Aboriginal data in such a way that a bridge would be built between two disciplines, psychology in its psycho-analytical developments, and the comparative sociology of social systems. Each of these men has an unusual observational skill and field ability. But they abstracted differently from the same or comparable facts; they abstracted to different levels of generality; and they projected their abstractions onto different schematic devices. The consequence is that to relate the work of any one to the work of any other is always difficult and at times impossible. We now need new minds and new points of view, even if only about old ideas.

1958

The Boyer Lectures: After the Dreaming (1968)

LOOKING BACK

The subject of these lectures will be ourselves and the Aborigines and in particular the new relations which have been growing up between us over the last thirty years. The changes from former times have been so great that some people speak confidently of a 'revolution'. I will find cause later to ask if that judgment is justified and if indeed the revolution has yet arrived, but for a particular reason the first thing I want to do is to look back a long way to the first five years of Australian history. It was over that period that there came into existence between the two races a basic structure of relations which ever since has formed a part of the continuing anatomy of Australian life. It is of course a much-told story, but I think it will withstand another telling, this time in seven brief chapters.

The first chapter starts with the landing in January, 1788, and covers a few weeks only. Phillip, the Governor, brings with him a hopeful theory of human affairs: that an offer of friendship and trust will bring friendship and trust in return. He hopes to coax the Aborigines into close relations with the settlement and to give them 'a high opinion of their new guests' (the words are his) by refraining from any show or use of superior force. For a while the theory seems to work: a writer of the time speaks of a stage of 'cautious friendship'. But things go wrong before a month is out and it is plain that the policy of 'amity and trust' is miscarrying.

The second chapter opens with the Aborigines holding aloof. The encounters of black and white are 'neither frequent nor cordial', and the background is one of nasty or violent incidents. No one has any clear idea what is the matter.

Phillip and other officers suspect the convicts and to a lesser extent the Aborigines, but not themselves or the fact and design of the colony. By the end of May the rift is so wide that Phillip feels he must force a confrontation in order to explain how much he disapproves of harm being done to the Aborigines, and how many good things he wants to do for them.

In the third chapter, which covers the period from May to October in the first year, we find him going around trying—without a word of the language—to convey his good intent. His failure is complete, and by the end of October, with the violence continuing and a real fear growing within the settlement, he reverses his first policy. He now thinks it 'absolutely necessary' (again the words are his) to force the Aborigines to keep at a greater distance. He responds to fresh Aboriginal violence by sending out a firing party. Whether they kill or wound anyone we do not know, but he succeeds in his purpose: not one Aborigine comes near them for months.

The fourth chapter opens towards the end of 1788. Within the settlement affairs have become desperately bad. Starvation seems not far away. Phillip seems to conclude that he has made a mistake and now decides that it is 'absolutely necessary' (his words again) to force the Aborigines *in to* the settlement, not *away* from it, and makes a plan to kidnap some of them. His own disclosed motive is to make them see the advantages of joining their lives with those of the settlers. Another man, Watkin Tench—someone has called him 'that liberal and candid mind'—discloses a second motive—to find out through them what resources the country has that might prolong the colony's weakening vitality.

Our fourth chapter, then, is mainly the story of a second turnabout, a rather crazy story of three kidnaps—of Arabanoo, Colby and Benelong. The first, the gentle, confused Arabanoo, dies within the settlement from smallpox, and Phillip feels 'utterly defeated', but six months later he tries again with Colby and Benelong. Colby, a wily fellow, escapes after a week. Benelong, a bouncing, ebullient man, and a bit of a rogue, escapes after five months.

The first three of Phillip's policies are now in ruins. He has gained nothing, and lost something—that is, all chance now of winning Aboriginal confidence, because Colby and Benelong have spread their tales—of what, we do not know, but certainly including a warning that behind any soft-seeming approach there is the possibility of sudden force and treachery. Phillip himself seems empty of ideas and divided between two half-expressed feelings: a falling confidence in the Aborigines, and a rising fear of them.

For month after month there are no significant relations until the fifth chapter opens in September, 1790, when Phillip—brave, magnanimous and good-hearted as ever, but, we must now conclude, rash and rather wrong-headed—very nearly meets his death by a spear thrown during a chance encounter with Benelong and some 200 other Aborigines at Manly Cove. A study of the background and conduct of this affair shows the Governor to have made one mistake after another. After almost three years' experience it is obvious that he had learned nothing of Aboriginal mentality or tendency.

We thus come to the sixth, the climactic chapter, at the end of 1790. Three themes are now starting to weave themselves together in a way that will have a signal bearing on Australian history.

Something breaks in the fabric of native life around Port Jackson, and from every side the Aborigines, unforced, begin to flock into the settlement. Phillip can now write: 'from this time on our intercourse with the Aborigines, though partially interrupted, was never broken off.' The break is one that never mends and will eventually reach right across the continent in every direction. Within the settlement the worst of the troubles seems to be over. A second theme thus comes into view: the colonists no longer need to know if the Aborigines can help; they can get along by themselves. The history of indifference thus begins and with it a dark and sombre third theme. At the end of 1790 Phillip's personal huntsman, a convict named M'Entire, is speared at Botany Bay. He is a villainous man, and almost everyone knows or suspects it—some of the colonists and the Aborigines certainly do.

The murder puts Phillip in a great passion. He throws away all his earlier scruples. He wants blood—anyone's blood, except that of women and children. At first he demands ten heads, and two live captives whom he will then hang 'in the presence of as many of their countrymen as can be collected after having explained the cause of such a punishment', no doubt by signs, for no one yet has a sentence of the language. At the suggestion of a squeamish officer Phillip makes it not ten heads, but six persons, to be captured or shot; if captive, two will hang; the rest will be gaoled for a time at Norfolk Island, the place set aside for the very worst of the convict desperadoes. So, carrying axes to lop the heads and bags to hold them, the punitive party (the first in our history) goes out, not once, but twice, ten days apart, but on both occasions the enterprise is fumbled and collapses in failure.

There can be no doubt that the affair leaves Phillip damaged in credit. He has shown himself an easy victim of pique, whose nerve and judgment can both go wrong at the same time, who reacts quite disproportionately to cause, and who, having been given ample time to cool, for a second time goes well beyond the edge of intent to commit judicial murder. Perhaps he continues to stand, in the frame of his relations with the colonists, as one historian has described him—as a man who 'with grace, dignity, industry and great self-control had won the battle for survival', but in the frame of his relations with the Aborigines there is now a different cut to his jib, and at least one young officer of his command sees it. In the whole of his record with the Aborigines there is little that suggests wisdom or even a great deal of commonsense, and half a dozen episodes reveal him as a rather eyeless, uninventive man.

The M'Entire affair happens at the very time when the Aborigines, in the main, are doing exactly what he has most wanted them to do under his three policies, that is, thronging into Sydney. But it is a Sydney that now neither needs nor fears them and exactly then Phillip is least like the man history reputes him to have been.

He still has two more years to serve as Governor. Over that period, which is our seventh chapter, he seems to pass beyond consideration of native policy. At all events we hear little about it from him, but others tell us a fragment or two of what is happening to the Aborigines. One writes that 'a great many of them have taken up their abode entirely among us' and another that 'every gentleman's house was now become a resting or sleeping place for some every night; whenever they were pressed for hunger, they had recourse immediately to our quarters'. It is the denouement of the policies of amity and trust, forcing away, and forcing in. The streets of Sydney are filling with the dispossessed, the homeless, the powerless and the poverty-stricken from all over the County of Cumberland and, before long, from places beyond.

The story tails away without a clear, sharp finish, so I suppose I cannot do better than to allow the historians, who know how to handle such things, to have the last word. From this time on, according to one of them, 'the native question sank into unimportance', which I understand to mean that no one bothered any more about it. According to another, the Aborigines became a 'melancholy footnote to Australian history' and, to yet another, 'a codicil to the Australian story'.

I have thought it worthwhile to retell this old tale from a particular point of view because more recent history suggests that the native question is rising into great importance, the melancholy footnote is turning into a whole chapter of Australian history, and the codicil is becoming a major theme in the Australian story. It has been my good fortune to have had something to do with that process over the last thirty years from a time when one could still go out in Australian space and, in so doing, in a certain sense go back in time so as to see the living reality of the things that occurred immediately after Phillip's seventh chapter. The clothes were modern, the body different-seeming, but the skeleton was the same. The fundamental structure of racial relations was as near to that of the early 1800s as made no difference.

This part of what I have to say will therefore to some extent be a personal history but it is sometimes useful to look at a piece of history—the development of attitudes and relations since the 1930s—through the eyes of someone who took part. What participant or bystander saw, felt, thought, or said at the time can help to put past happenings in a proper light. That must be my excuse for the element of personal reminiscence.

In 1932 I went to a remote place in the Northern Territory to study some little known tribes. It was a broken-down settlement which might well have been the Illawarra or the Hawkesbury of a hundred years or so before. There was an exiguous scatter of farmers, cattlemen and miners with leaseholds over lands still lived on by the remnants of the local tribes, which nevertheless still felt that they had an ancient and unbroken title to the lands.

On the outskirts of the settlement there were a few groups of 'myalls' (bush natives) who were as wild as hawks, timid and daring by turns, with scarcely a word of English, and in two minds what to do: drawn towards the settlement because the break in the tribal structure had reached them too, but unreconciled to the prospect of a sedentary life. Some of them were being tempted in, others pushed away, as the need, fear or expediency of the Europeans dictated in almost Phillipian stops and starts. There was bad blood, frequent fighting, and much talk of sorcery and poison, between the bush and the sedentary groups, and no love between any of them and the Europeans, so that cautious friendship alternated with covert or open hostility. In the space of a couple of years two Europeans in the vicinity were speared to death, and several Aborigines were killed or wounded by others of their own kind.

No one liked to walk alone too far from habitation except along the main tracks. In the settlement itself there was extreme poverty: I had never supposed that men could live so hard and think it worthwhile to battle on; everything was run-down and ramshackle; there was not a doctor, a teacher, a school, a store, or a church within a hundred miles. The Aborigines were looked on and used almost as free goods of nature. For such work as they did they were given a little payment in kind. It was a sort of peonage. I do not think there was a single element in the whole system of life—land, food, shelter, jobs, pay, the safety of women and children, even access to and protection by the law—in which they were not at great disadvantage, and without remedy. The dominance of European interests was total, unquestioned, and inexpressibly self-centred. Here, only thirty-six years ago, was the still living reality of 'the codicil to the Australian story'.

How did people regard such conditions at the time? It is an interesting question if the answer is given without anachronism. I suppose the first thing is: how well and widely known such conditions were. The authorities in the Northern Territory were certainly well-informed; indeed, they had warned me what to expect, at least in general. I would say the facts were the open knowledge of the countryside. I would not say that anyone actually approved but, just as plainly, no one with the exception of the devoted mission societies thought very much could be done, or had a visibly high impulse to try. That was certainly true of the law. The police turned a blind eye, and they were the local Protectors of Aborigines. My own personal response seems to have been mixed. I remember recoiling in dismay from the poverty, neglect, illhealth, ill-use and exploitation. But let me pause. It is easy to trade on memory, and I said there was to be no anachronism; so I have to say 'I think I remember'; but I could not prove that I remember aright. But I have some letters and reports which I wrote at the time. They help to bridge the gap a little, but not wholly. The letters are filled with sympathy for the plight of the natives, with respect for their quality of mind and social personality, and with real affection for several who had become personal friends. But they show very much the same attitudes towards the bushmen I had met, many of whom also had befriended me. It is clear that I gave a lot of weight in the scales of judgment to the hardship, loneliness and privation of their lives, and to their unyielding struggle to keep going. The reports are rather different. Somehow, in them, I seem to have managed to draw a screen over at least the worst things of that frontier. There is no obvious sign of trying to put a good face on things; no indication of saving the eyes or ears of those to whom I was reporting; no palpable effort to write, as it were, for history; but on the other hand a very interesting absence of declamation. The tone of my comments is rather reminiscent of the flat, emotionless remark that Spencer and Gillen had made thirty years earlier when they said that '...taking all things into account, the black fellow has not perhaps any particular reason to be grateful to the white man'. Apparently what lay before my eyes seemed to me a natural and inevitable part of the Australian scene, one that could possibly be palliated, but not ever changed in any fundamental way.

Of course personal limitations, training, and narrow concerns explain a lot of this. In particular, the interests of anthropology as it was at that time certainly had much to do with it. I was steeped in the outlook of Spencer and Gillen, but not long since, under the influence of Radcliffe-Brown and Malinowski, I had been taught to turn my back on the speculative reconstruction of the origins and development of primitive institutions, and to have interest only in their living actuality. The young anthropologist now wanted to understand what was then being called the 'functional system' of social life, how institutions help to maintain each other, and contribute to the whole process of human society. We were beginning to speak about 'social structure', the system of enduring relations between persons and groups. Where a society was breaking down (as with most of the Aborigines) we thought it our task to salvage pieces of information and from them try to work out the traditional social forms. Such were my interests. They help to explain why an interest in 'living actuality' scarcely extended to the actual life-conditions of the Aborigines, and why in referring to those conditions I did so in a sidelong way and in anything but a firebrand's words. But it will hardly do as a sufficient explanation. What was missing was the idea that a major development of Aboriginal economic, social and political life from its broken down state was a thinkable possibility. How slowly this idea came to all of us.

Aboriginal affairs had begun to cause a certain public concern in the middle of the 1920s, because of a series of clashes and atrocities. There had been several inquiries from which authority did not emerge at all well. Our international reputation, which had never been very good, went farther downhill. Humanitarians, mainly in the cities, pressed the authorities hard, and their tracts and pamphlets today make interesting reading: all they ask for are palliatives, better protection, better health measures, better conditions of employment. Few people could think beyond 'protection' and 'segregation'.

Judged by the way in which today's demonstrations go, ours were mild and decorous affairs—beardless too, that is, middle-aged and elderly; youth then could not be dragged to the barricades. They were vigorous for their time but Governments scarcely responded; indeed, in the Northern Territory, as late as 1933, after there had been several murders, including that of a policeman, there was immediate talk—official talk—of sending a punitive party to Arnhem Land to 'teach the Aborigines a lesson'. Public indignation prevented that from happening because now almost everyone sensed that the era of an eye for an eye had come to an end. Some sort of new spirit was in the making, but it did not discern at all well where to go. A really clear breakthrough did not come until 1934 when A.P. Elkin and others spoke in downright words of the need for a change from the negative policy of protection and segregation—which, anyway, was obviously failing—to a positive policy. There are many names which deserve honourable mention from this decade—Bleakley, Duguid, Warren, Albrecht, Love, Strehlow, Thomson, Piddington—far too many for me to list on this occasion. Men and women from all walks and levels of life made their lasting contributions.

I should like to make two things as plain as I can. It had not been up to this time a matter of people looking without being able to see: far from it; many had seen, described, and analysed extremely well what was the case; the public documents after 1926 are full of really excellent accounts of Australia. Secondly, the idea of a 'positive' policy had not come out of the blue. Many people had been working up to a change of perspective, especially after a meeting of the Association for the Protection of Native Races in 1931. What was radical and startling was the putting into words of the first notion of a 'positive' policy, obvious and unadventurous as it may seem now.

If we could have foreseen in the 1930s what an inch by inch affair the acceptance of the new outlook would turn out to be, we might all have felt despair. My own higher education in the snail's-pace of change began in 1934. I went overland to central Australia and was there in time to see part of the rush to the gold-strike at Tennant Creek. In a small way it must have been very like some of the 19th century goldfields in their first stages: a true Never Never landscape, a stretch of bush pock-marked with scattered shafts; a lot of ore at grass; little food, less water, almost no ready money; rough humpies and scores of hard customers with that worst of fevers, gold-fever. I had to keep a gun hard by to guard my stores, which just then were nearly as good as gold. There were no police: I remember the first trooper coming, with some savage dogs, after there had been a shooting. Some of the miners suspected me of being a Government agent of some kind. A party came one day to offer, in a firm but civil way, to throw me off the field if I tinkered with their affairs. The men were mollified when they learned that I was working on strictly anthropological matters. But the affair nettled me, and I was upset—more so than in 1932, so the yeast was working—by some talk of moving the Aborigines, the last of the Warramunga, out of the way of the mining into a stretch of bush in which, incidentally, I almost perished from lack of water, even though I had Aboriginal guides. I wrote a report on the whole situation for my sponsors, the Australian National Research Council. It may have been used; I never found out; but as for its effects—there were none; not enough spark, or not enough tinder in the right places. The miners won and the Warramunga lost.

It is clear to me now, though it was not then, that the new 'positive' thinking, advanced though it was, left a hole in the very centre of our social thinking. Most of that decade had to pass before the idea of a true development programme for the Aborigines came into anyone's mind. That is, an organised national programme for their social, economic and political advancement in a major and not a minor degree, and in a structural and not a merely ameliorative sense. To be sure, that basic idea was writ small throughout the 1930s, but it was never writ large and plain, so as to become a sort of committal, until 1938–39, and we had to wait for another ten years before the policy of 'assimilation' even began to be put into effect. One would like to think that its coming, late or soon, was a case of virtue at long last working on Australian hearts from Australian causes. But that would be a hard thesis to sustain. By the end of the 1930s the whole world had changed its attitude towards dependent peoples, and we responded at least as much to events and sentiments outside Australia as to events and sentiments within it. I know that in my own case the first proof I can show that I was thinking towards a national development plan for a native people did not come until 1938, and it had nothing to do with the Aborigines. I was at work in Kenya: and the new stimulus came from such works as McMillan's *Warning from the West Indies* and Ley's *Last Chance in Kenya,* from talking to men like L.S.B. Leakey and Jomo Kenyatta, from the strength of the African protest, and from the dawning insight that Kenya was a Land of Cloud Cuckoo that could not long endure.

In this lecture I have wanted to say four leading things. First, that only a generation ago in a part of Australia one could live within a real structure of life—a racial structure—akin to that of Phillip's day. Secondly, it was for everyone a very difficult struggle to escape from a style of thinking that unconsciously ratified that order of life as natural and unalterable. Thirdly, even when the break came, we moved by little arithmetical steps in the face of problems which even then were looming up geometrically: there was no straightline transition to a modern type of development policy. Lastly, the credit for our change of attitude is not by any means wholly ours, but rather a case of '...for not by eastern windows only, when daylight comes, comes in the light'.

I will go on in my next lecture to discuss some of the questions which arise now that something very remarkable has happened: the fact that the Aborigines having been 'out' of history for a century and a half are now coming back 'into' history with a vengeance. I wrote that sentence without thinking how two-edged it is. Even so, I think I should let it stand.

THE GREAT AUSTRALIAN SILENCE

In my first lecture I spoke about a structure of racial relations that had come about between us and the Aborigines in the early days and had stayed more or less unchanged for one hundred and fifty years. I tried to sketch something of the frame of mind and vision we had when we saw the skeleton beginning to walk in the early 1930s.

Why it began to walk then, and not earlier, or later, is a question to which I cannot give a very satisfactory answer. There was scarcely any interest in the Aborigines of the settled areas of the east and south. Concern over them is a very recent development indeed. What had aroused public feeling in 1926 and afterward were reports of atrocities in the outback and the subsequent disclosure of many bad practices. But I do not think that pastoralists, miners and other employers had suddenly become harder on their Aborigines than in the past. I doubt if authority had suddenly become more observant or active; indeed, one of the great difficulties of the time was to get the executive, administrative and legal arms of authority to notice what was afoot, let alone to move. The people whom W.K. Hancock acknowledged in his book *Australia* (1930) as ever-present—'the enthusiastic friends' of the Aborigines—were active but I doubt if their ranks were any stronger. Perhaps there had been a true rise of public sensibility but I find it hard to pin down any changes of conditions that may have brought it about. The explanation may simply be that just as in earlier times the view from Exeter Hall had been clearer than the view from Sydney, so now it was clearer from Sydney than from a town like Alice: and there was now much more to see. The road, the motor car, the aeroplane and the radio had put an end to the old isolation of the bush. It was a humdrum affair to drive from Sydney and Melbourne to Cape York and the Kimberleys. There was a piling up of evidence or near-evidence into a presumption that intolerable things were happening in the lonely places, and a certain taint of hugger-mugger about some of the official disclaimers did nothing to allay suspicion. What I am suggesting then is simply that people heard more, and heard more quickly, about a pattern of outback life that probably had not changed greatly for the worse.

Some people consider that 1934 was the main 'turning point' of Aboriginal policy. I cannot say that I recall anything about that year that suggests a sudden access of public virtue or a new vision at all widely shared. It seems to have been just another year on the old plateau of complacence.

In 1931 the Prime Minister of the day, Mr Scullin, still showed little inclination to credit that much could be amiss in Commonwealth territory and seemed not ill-content to plead the constitutional limit on his responsibility for events in the States. In 1932 the Federal Minister for Home Affairs, Mr

Parkhill, went very close to giving the Northern Territory a coat of whitewash. Even after the Arnhem Land affair of 1933 and 1934 the Prime Minister of that time, Mr Lyons, thought it appropriate to continue substantially with the existing policy. There was, perhaps, a certain softening of official attitudes and if so I do not think we can altogether dissociate the fact from inquiries which had been made by the Dominions Office through the High Commissioner in London. But we are hardly justified in placing the 'turning point' before 1938 when Mr McEwen, the then Minister for the Interior, placed before the Commonwealth Parliament the proposals which later became known as 'the New Deal for the Aborigines in the Northern Territory'. It was then that the new concept of 'assimilation' came into use although another ten years had to pass before its effects became at all noticeable.

 It is an interesting question whether we should connect the change with another 'turning point' which is supposed to have taken place at that time. I refer to R.M. Crawford's theory that a 'New Australia'—the phrase is Peter Coleman's, not Crawford's—came into being in the second half of the 1930s, and that from then on the whole stream of Australian life and thought, in public policy, social and economic attitudes, culture and letters, took a new course. The new and the stretched ideas and activities that have been cited in evidence do make an impressive list. The writers who have discussed the matter would include the great expansion of CSIRO, the recruitment of graduates to the Commonwealth Public Service, the generous patronage of culture, art and letters by the ABC and the Commonwealth Literary Fund, the formation of the Literature Censorship Board and the Contemporary Arts Society, the welcoming of Jewish refugees from Europe and the new liberalism towards immigration in general, the new confidence in industry and trade, and even such developments as the penetration of key unions by the Communist Party and the establishment of the National Secretariat of Catholic Action. These are perhaps the leading items from a catalogue which could of course grow to almost any size by the same principle of selection, that is, to take a handful of roughly contemporary things and regard them as a connected bundle.

As far as I am aware, no one yet has put the new Aboriginal policy into the bundle. The omission is surely significant. But of what? Part at least of the answer, I suggest, can be given by extending the examination into the war years. So far as domestic affairs were concerned the main power-house of progressive social thought was the Department of Post-War Reconstruction. I have good authority for saying that the idea of taking the Aboriginal situation as a challenge simply never occurred to the collective mind of that exciting and vital department. That more than anything else confirms me in my view that for all the quickening and deepening of the national stream only a trickle of new thought ran towards the Aboriginal field, and it ran around the edges, not through the middle. The only natives we were prepared to think about at all seriously at this time were those of New Guinea.

The Aborigines came a bad second. This is not to say that the war years were a blank. There was some progressive thinking in the Northern Territory, where some excellent men found themselves too far ahead of government to make their ideas felt, and the new Commonwealth Department of Social Services also made some useful advances in association with Federal and State Aboriginal agencies and with missionary bodies. But Aboriginal Australia simply could not compete with New Guinea either for public resources or for public interest. What with one thing and another the new policy of assimilation hung fire for more than a decade. I know that even in 1952, when I returned to the Northern Territory after a long absence, I could start to work very much where I had left off without any acute sense of change in the Aboriginal life around me or in their relations with white Australia. There were some changes but they were more the effect of war and the new priceinflation than of policy.

I am therefore inclined to argue that the two 'turning points' had precious little to do with each other. I suspect that the achievement of the new policy of assimilation was the product of a compartment of Australian thought and experience quite separate from and much weaker than that which led to the great energising of the rest of Australian society and culture. The 'feedback' from the greater into the lesser movement—the 'trickle' I spoke of—was entirely minimal. There is small doubt in my mind that that continues to be the case, and that it is one of the main reasons for the slowness with which we are mastering our Aboriginal problems. It is absurd that so small a part of the talent and ingenuity that exist in our departments of state, our great private industries, our universities and our research organisations should be turned toward these problems.

I will not pursue that theme further for the moment, although I will come back to it. I want instead to pick up a dropped thread. It seems clear to me now that the change of attitude and policy towards the Aborigines which we trace back to the 1930s was confined very largely to a rather small group of people who had special associations with their care, administration or study. Outside that group the changes made very little impact for a long time and, within the group, it was a case of the faithful preaching to the converted about a 'revolution' which in fact had arrived only for them. The situation has altered very considerably in the last five or six years—witness, for example, the Referendum of 1967—but has a long way to go before we are justified in using words which, like 'revolution', suggest a total change of heart and mind.

Turning this thought over in my mind the other day I asked myself whether it could be tested for truth-value even if only in part. If, for example, the two 'turning points' were not as I suggested distinct and separate, but were connected in some vital way; that is to say, if more than a very few people had been aware of a struggle waged and won in the Aboriginal field, surely (or so I argued) there should have been a marked response from the 'New Australia' that was coming into being after the late

1930s; surely the serious literature from that time on should show some evidence of a consciousness that here was another old, cluttered field to renovate by the new progressive thought. I put to one side the large array of technical papers and books expressly concerned with the Aborigines, such as Paul Hasluck's *Our Southern Half Castes* (1938) and *Black Australians* (1941) and E.J.B. Foxcroft's *Australian Native Policy* (1941), and looked instead at a mixed lot of histories and commentaries dealing with Australian affairs in a more general way. They seemed to me the sort of books that probably expressed well enough, and may even have helped to form, the outlook of socially conscious people between say, 1939 and 1955, by which time some objections of a serious kind were beginning to be made to the idea of assimilation.

The first book I looked at was M. Barnard Eldershaw's *My Australia* (1939). The Aborigines figure quite prominently in it; their affairs, indeed, make up nearly one tenth of the book; but it is only too clear that they are marginal, and in a deeper sense, irrelevant to the author's story. Hardly a word on the other 280 pages would have to be changed if they were dropped from the prologue ['A mask of Australia for inaudible voices'] and if one chapter ['The Dispossessed'] were snipped out.

The writers take over from W.K. Hancock his thesis that 'in truth, a hunting and pastoral economy cannot co-exist within the same bounds', but they do not like his plain language, and they prefer to say that 'the twentieth century and the Stone Age cannot live together'. They also have it that the white man did the black man 'very little wilful harm' and that the rest was 'inevitable'. The revolution of attitudes had certainly not arrived for these writers. In the next book, Hartley Grattan's *Introducing Australia* (1942), we are given a good thumbnail sketch of old, familiar facts. I could not deny that Grattan has a sense of change: he mentions it in one sentence on one of his 300 pages. But Brian Fitzpatrick's *The Australian People* (1946) does not show even this degree of awareness.

Only one or two of his 260 pages makes any mention of the Aborigines and, although it says well what it has to say, it is all backward-turned.

Much the same is the case with H.L. Harris's *Australia in the Making: A History* (1948). There are some fragments about Dampier, Banks, Cook and Sturt, but there it ends. The next book, Geoffrey Rawson's *Australia* (1948), has a chapter entitled 'Aborigines', which also deals with wild life, so the title could as well have been 'Aborigines and Other Fauna', after the style of John Henderson, who in 1832 wrote some 'Observations on Zoology, from the order Insecta to that of Mammalia; the latter including the Natives of New Holland'. I then turned to the 1950s, hoping for rather better things. My hand fell first on R.M. Crawford's splendid little book *Australia* (1952). There is a chapter on the Aborigines; not the shortest chapter, and not a tailpiece, but one full of good information and well-moulded general statements, and—a great novelty, this—a lively awareness of questions which historians ought to have but apparently had not, asked; for example, what were the relations between the squatters and the Aborigines? But there is little that bears on either of the 'turning points'. The next was George Caiger's *The Australian Way of Life* (1953), in which the word 'Aboriginal' is not to be found; no, I am wrong; it does occur—once, in a caption under a photograph which displays two of Australia's scenic attractions, the Aborigines and Coogee Beach. To the next book, W.V. Aughterson's *Taking Stock: Aspects of Mid-Century Life in Australia* (1953), there were ten contributors. Only one of them, Alan McCulloch, the art critic, has anything to say about the Aborigines, some passing but perceptive observations on their art. Incidentally, the book opens with a chapter entitled 'The Australian Way of Life', written by W.E.H. Stanner, who can safely be presumed never to have heard of the Aborigines, because he does not refer to them and even maintains that Australia has 'no racial divisions like America'. [At this point in my reading I could hardly resist feeling that all the authors so far mentioned should surely have used M. Barnard Eldershaw's title *'My Australia'*; that, clearly, was what they were writing about.] The intense concentration on ourselves and our affairs continues in Gordon Greenwood's *Australia: A Social and Political History* (1955). The other books by comparison are in the light or middleweight divisions; this one is nearly a heavyweight. It sets out to give a broad but comparatively detailed study of our history; to discover significant elements and the organic relations between them; to reveal the essential spirit and the dominant characteristics of each stage; and more, to show 'what gathering forces transmuted the existing society into another, different in outlook and constitution'. It is written by six eminent scholars and has been reprinted half a dozen times, so it seems to have been influential. How does it deal with the Aborigines? It mentions them five times—twice, quite briefly, for the period 1788–1821; twice again, as briefly, for the period 1820–1850; once, in sidelong fashion, for the period 1851–1892; and thereafter not at all.

Here I was, then, seventeen years after the 'turning point' in Aboriginal policy, only to find that some of our most perceptive thinkers seemed to be unaware of it or if they were had nothing to say about it. Perhaps they were right; perhaps in 1955 there were still no 'gathering forces' seeking to 'transmute' Aboriginal–European relations; perhaps my theory of two unrelated compartments of Australian life and thought could have something in it. By picking and choosing a little I went on to persuade myself that for a number of writers the lack of interest ran on even into the 1960s. For example, Peter Coleman's *Australian Civilization* (1962) leaves little of our life and thought unexamined but by its total silence on all matters Aboriginal seems to argue that the racial structure which is part of our anatomy of life has no connection with our civilisation past, present or future.

I need not extend the list. A partial survey is enough to let me make the point that inattention on such a scale cannot possibly be explained by absent-mindedness. It is a structural matter, a view from a window which has been carefully placed to exclude a whole quadrant of the landscape. What may well have begun as a simple forgetting of other possible views turned into habit and over time into something like a cult of forgetfulness practised on a national scale. We have been able for so long to disremember the Aborigines that we are now hard put to keep them in mind even when we most want to do so. It might help to break the cult of disremembering if someone made a searching study of the moral, intellectual and social transitions noticeable in Aboriginal affairs from the 1930s to the 1960s. It seems to me to beg to be written.

I am no historian and I should stick to my last but the history I would like to see written would bring into the main flow of its narrative the life and times of men like David Unaiipon, Albert Namatjira, Robert Tudawali, Durmugam, Douglas Nicholls, Dexter Daniels and many others. Not to scrape up significance for them but because they typify so vividly the other side of a story over which the great Australian silence reigns; the story of the things we were unconsciously resolved not to discuss with them or treat with them about; the story, in short, of the unacknowledged relations between two racial groups within a single field of life supposedly unified by the principle of assimilation, which has been the marker of the transition. The telling of it would have to be a world—perhaps I should say an underworld—away from the conventional histories of the coming and development of British civilisation. I hardly see that it could afford two assumptions. One is that it satisfies the canons of human relevance and social influence to allow men of the kind I have mentioned to flit across the pages as if they were the Benelongs and Colbys of the day. The other is that the several hundred thousand Aborigines who lived and died between 1788 and 1938 were but negative facts of history and, having been negative, were in no way consequential for the modern period. In Aboriginal Australia there is an oral history which is providing these people with a coherent principle of explanation of which I will speak later.

It has a directness and a candour which cut like a knife through most of what we say and write. We would have to bring this material—let me be fashionable and call it 'ethno-history'—into the sweep of our story.

One consequence of having given the Aborigines no place in our past except that of a 'melancholy footnote' is both comical and serious. Comical, because one of the larger facts of the day is the Aboriginal emergence into contemporary affairs but about all we can say, on the received version of our history, is the rising twin of that immortal observation, 'from this time on the native question sank into unimportance'. Serious, because the surfacing of problems which are in places six or seven generations deep confront us with problems of decision, but we are badly under-equipped to judge whether policies towards the problems are slogans, panaceas or sovereign remedies, or none of them.

In one sense, of course, the historians have been right. It is incontestable that few of the great affairs of the past took any sort of account of the continued Aboriginal presence. It is also the case that some great affairs of the present—the plans for the development of subtropical Australia—take all too little account of the continued Aboriginal presence there. But it is precisely this situation which calls for a less shallow, less ethnocentric social history. Fish swim in water, and what we do with our fins, gills and tails is not unrelated to the permissive-resistant medium in which we move. For example, it occurred a long time ago to W.G. Spence, that father-figure of trade unionism, that the weakness of our system of local government was connected with the rapid decimation of local native populations. As he saw it we did not devolve protective and other powers locally because there was no need to do so. The medium was in that respect permissive. But a poorly working parish pump is at one end of a scale. Let me go to the other end. All land in Australia is held in consequence of an assumption so large, grand and remote from actuality that it had best be called royal, which is exactly what it was. The continent at occupation was held to be disposable because it was assumed to be 'waste and desert'. The truth was that identifiable Aboriginal groups held identifiable parcels of land by unbroken occupancy from a time beyond which, quite literally, 'the memory of man runneth not to the contrary'. The titles which they claimed were conceded by all their fellows. There are still some parts of Australia, including some of the regions within which development is planned or actually taking place, in which living Aborigines occupy and use lands that have never been 'waste and desert' and to which their titles could be demonstrated, in my opinion, beyond cavil, to a court of fact if there were such a court. In such areas if the Crown title were paraded by, and if the Aborigines understood what was happening, every child would say, like the child in the fairy-tale, 'but the Emperor is naked'. The medium, in this matter once permissive, is not turning resistant, and the fact is one of the barely acknowl edged elements of the real structure of Australia which is working its way towards a more overt expression. Like many another fact overlooked, or forgotten, or reduced to an anachronism, and thus consigned to the supposedly inconsequential past, it requires only a suitable set of conditions to come to the surface, and be very consequential indeed.

I hardly think that what I have called 'the great Australian silence' will survive the research that is now in course. Our universities and research institutions are full of young people who are working actively to end it. The Australian Institute of Aboriginal Studies and the Social Science Research Council of Australia have both promoted studies which will bring the historical and the contemporary dimensions together and will assuredly persuade scholars to renovate their categories of understanding. If we could have done this in the 1920s and 1930s, perhaps we would not have had to wait until the middle 1950s to see any real product of the new 'positive' policy. For example, the effort to preserve the Aborigines within inviolable reserves was the last ditch of an older policy, and we were then beyond the last ditch. I do not recall that we asked ourselves at all clearly: what comes *after* a policy which *by definition* is one of *last* resort? The inability to ask the question in that way left us, not rebels without cause, but doctors without a diagnosis, and it is interesting to recall how few people then thought in terms of some of the notable advances that have in fact come about—the grant of equal political status, the suffrage, the extension of civil liberties, the ending of legal discrimination, the right to social services, and other things of the kind. One wonders what equivalent astigmatisms may affect our contemporary vision. I will suggest later that one of them is a certain inability to grasp that on the evidence the Aborigines have always been looking for two things: a decent union of their lives with ours but on terms that let them preserve their own identity, not their inclusion willy-nilly in our scheme of things and a fake identity, but development within a new way of life that has the imprint of their own ideas. But that is a topic for another lecture, and I want now to round out what I have been saying.

The impulse to make radical changes in the Aboriginal situation had little force or product until the last decade. Twenty years of the 'revolution' were thus years of the locust. The ideal of assimilation took shape when no one dreamed that galloping development would overrun all of Aboriginal Australia, and no one devised a very convincing human strategy or technical method even for the older circumstances. We thus enter on a new time with a heavy backlog of unsolved older problems. A glance at the human map of Australia still shows one of the worst of them. The map is disfigured by hundreds of miserable camps which are the social costs of old-style development that would not let any consideration of Aboriginal interest stand in its way. Development over the next fifty years will need to change its style and its philosophy if the outcome is to be very different. I have begun to allow myself to believe that there is now a credible prospect of that happening. A kind of beneficial multiplier could be starting to have effect. One notices the coming together of things from different starting points. The private industries which use and in some measure may depend on Aboriginal labour do not all resist as they once did the idea that it is in their interest to habilitate this broken society. We may see a market take shape in private industry for workable proposals. The public instrumentalities concerned with Aboriginal affairs have a head of steam towards their tasks which was not the common rule a few years ago. The flow of public funds specifically earmarked for Aboriginal advancement is relatively generous. Some very worthwhile ideas are starting to come forward from some sectors of the Aboriginal population. Perhaps the one thing now needed to increase the power of the multiplier is a projection of the costs, monetary and social, that will be a charge on the national pocket in default of a rapid advance of the Aboriginal people to self-support. A native population which promises to double itself well within twenty years will otherwise become a fiscal problem of magnitude.

One cannot talk of everything, even in a generous series of lectures of this kind, and I must now narrow my span to one of the things that interfere with our judgment of a scene that is being transformed under our eyes. That is to say, our folklore about the Aborigines. It had a lot to do with the making of our racial difficulties and it still has a lot to do with maintaining them.

THE APPRECIATION OF DIFFERENCE

I was asked the other day whether I did not agree that the Aborigines must have originated and evolved within Australia. My questioner was an earnest and sensible man and I asked him why he thought so. His answer was: 'because they are in every way so unlike any other people in the world'. He was quite unaware that he was expressing a view common in Australia more than 130 years ago which has stalwartly withstood all the biological, anthropological and archaeological information built up since that time. Popular folklore is like that, and our folklore about the Aborigines shows the qualities which distinguish it everywhere, a splendid credulity towards the unlikely and an iron resolve to believe the improbable. It mixes truth, half-truth and untruth into hard little concretions of faith that defy dissolution by better knowledge.

Sometimes self-contradictory mixtures lie about side by side. The Aborigines were masters of mental telepathy or, alternatively, had no minds at all; their morals were deplorable or, alternatively, superior to ours; they sent complex messages by smoke signal but had no true language, only a kind of bird-talk; they did not suffer pain as we do; they practised communism of property and women; they were incapable of abstract thought; they had no religious ideas—these are but a few of the more genial pieces of folklore that are still current. One of the hardiest perennials is the notion that any person of Aboriginal descent from time to time feels an overpowering urge to 'go walkabout' for some instinctual or biologically-imprinted reason. In their traditional life of course the Aborigines 'walked about' for practical reasons. Water and food were distributed unevenly and people who lived by hunting and foraging had to be mobile to survive. But both water and food usually had a seasonal distribution too. Aboriginal life thus had to be rhythmical or patterned as well as mobile. They sensibly adapted weapons, chattels and the institution of property to these basic conditions. In the same way, and with as good sense, they shaped ordinary activities so as to accommodate to the mobile-rhythmical mould: meeting friends and relatives, conducting ceremonies, trading, settling grievances, jollifying humdrum, and much else besides. The pattern of mobility and rhythm thus took on a premial emotional and aesthetic appeal. It seems to have been a law of Aboriginal life to embroider the unavoidable. In this their true humanity was well revealed. There is no need to search for hidden or mysterious causes of 'walkabout', especially phylogenetic causes. It was in the first place an ecological adaptation which was worked into the ordinary system of life and at the same time used to lift life, and to lift it zestfully and rewardingly, above the level of biological survival. The urge to 'go walkabout' seems to vanish in direct ratio with the attractions of new conditions of life. It drops away to about our own level of industrial absenteeism with decent wages, fair working conditions, and jobs which are not overpoweringly tedious. Phylogeny is made of sterner stuff than that.

There is a learned as well as a popular folklore, and hardly more sensible. It is made up of simple-cause theories about the proper policies to pursue towards the modern Aborigines. I will mention some of them in a later lecture, but I would first like to say something of the extraordinary intellectual struggle which we have had to live through before seeing the Aborigines in a perspective that is at one and the same time well-informed, humane and respectful.

Roughly speaking, there have been two periods in the development of our appreciation of them: the ninety odd years before 1880, and the ninety odd years after it. Over the greater part of the first period interest in them was at best casual and incidental to other things whether the observer were official, explorer, traveller, settler, missionary, convict or bushman. That is not to say the information thus garnered was of no value. Much of it was knowledge by direct acquaintance, and for that reason alone is not to be dismissed out of hand. Some at least was rather better than in later times we have been disposed to admit, for example, our knowledge of the absolute dependence of each local band on a particular tract of country. But the general picture was sketchy, ill-proportioned and often malevolently drawn. It was also vague or blank about matters on which we would now give almost anything to have even fragments of solid fact. Yet it does not seem to me notably worse than the pictures we have of other native peoples in other countries at about the same time. From the better writings one can form at least an outline understanding of some important things: the apparent similarity of physique, language and custom over a large part of the continent; hunting methods and weaponry; the bond between hunter and hunting-ground; the love of music, song, dancing, and jollity; the public aspect of some striking customs such as initiation, grievance-settlement and trade; some of the notions of property and government; and even a few tantalising glimpses of social and religious complexity. We should give the early work its due not only to honour men who should be honoured—Collins, Tench, Threlkeld, Grey, Taplin, Ridley and others—but to counter the common argument that a simple ignorance of Aboriginal ways of life and thought sufficiently explains our early mishandling of racial relations. The argument washes, perhaps, until the 1830s; thereafter, the threads show too plainly. By then sufficient good information was at hand to have made a difference if the compulsive structure of Australian interests had been open to it.

One trouble was that the sound if limited information was the possession of the few. What replaced it among the many was the folklore I have mentioned. The motive of folklore about others—especially if they lie across racial and cultural barriers—is seldom generous. Yet, especially in the very early days, there were some excusable ignorances at the bottom of it. There was no idea of the high antiquity of man in Australia. The basic classification of the races of man was so confused until the third quarter of the 19th century that the ethnic affiliations of the Aborigines were truly puzzling.

These two things alone lent some plausibility to the old theological notion that the Aborigines were one of God's special creations, outside the line of true man. The folklore thus served easily as a natural vehicle of popular ignorance, self-interest and prejudice—and of prejudice there was no end.

After the 1880s, the casual and incidental studies were replaced by others closer to the spirit and style of modern research. This happened less from local causes than from causes outside Australia. In England, Europe and America, over the generation from the 1860s to the 1870s, there was a remarkable flowering of intellectual interest in the widest possible world of human customs, ancient and contemporary.

At first only slowly and in a marginal way, then rapidly and centrally, the Aborigines began to come within the sweep of disciplined and scholarly visions. The new interest took to itself the name 'ethnology'. The first solid work in Australian ethnology was Fison and Howitt's *Kamilaroi and Kurnai,* which was published in 1880—the dividing line I have mentioned—under the direct influence of Lewis Henry Morgan, the great American ethnologist whose monumental work *Systems of Consanguinity and Affinity of the Human Family* (1871) seems to have had rather more impact in Australia than other classical works of that wonderful decade, including McLennan's *Primitive Marriage* (1865) and Tylor's *Researches into the Early History of Mankind* (1865). I do not overlook the fact that during very much the same period there were attempts within Australia, for which we gratefully remember such men as R. Brough Smyth, the missionaries Taplin and Ridley, and a few others, to collate old and collect new information. Some estimable books were the result and parts of them showed a little of the thrust and quality of Fison and Howitt's. But too much lay in the old style, and their motive was less to explore new dimensions of fact in the light of new general ideas about human institutions than to put order into what was already known against a day, which everyone, including Morgan, supposed must come very soon, when nothing more would be discoverable. At least, however, external and internal causes made a happy junction, and some Australian scholars responded to the exciting new vision held out by ethnology—a universal and comparative science of human social institutions.

It is not my intention to try, even in a summary way, to trace from these beginnings the development of modern anthropology, as an autonomous academic discipline or collection of disciplines to which the world owes a great deal of the new insights across the borders of race, language and culture. At the most I can mention only fragments and episodes, but I can appropriately remark at this point that when at long last, as an outcome of the early developments I have mentioned, a few Australian scholars were intellectually ready to make a rigorous study of what they took to be the true distinctiveness of the Aborigines, circumstances could scarcely have been less propitious. We were then well into a secular phase of life in which the denigration of the Aborigines deepened into a real vilification.

In most of Australia Aboriginal affairs were now—that is by the 1880s—out of the urban sight, and for that among other reasons, out of the urban mind. A good half of the continent's 600 and more tribes, including those within the 20-inch rainfall belt, had been more or less obliterated.

The great wrecker had been the pastoral industry. In some places farms, mines, the formation of villages and other forms of settlement may have played an opening role, here and there perhaps even a decisive role, but pastoralism easily wins and must wear the laurels both for the number of tribes dispossessed and dispersed and the expanse of territory over which this happened. The industry was still expanding in the 1890s and was carrying the chain of like causes and like effects out into the dry zones of the west and centre and into the Northern Territory and the Kimberleys.

Over this long period the depreciation of the Aborigines—or to put the matter the other, and possibly the more correct way, the justification of what was being done to them—was more violent and moralistic than before or since. The correlation, I would say, was high and positive. This was the time of greatest talk about the law of progress and the survival of the fittest. What was happening in the remoter parts of the continent was at best peripheral to the great affairs—the trade union struggles, the debates over social justice, the industrial disturbances, the approaches to Federation—which so occupied the urban public mind of the time.

Fison and Howitt seem to have been insulated from all this. They did much, though not all, of their work in the long-settled areas and much, though again not all, by correspondence, questionnaire and interview rather than by the protracted field expeditions and the face-to-face observations of actual tribal life that later were to become the hallmarks of professional anthropology. The work of these two pioneers, one a missionary, one a magistrate and naturalist, had all of its mind on scientific questions, and it was they and their immediate successors—men such as Baldwin Spencer, F.J. Gillen (whose diary has just been printed), W.E. Roth, and R.H. Mathews—who brought the Aborigines to the prominence they have had in the world of anthropology ever since. One can but record that this happened over the period during which the life-situation of the remaining Aborigines was drifting to its nadir.

Spencer and Gillen became very famous. I intend no slight to others left unmentioned but it was they, with Roth and Mathews, who typified the best tradition of 19th century natural science which, in its possible applications to the study of human affairs, was not yet in the disrepute into which it appears to have fallen among some latterday anthropologists. But in a perverse way their work deepened the plight of the Aborigines by strengthening the impression of their singularity. Spencer and Gillen's publication in 1899 on the central Australian tribes created a profound sensation. It was hailed not only as a jewel of science which, for its day, it surely was, but also as the first really adequate ethnography of a savage people. The word that mattered was 'savage'. It made nearly inevitable the identification of 'contemporary Aboriginal man' with 'Stone Age man', with 'early man' in the sense of ancient and prehistoric man and, as Sir James Frazer was to put it, 'mankind in the chrysalis stage'. This atrocious muddle appeared to give scientific warrant for the judgment of Australian practical experience that nothing could be done for the Aborigines but to immure them in protective isolation within inviolable reserves. Unintentionally, the anthropology of the time underwrote what I called the 'last ditch' policy. It was, incidentally, on Spencer's advice that the Commonwealth later adopted its system of reserves in the Northern Territory.

I would make a distinction here between the men who did the ethnographic fieldwork and the men who interpreted it. One of the most interesting things about the local pioneers, especially the four I have mentioned, was their down-to-earthness at a time in which highpiling speculation was prevalent. The substance of their work was matter-of-fact in style, and unphilosophical, not in the sense of being untheoretical, but in that it was more akin to natural history than to natural philosophy in the old 19th century sense. It had little of the grand philosophical furniture that crammed the studies of so many other men, the great interpreters, who had so much to say about the Aborigines—J.G. Frazer, Andrew Lang, Emile Durkheim, Freud, and others. Of course there was some furniture: few people who wrote at that time doubted that men and institutions everywhere must have developed through a fixed sequence of set stages from savagery and barbarism to civilisation, or that history must be the grand interpretation (and the historian, therefore, the great interpreter) of all human affairs. This genetic-historic bias suffused the atmosphere of the time. It was so pervasive—and not, of course, only in anthropology—that all thinking seemed to be at bottom a thinking about causes, origins, and development. I do not think it right to criticise our local pioneers too heavily on such grounds. Their practical working emphases were on sounder principles, and the damage to our appreciation of Aboriginal life really came from the men of the armchair, who wrote from afar under a kind of enchantment. I have mentioned the fascination of the early ethnologists with the supposed origins of human social institutions, such as the family, marriage, property, government, religion and the like, and their obsession with hypothetical reconstructions of the path of human development. A line of men of this mentality runs from McLennan, Tylor, Morgan, Lubbock and Frazer in the 1860s, '70s and '80s to Westermarck, Hobhouse, Freud and Durkheim in the first decades of this century. To them, the new ethnographic material was manna from heaven, and in the twenty years after the middle 1890s a large literature grew up about topics which took on a curious independence of the people to whose life they referred—the Aboriginal family, clan and tribe; the systems of kinship, marriage and descent; exogamy, incest and promiscuity; totemism, ritual, magic and myth. Nowadays we do not take much of it seriously, although some of the subjects cling like old men of the sea. But we are ruefully aware of the extent to which the literature fastened on the Aborigines a reputation of extraordinary primitivity.

They were made to appear a people just across, or still crossing, that momentous border which separates nature from culture, and trailing wisps of an animalian past in their human period. It was through this interpretive literature, which in some notable cases—for example, Freud and Durkheim—used the primary data mainly as a crystal ball for private visions, that other disciplines, such as jurisprudence, economics, political science and psychology, picked up and propagated many falsities into wider scholarship. Well after my own student days text-books were in use which illustrated particular theories of human development by mangled versions of Aboriginal customs, ideas and attitudes given in sources that anthropologists themselves had discarded as unsound.

At or soon after the turn of the century a revulsion set in against this pseudo-historical outlook, and what we like to think of as the modern types of empirical study, guided by less flighty theoretical ideas, and certainly using more stringent methods, were under way before World War I. I will not embark on a discussion of the modern work because we are now making a fundamental revaluation of the most basic structures of Aboriginal thought and culture. Our most exciting concern is with what may be called the syntax of the codes that lie within Aboriginal symbolic systems. These are at least as basic to life on the social as the genetical codes are to life on the biological plane. From this newer point of view the work of the last fifty years may show many defects, but it has helped to fertilise a richer human scholarship than may appear, and in season and out it never wavered from the view that across the borders of race, language and culture there are human integrities and valuable patterns of life, experience and thought that we ought to understand.

I doubt, for reasons already mentioned, whether the work had much direct effect on our treatment of the Aborigines but I like to think that indirectly it may have contributed something to the changing attitudes of more recent years. Australian governments and other authorities seem always to have thought the information too specialised to be relevant but as long as the extinction of the Aborigines was assumed to be inevitable (and as late as 1930 the historian Hancock could still speak of their 'predestined passing') no information could have had much more than a poignant irrelevance. But this does not state the situation rightly. It was not so much a case of no suitable information as of no place at all for scientific information in the dealings of public and private authorities with the Aborigines. For example, if there are three subjects which anthropologists have understood quite well for a very long time, they are the initiation rites, the marriage systems, and the delicate intimacy of a kinship-bonded social life. The suppression, interference, or ridicule by public and private organisations of these Aboriginal preferences of life was both sad and bad in the light of the known information recorded by anthropologists from the 1880s onward. Only in the present generation have the various authorities moderated their once imperial way with these private Aboriginal concerns. Even in the first phase of the assimilation policy there was still some impulse to break up the bonds that made Aborigines cling together for mutual support and comfort long before any true alternatives were really open to them.

Nevertheless there are evidences of a large swing from depreciation towards appreciation. I myself would not call them plain evidences because they are difficult to interpret. In 1967 nearly nine people in every ten who voted at referendum declared that the Commonwealth should have full power to legislate for all Aboriginal citizens wherever situate. No one knows or can say exactly what message that signal sent. The great reforms of the recent past—the full suffrage, the end of discriminatory laws, and other such things—all real, all valuable, all in their way courageous, did not damage real interests or pockets to an alarming extent, and hardly a nervous voice was heard. The psephologists missed their biggest bus in not analysing what the voters had in mind. Then there is the remarkable market for all things Aboriginal. Their art, music, dancing and articles of handicraft have been given a new value by an institution that does not deal in sentiment. The demand for the spoken or the written word about the Aborigines, or the film in any form, is insatiable. The old books have become collector's treasures. But the market wants only a cult that could end as rapidly and as strangely as it began. Exactly where the market came from I do not know, but I question whether we would be right in reading from the fact of its existence to a proof of any deep-seated change of heart or mind towards the living Aborigines. I see it rather as the sign of an affluent society enjoying the afterglow of an imagined past and as a reaching out for symbols and values that are not authentically its own but will do because it has none of its own that are equivalent. But for all that the market may turn out to be one of the indirect, and therefore the more permanent, forces making for an appreciation of the authenticity of the Aboriginal past and of their complications of life in the present. I think it would unduly flatter anthropology and archaeology to credit them with having made the market although they and other research disciplines have fed and strengthened it. Thirdly, there is the fact, as hard as the market, that Aboriginal affairs are news as never before. Aboriginal leaders have become men of the headlines and I have a strong sense that what they say and do will much affect the future of causes that have come into a delicate poise.

Of course I like to think that anthropology has had something to do with all this. I even like to think that just as in the 19th century a sense of physical and biological principle steadily permeated the public mentality so a sense of what I will broadly call 'anthropological principle' may be permeating our own country's mentality. I mean by that a steady awareness that there are no natural scales of better or worse on which we can range the varieties of men, culture and society, and that we are dealing with individual integrities. By speaking of it as 'anthropological' principle I am not suggesting that the academic discipline invented it. We were somewhat anticipated by certain scholars 2,000 years ago, and at any moment the genius of a Sidney Nolan, or another artist or writer or poet of his order will disclose facets of the Aboriginal integrity which our professional style can scarcely encompass. But I feel entitled to say that the method, and perhaps even the motive, of insight would be weaker but for the steady drive that anthropology has maintained during the last century across the borders of race, culture and language into other countries of the human mind.

I have tried in this lecture, without becoming lost in the technical recesses of anthropology, to show that scientists too have had their struggles to attain perspective towards the Aborigines. Research has been conducted against a moving tableau of shifting previsions of the people under study. In view of the criticisms which I allowed myself at the cost of historiography I should not omit to say that anthropology could be, and assuredly will be, criticised more severely. It has shown itself over much the same period to have been very susceptible to intellectual fashions exotic to itself, and especially to the particular science, philosophical school, or general mode of scholarship that happens to be attracting attention. We shall probably now, under the impress of the new biology, see an enthusiastic exploration of the possible phylogenetical bases of Aboriginal culture, and no doubt be able to discuss with our Aboriginal friends our respective territorial imperatives and which cuckoo is in whose nest.

But in another direction too the suggestibility has been apparent. Once upon a time the Aborigines were to many anthropologists, as Toynbee said rather brutally of certain peoples, 'mere ethnographic material', and the best research of the day was the unwitting underwriter of an extreme social negativism. At present anthropology is perhaps rather too identified with the new positive social policies. Fortunately, within these large swings there is always a steady thrust of study along a central line. The great event in the modern period of research was the foundation in 1961 of the Australian Institute of Aboriginal Studies. It came late upon the scene, especially when one remembers that as long ago as 1880, in his preface to Fison and Howitt's book, Morgan was already saying that 'in a few years nothing will be known of the arts, institutions, manners, customs and plan of life of savage man, except as they are preserved in memoirs like the present'. But in the seven years of the Institute's life the work it has made possible in biology, prehistory, linguistics and anthropology has immensely deepened our perspectives. I use the plural advisedly. We have by no means made a single pattern from the record of the people or peoples who arrived here perhaps 30,000 years ago, and it remains to be seen whether we shall now ever do so. Our full interest has been aroused rather late. But even so we have built up a treasury of good knowledge that ought not gather dust on library shelves or in museum basements.

Given all the years of the locust, and the debris of folklore they left behind, it continues to surprise me that we have not found a way to put our treasury of good knowledge to full educational use. If we began with the first primary classes in schools there would be a real prospect, within a single generation, of transforming the public mentality towards a people who by that time will be a much larger, more visible, and I have no doubt a much more demanding segment of our population. I am not concerned with the scientific questions; they will look after themselves; but I will say in passing that there is stuff in Aboriginal life, culture and society that will stretch the sinews of any mind which tries to understand it. I am concerned about the risk that we will not manage to convey to younger people an appreciation of what is coming about after, not two centuries, but three hundred centuries, of human affairs in this country.

CONFRONTATION

One of the remarkable things about the Aborigines is the mildness which they showed once the main clash was over and their lot was cast. We have been able to count on that quality of response in most of our dealings with them and quite often to trade upon it to their disadvantage: Wattie Creek is only one of several episodes with a strong family likeness.

I would like to spend part of this lecture in discussing why they have responded so quietly to being worsted, but before doing so I must dispose of a piece of white man's folklore about the subject.

A tradition of writing since Banks and Cook insists on describing the Aborigines as an 'inoffensive' people, or uses some other adjective to hint at innate docility or submissiveness or weakness of temperament or character. From this vein of thought one often hears it argued that they would have had a better fate if like the Maori, the Zulu, or some of the American Indians they had stood their ground and given battle. It is one of the least probable might-have-beens of history, and the whole line of thinking is badly mistaken.

The Aborigines were originally a high-spirited and in their own way a militant people. They were not, however, an organised martial people, and that was why we broke them up so easily. The genius of their society lay in other directions and it was this otherness, fundamentally, that led to their undoing. They had had no need for the larger social and political organisations, the executive leadership, and the skill or wherewithal for operations of scale that channel militancy into martial capacity to serve a flag and a cause. When the time of need came they were at a loss.

It may seem that I pass over too lightly the immediate sinews of war. I concede that they had only spears, clubs, throwing sticks, and in some places boomerangs (which were not used everywhere) and—the weapon they used against Cook at the Endeavour River—fire, and that even with such poor arms they threw panic into many a settlement and imposed a reign of fear on some regions for a long time. But if they had had guns it could only have spun out the story to the same end. A population so sparse that its average density was one person to a square mile made the concentration of a sizeable force difficult, and commissariat by hunting and foraging made more difficult still the holding together of a sufficient force long enough to be effective. In the long run the situation was a hopeless one. The continent was lost and won, not by campaigns and operations of scale, but by local attrition. It was inched away, locality by locality. The marvel is that the defenders did so well.

It is high time that our histories were renovated to do justice to the other side of a struggle that was still going on in the Northern Territory in the early 1930s. There were then several regions through which police, cattlemen, and prospectors were reluctant to go, if they cared to visit them at all. In the archives of all the States there is ample material to prove that the Aborigines fought a very vigorous if unavailing battle. What has prevented the story from becoming better known is simply the ethnocentrism of our outlook.

We have conclusive evidence from the beginning that they did not—and do not—lack courage, intelligence, endurance or indeed any of the cardinal soldierly virtues. I am not speaking of the military skills, but it is worth saying in passing that as far as minor tactics are concerned there was remarkably little that they had to learn. In other days I was an eye-witness of many fights in which more than a hundred men came to an appointed field. I went away, as I am sure anyone else would, in no doubt whatever about either their personal valour or their battle-spirit. There would be a warming-up period given over to threat-signals and other ritualised gestures of hostility but once the true fighting started it might go on fiercely for hours. The very last thing a man would do would be to leave the battle-line except for honourable cause, such as to get more spears, and then as like as not he would meet his wife rushing up with them. Man for man, under equal and familiar conditions, they were a people who would withstand any comparison.

One of our most difficult problems is to overcome our folklore about them. It tends to run to extremes: canard on one side and sentimentality on the other. There is no point in making them appear better or worse than they were or are. Depreciating them is a way of justifying having injured them in the past and an excuse for short-changing them in the present and future. Sentimentalising them is to go too far in the other direction. We can neither undo the past nor compensate for it. The most we can do is to give the living their due.

What we think of as mildness or passivity is neither of those things. What we are looking at is one of the most familiar syndromes in the world. It is a product mainly of four things—homelessness, powerlessness, poverty and confusion—all self-acknowledged and accumulated over several generations. I will deal briefly with each.

No English words are good enough to give a sense of the links between an Aboriginal group and its homeland. Our word 'home', warm and suggestive though it be, does not match the Aboriginal word that may mean 'camp', 'hearth', 'country', 'everlasting home', 'totem place', 'life source', 'spirit centre' and much else all in one. Our word 'land' is too spare and meagre. We can now scarcely use it except with economic overtones unless we happen to be poets. The Aboriginal would speak of 'earth' and use the word in a richly symbolic way to mean his 'shoulder' or his 'side'. I have seen an Aboriginal embrace the earth he walked on. To put our words 'home' and 'land' together into 'homeland' is a little better but not much. A different tradition leaves us tongueless and earless towards this other world of meaning and significance. When we took what we call 'land' we took what to them meant hearth, home, the source and focus of life, and everlastingness of spirit. At the same time it left each local band bereft of an essential constant that made their plan and code of living intelligible. Particular pieces of territory, each a homeland, formed part of a set of constants without which no affiliation of any person to any other person, no link in the whole network of relationships, no part of the complex structure of social groups any longer had all its co-ordinates. What I describe as 'homelessness', then, means that the Aborigines faced a kind of vertigo in living. They had no stable base of life; every personal affiliation was lamed; every group structure was put out of kilter; no social network had a point of fixture left. There was no more terrible part of our 19th century story than the herding together of broken tribes, under authority, and yoked by new regulations, into settlements and institutions as substitute homes. The word 'vertigo' is of course metaphor, but I do not think it misleading. In New Guinea some of the cargo-cultists used to speak of 'head-he-go-round-men' and 'belly-don't-know-men'. They were referring to a kind of spinning nausea into which they were flung by a world which seemed to have gone off its bearings. I think that something like that may well have affected many of the homeless Aborigines. We are watching a little miracle when we see men who, having been made homeless, again pull their world together sufficiently to try to make another home for themselves, like the Gurindji at Wattie Creek. It is something which people brought up on ideas of land as 'real estate' or 'leasehold' find difficult to understand.

The second part of the syndrome is powerlessness. This condition is anything from three or four to seven or eight generations deep, depending where one goes. The Aborigines did not lack men and women of force and of outstanding, even of commanding, character and personality. I am not thinking of mercurial upstarts like Benelong but of innumerable others who, having no office or title or rank, nevertheless had sway over large regions and numbers—men such as the great warriors Yagan and Midgegooroo of Western Australia, or Durmugam of the Northern Territory. Some were military leaders, some leaders by their religious wisdom and authority in sacred matters. That there will be others like them I am entirely confident. We do not know exactly what happened to such men in most of the older-settled parts of Australia. Yagan of course was shot and Midgegooroo was executed. Few Australians realise the number of men who were probably potential leaders but who, being seen as trouble-makers, were quietly whisked away to places where they had no influence. This was done until quite recent times. Many of us have talked to men and women whose tribal life broke up in the late 19th and even during the present century. From what they said there came a time for all of them when they saw there was nothing else to do but to accept whatever life we offered on our terms. Under those terms it was exceptionally difficult for them to keep or find leaders. It meant unifying heterogeneous and accidental collections of people, who usually felt no reciprocal obligations to each other, for ends few can have seen clearly and by means no one really commanded. To thrust himself forward as a leader is a hard thing for any Aboriginal to do. The idea of a man of authority with right and title to command them over a wide range of many things is foreign to their idea of social life. In this respect their tradition left them very exposed to leaderlessness. I will risk being aphoristic and say that whereas they may tolerate a leader they hate a boss. In their broken life any man who sought to lead them to new things, which had by definition to be European things, risked being thought a boss. It reminded them too much of Europeans: at least they have told me so. I have heard many an assertive would-be leader twitted and publicly ridiculed for trying to be 'like a white fellow'.

Given such a background, when potential leaders do appear we should welcome and develop them with at least the enthusiasm, say, with which we welcome and develop the precious metals and valuable minerals we are finding in their reserves. On the occasions on which Aborigines do show an impulse to strike out for themselves, and throw up possible leaders, we should treat them as the rarest of rare metals.

Homelessness, powerlessness: there is a third and fatal element. In a hundred local patterns they drifted into a vicious circle of poverty, dependence and acceptance of paternalism. Every act of paternalism deepened the poverty into pauperism and the dependence into inertia. The situation was self-perpetuating and self-reinforcing.

Not many people realise that those whom we least respected—the fringe-dwellers—were precisely those who deserved respect most because they were trying to break out of the circle by refusing to go into institutions. In the conditions of the 19th century and the first half of this century any Aboriginal who could go much farther had to belong to the Nobel Prize class of human spirits. Astonishingly enough, there were some who did.

I began by speaking of conflict so I will use that theme to try to bring out the fourth element—the Aboriginal inability to grasp the European plan of life.

I spoke of them as originally a high spirited and militant people. Their lives together certainly had a full share of conflict, of violent affrays between individuals, and of collective blood-letting. But in some ways they were more skilful than we are in limiting the free play of men's combative propensity.

If we judge by their settled customs, they admitted to themselves that people simply *are* aggressive and that it was no bad solution to allow what could not be avoided, and to ritualise—and thus be able to control, approve and enjoy—as much as possible of what has to be allowed. It is hard to fault their psychology. The subject is a fascinating one but unhappily the research we have done upon it in Australia has neither been plentiful nor distinguished. I cannot, therefore, take it very far, and I can mention a few points only.

The impression I received in watching their large-scale fights was that an invisible flag of prudence waved over the battlefield. There was a tacit agreement to call a truce or an end when a few men on each side had been grievously wounded or at the worst killed. Each life in a small group was a great treasure.

That is not to say there were never occasions on which whole groups were put to the spear, or that there was no lasting bad blood between groups at enmity. It was often so, especially when, by migration or some other cause, neighbour tribes spoke unrelated tongues, or had very distinct customs. But the conquest of land was a great rarity: I do not know personally of a single case. And the war of extermination, with one group bent remorselessly on the complete destruction of the other, as far as I have discovered, was so rare as to be all but unknown. In this sense there were few or no 'total' enemies. It was much more commonly the case that groups which fell out contained a proportion of people who were closely tied by kinship, marriage, friendship, trade, or some other precious bond.

In such cases, a man could stand aside—honourably, and with social approval—or play only a token part if he had to oppose and might injure people who were precious to him. The ties that bound overrode the conflicts that divided. Prudential and countervailing forces of these kinds went with many conventions and canons governing the actual conduct of conflict. For example, in the great public fights which, as I have said, were ritualised affairs, it would have been bad form to use a heavy killing spear against an opponent armed only with a light duelling spear. I can recall one fight where a man with boomerangs, which were simply not *de rigueur* in that region, was received very much as a knight in armour might have been if he had come armed with gunpowder and shot.

There was a distinct canon of equality at arms, a norm of sufficient—but just sufficient—retaliation, and a scale of equivalent injury. One could see them working in the case of a man who, knowing that a mortal wound would not be given, would offer his body to the spear of another man he had wronged; or in two men, both with a grievance, each clasping the other with an arm, and using the free arm with equal opportunity to gouge the other's back with a knife; or in two unreconciled women, giving each other whack for whack with clubs, but in strict rotation. I must not overdraw the picture. A lot of this restraint and limitation went by the board when passions got out of hand, as they often did, especially when old or sudden new quarrels flared up, as they might, over the most trivial things. One could then be in a donnybrook in no time. And I could not find rules that applied in the raids, ambushes and cutting-out expeditions for which the young bloods had a liking.

But what I have led towards saying is that some sorts of conflict—those at which we are particularly skilled—were unknown or rare, and that in their adversary system at its best there was a strong institutional bias towards the limitation of conflict and the deflection of animosity into forms that acknowledged it but controlled the sting through convention and ritual. Always at hand there was an immense catalogue of formal symbolic usages—in play, language, gesture, bodily movement, facial expression, avoidance, ceremonious forms, juridical procedures, to mention only some—which deflected, redirected and softened the difficult, awkward, injurious and dangerous natural oppositions of social life. Not all, not always, and not always successfully; but enough to make for an expected style of conduct, a set of values, and a habit of thought between people which made European conduct, values and thought in outwardly similar situations barely intelligible and sometimes not at all. From their point of view we were men from Mars. It was a nightmarish world in which every code of communication and transaction between people was made topsy-turvy. Incidentally, from these sources an Aboriginal folklore about us came into existence. Some of it is comical—that we have no morals, and that our marriage system is incestuous; some of it is sardonic—that we are 'like sharks', meaning that we pursue land, money and goods as sharks pursue little fish; some of it perhaps very near the bone—as one old man said to me: 'You are very clever people, very hard people, plenty humbug.'

I myself think that these four things—homelessness, powerlessness, poverty and the continued disparity between plans and styles of life—had much to do with producing the syndrome we have seen for a long time: the inertia, the non-responsiveness, the withdrawal, the taking with no offer in return, and the general anomie that have so widely characterised Aboriginal life during their association with us. No doubt there were contributions from the Aboriginal side also. We hardly know what we may yet conclude from the new biological, genetical, psychological and sociological researches which are under way. In the meantime there is a simple device that is worth using. That is, to hold up a mirror to our own record and study what is reflected.

I have perhaps given the impression that these things all happened long ago and far away. Take the last element which I discussed—the incomprehensibility of our plan and style of life. Only the other day I went to the corner of Arnhem Land where a great mineral industry is taking shape within an Aboriginal reserve. I thought it would be interesting to see at first-hand the response the Aborigines are making to it, and whether they grasp what it may hold in store for them. On the few evidences I could gather in a brief visit they could not be said to be opposed to it in an outright way. I would say, rather, that they were simply overborne by the weight of external initiative, authority and advice that all will be well. But, for all that, those I spoke to or listened to were perplexed and worried in spite of a hope that great things would come to them.

Perplexed, understandingly enough, because none of them can really grasp the scale and complexity of the enterprise; or gauge the changes it will bring into their lives at its peak; or foresee the place they will have in the new world it will bring. A new world indeed! Apart from a very large industrial complex which, according to published statements, will cost several hundred millions of dollars, there will be a new port, a new township for several thousand Europeans, not all directly concerned with the industry, and a whole new infrastructure to carry the developments. The Aborigines of course have no comprehension of what lies ahead. The adjustment they will have to make will be greater relatively than that which the Aborigines of Botany Bay and Port Jackson had to make to the smaller and more leisurely events of Phillip's time. At present they are shielded by a little distance from the immediate hurly-burly of first-stage development, but before long a wave will burst over their heads. The Industrial Revolution engulfing 18th century rural England could not have been more devastating.

They were worried by one fact already patent to them: that some large tracts of country which they believe, in their innocence, to belong to them, will be foreclosed for a long time, perhaps lost forever.

I listened to one elderly man speaking on the matter. He was something of an orator, with a power of words, a sense of pause and gesture, and very evident ability to phrase the conventional wisdom of his audience. I had the sense that he expressed well what many of his fellows were feeling and thinking. He turned his back to the open waters of Carpentaria, and looked north, west and south to the great stretches of Arnhem Land which no one—no one, that is, except the Aborigines—wanted only a few years ago when we knew nothing of the mineral riches that have been discovered. In a dramatic way he pointed to and declaimed the names of territories and places within the tribal domain. 'All of them,' he said, 'are our country.' He then named the places already or soon to be lost under the special leases created over them. I could not follow all he said because I depended on an interpreter but there was no mistaking the substance of his remarks or the fact that he was unhappy and unreconciled. Were they to be compensated? Would yet more land go? Would the sacred places really be protected? These were among the questions he asked, but no one present could answer him with the scruple and certainty that alone could set his doubts at rest. The upshot was that he and others made the response that must have happened a thousand times since 1788. They said, in effect: our homeland is being whittled away; we have no power to control what is happening; we do not understand; we are in your hands; by ourselves we can do nothing. There was no long ago and far away about all this: it happened in August 1968.

Like causes, like effects. The development explosion of the 1960s and '70s is the pastoral expansion of the 1860s and '70s vastly intensified. It will take all the ingenuity of which we are capable to avert similar effects on the Aborigines. Nothing of course can arrest development. If the Aborigines have no prospects within it they have no prospects outside it, but some of us would like to think that we can devise something better for them than to be hewers of wood and drawers of water on the fringes of these vast new enterprises. Otherwise, I think that in this and similar situations—and there are now many of them—a good deal of combustible material awaits a spark. One of the most striking developments in the world in the last generation is the rapidity with which peoples who but a short time ago were powerless, dependent and voiceless found power, independence and voice and through them began to make an impact on history in their own right. Externally that kind of confrontation is going on all around us. It increasingly takes on a racial façade, though race is seldom if ever the real issue but only a language which is conveniently symbolic and expressive of other grievances. It is a language increasingly used alongside, across and within the confrontations of the nation-states and increasingly projects itself into every major issue. I think it would be self-illusion to suppose that a confrontation using that language may not reach eventually into the very last corner of Aboriginal Australia. I believe that the path of statesmanship is to work while there is still time towards a grand composition of all the troubles that lie between us and the people of Aboriginal descent. Much effort and wisdom have already gone into the welfare and advancement policies of the last generation. But, as I said in an earlier lecture, the freshening flow from the great river of national imagination, private and corporate, into this little muddied stream is still only a trickle.

COMPOSITION

I began these lectures by speaking of a structure of racial relations that formed a continuing part of the anatomy of Australian life. I used the word 'racial' in a descriptive sense to refer to the fact that we and the Aborigines are of distinct racial stocks. The 'relations' are the affairs of life that go on between us. It is these affairs that have structure. I pointed out that some long-lasting patterns founded on inequality and disadvantage had kept on repeating themselves. I chose to begin by drawing attention to the fact because although the whole structure is creaking and has even shifted on its base, some of the main affairs of life are not yet radically different from what they used to be. I suggested therefore that the 'revolution' of attitudes and relations had not yet arrived in a general way, one of the reasons being that we had been caught up for so long in a cult of forgetfulness or disremembering. One consequence was the growth of a syndrome of coiled and tangled problems of which homelessness, powerlessness, poverty and confusion are main constituents. I expressed the opinion that in more recent years two forces have been at work concurrently. One is a real and growing appreciation of the distinctive qualities of Aboriginal culture, thought, and problems of life. The other is the surfacing of old and new tensions between us. I said that in my judgment the two together are shaping into a wider confrontation between black and white. I argued that there are enough imagination and inventiveness within the country to find a way to compose the troubles. The price of failure may be 'racial' relations in a sense all too familiar elsewhere.

I can well understand that these views may not commend themselves to everyone. We are all in some sense prisoners of personal experience, and my views rest on associations with Aborigines who first met Europeans two or three generations ago. It would be wrong to make a direct comparison between them and the people in the cities, or in country towns, or in institutions in the older settled areas, who are mainly now of mixed descent and whose associations with us are older and deeper. Some false assimilations of this kind are already being made by both sides in the debate on Aboriginal rights. There is no one 'Aboriginal problem' and much of the talk about 'the Aborigines' is itself misleading. We are looking at a spectrum that is almost indefinitely divisible. A problem, such as housing, at one end is not identical with what may seem to be the same problem at the other end.

In practical affairs one has to make some division, and one will come to no great harm by assuming that most of the spectrum is covered by four broad divisions. In the first I would put the 'bush people' with whom I have had most to do. In varying degrees they still have a sense of local and corporate identity and are substantially in touch with their traditional life, but they have no real grip on modernity even though most of them live on mission or government stations. I would call the second group, the 'outback people'. In the main they are to be found in residential camps on the pastoral properties, where they are tangling with modernity in a more disturbing way and from a less traditional background than the bush people. The third group is a double one: the people who have made their own shanty-settlements on the fringes of country towns, as distinct from those in the older settled areas who prefer, or feel there is no alternative to, life in government or other institutions. They are both shifting and unstable groups which often neither know nor care about traditional things. They gain or lose members as individuals or families fail or succeed in the struggle towards assimilation. They are the main source of recruits into the fourth group, the city dwellers, who are growing rapidly in numbers, and include people at all stages towards, within, or beyond that rather indefinable state of life we describe as 'assimilation'. It is a rough-and-ready division but it points to different states of life which I have touched on all too lightly because my purpose has been to suggest that whatever their state of life the people themselves are the products of life-experiences which have had a pronounced pattern, and I thought myself justified in trying to generalise the experiences and pattern.

It has seemed to me for some years that two aspects of the Aboriginal struggle have been under-valued. One is their continued will to survive, the other their continued effort to come to terms with us. I will illustrate both by the last two men I met who knew that they must give up the bush life and come more than half-way to strike a bargain with us. One of them, whose tribe had scattered to a dozen places, was an elderly widower whom I saw destroying something in a fire. I asked him what he was doing and he told me he was 'killing his dreaming'. I had never seen nor heard of anything like it before. There is nothing within our ken that remotely resembles it. He was destroying the symbol that linked him with his country, with the source of his own life, and with all the continuities of his people. It was a kind of personal suicide, an act of severance, before he came in to find a new life and a new identity amongst us. The other man was in much the same situation. His people too had wandered away and he was left in solitude except for his wives and children. He told me that he wondered for a long time what it would be best to do. He was a supremely competent hunter and he could have stayed in the wilderness for the rest of his days. But he knew he was getting on in years and in the end he too came in to strike a bargain. What decided him, or so he said, was that he had heard about something called 'a school' and that it was good for children, so he took them in to let them find a new life and a new identity. Neither man was a good model for Henry Kendall's sentimental poem *The Last of His Tribe.* The poet knew and evidently liked the Aborigines but he created a dubious stereotype. Compare the image of his man and those of my two men. Compare also another man I knew who at one time seemed likely to be the last of *his* tribe. I talked to him often about their impending extinction. He had no tears, reproaches, or dramatics; instead, he would often laugh in a sardonic way. One day he poked me in the ribs and said: 'When all the blackfellows are dead all the whitefellows will get lost in the bush, and there'll be no one to find them and bring them home.' And he went off laughing. I wish I had the time to enlarge on Aboriginal humour, which comes in part from a wonderful gift, one they did not get from us, of taking us gravely but not seriously. Long may they do so. But I must not pass over the main point of my story about the two seekers after a new life and a new identity.

I conceive that what these men did must have happened untold thousands of times which make up an unwritten chapter of our unexamined history. There was an endless replication of that culminating event of Phillip's time—the voluntary movement of groups, family parties and individuals into our camps, stations, settlements and towns. I can, incidentally, remember seeing it happen at Wave Hill among the grandfathers and fathers of the present-day Gurindji, and of course it still goes on widely. The drift from country to city seems to be an extension of it. The fringe-dwellers are local moraines left by this—by us—unnoticed movement of humanity. I would interpret each such movement as two things in one—an offer, and an appeal; an implicit offer of some sort of union of lives with us, and an implicit appeal for a new identity within the union. To go near is always a sort of offer: the Aborigines, from Phillip's time on, came voluntarily as near to us as they could. Usually they ended in a fringe-camp or an institution, but just being there was a continued appeal. The trouble was that they made their offer on a hard market and their appeal at times when no one saw or heard very clearly.

Over the last thirty years we have been trying to attract them into some sort of union with us. We call it 'assimilation' and think of 'integration' as an intermediate stage or perhaps as a less complete union. But it is easy for us to overlook that a long humiliation can dull the vision, narrow the spirit, and contract the heart towards new things. Some of the Aborigines do not understand our offer; some think it is not genuine; some, that its terms are not very attractive; some prefer to cling to their old identity until they are more sure what identity they would have within our new proposals for them. There are deeper difficulties still. We are asking them to become a new people but this means in human terms that we are asking them to un-be what they now are. But many of them are now seeking to rediscover who and what their people were before the long humiliation. It is a search for identity, a way of restoring self-esteem, of finding a new direction for the will to survive, and of making a better bargain of life on a more responsive market at a more understanding time.

There are many, perhaps too many, theories about *our* troubles with the Aborigines. We can spare a moment to consider *their* theory about *their* troubles with *us.* Two of their strongest ideals are to be 'one company', to join with others for a purpose, and to 'go level', to be 'one company' on equal terms. Their theory is that we are unwilling really to be 'one company' and to 'go level' with them. It has an historical candour and simplicity that are hard to shake, and it makes an interesting comparison with many of the theories we have developed about them and their motives and capacities.

Some theorists maintain that we can do little or nothing because for reasons of race, culture and history the Aborigines lack the intelligence or capacity to advance. Others argue that for nearly two centuries few have sought to strike out for themselves, or to rise above the ruck, and that this must point to an innate disability of some kind, even if we cannot identify it. I consider these to be a folklore unfounded on good knowledge. More substantial are the theories that there would be a rapid general advance if only some one sovereign remedy were applied, such as better education or health measures, or modern sanitation, or improved housing, or higher wages, and so on. They are all in part right and therefore dangerous. If all these particular measures, with perhaps fifty or a hundred others, were carried out everywhere, simultaneously, and on a sufficient scale, possibly there would be a general advance. But who shall mobilise and command this regiment of one-eyed hobby horses? And keep it in line or in column? Then there are others who advocate community development or co-operatives in the belief that joint enterprises are especially suited to the Aborigines. I do not discount these ideas but some theorists are not at all troubled by the known facts that the record of experiment with such schemes is not impressive, and that Aboriginal groups, for all their ideals, are usually made up of factions. This divisiveness is supposed, somehow, to be certain to vanish within *any* joint enterprise. There is, certainly, a field for experiment, but the community scheme and the co-operative are not sovereign remedies, and any proposal in the field needs a very unsentimental study, no less in the interest of those who may have to take part than of those who will have to stand the cost.

Possibly the most dangerous theory, though it is scarcely that, is that things are now going well, that all we need to do is more of what we are already doing, that is, deepen and widen the welfare programmes, and the rest will come at a natural pace in its own good time. The trouble is that things are not going well. The gap between the average real conditions of the Aborigines and ours shows signs of widening, not narrowing. This appears to be one reason why there is such a steady drift from country to city. The composition of their population is also undergoing a startling change: it is now, in at least some groups, very much more youthful, and growing in size at a very much faster rate, than ours. It follows that their conditions will have to improve faster than ours if they are to stay even at their present relative disadvantage. This is a sobering thought. The bill for welfare expenditure will increase without offset until such time as Aborigines begin to make a contribution to the national product. At present they contribute hardly at all.

I should not overlook the philosophy of policy. Much time and thought have been given to working out the implications of notions like 'assimilation' and 'integration'. Events have brought us to a phase in which intellectual effort can probably be applied more usefully. These large ideas try to define states of affairs or general conditions of life which for most Aborigines are distant in time and necessarily can be spelled out only in vague terms. They have very little strategical value but they do invite us to develop a strategy and tactics to attain them. I have put the strategical problem in terms of union and identity. The tactical problems are those of invention and experiment on the technical plane. It is these which are now the great challenge to our best abilities.

Anyone who moves in Aboriginal Australia, at any point along the spectrum, instantly sees scores of interdependent problems that call for many essentially technical skills. For example, devising ways to get people and worthwhile jobs together in the same place: the jobs never seem to be where the Aborigines are; or opening sources of capital to men with ideas—and there are many of them; or giving them an interest and the chance of earning an equity in industries which will always dominate the localities they cling to; or making unstable families more stable; or reducing absenteeism; or giving young women real alternatives to prostitution; or discovering the precise reasons for disappointing educational performance; or finding a productive therapy for the many who are withdrawn, unco-operative, hostile and without selfesteem. I do not contend that there are no larger problems which still require larger thought but I feel that we are now within a period during which applied technical skills for identifiable problems are a first consideration.

If I am correct, and I believe I am, in saying that we have badly misinterpreted, as inertia and parasitism, what in fact were their opposites—a people's will to survive, somehow, under any conditions, and an offer of union which until recently we were not minded to take up—then the question of composing our differences with the Aborigines at once passes to an essentially technical plane. In scale Aboriginal problems are small to the point of triviality compared with the scale of problems with which many public and private corporations deal as routines of life. They may be intricate, but they do not amount to an India or an Asia of intricacy: there are but 150,000 people of any degree of Aboriginal descent in all Australia.

I mentioned larger problems requiring larger thought. I have time to refer to one only, but perhaps the greatest, of many. It is a problem in two senses, in that in one way or another it must touch a sensitive part of the structure of Australian life, and in that it promises to put a powerful symbol in the path of composition. I refer to the question of 'land rights for Aborigines'. I discuss it with trepidation because it is full of difficulty for both sides, but I cannot defensibly pass over it in silence in these lectures.

Every fence in Australia encloses land that was once the sole or the shared possession of a particular group of Aborigines. There are virtually no exceptions to that statement. But in most of Australia, especially in the long-settled parts, it is now impossible to connect the original possessors in an exact or definite way with any living persons of Aboriginal descent. Some people of Aboriginal descent nevertheless hope for compensation by a hand-out of Crown or other land to individual persons, or by cash payments from Crown Land revenues.

It seems to me that proposals of these kinds will wreck themselves on the rocks of entitlement or on the lee-shore of an electorate in which there are too many *non*-Aboriginal people who own no land. Entitlement would have to be shown exactly: a vague or inferential connection could not suffice. The people who have no land or no income from land would cry discrimination, and those who do, or hope to, own land or draw income would think and act self-protectively. A general settlement of this kind in such areas seems to me unattainable. A problem of choice may thus confront the Aborigines: whether to lose public goodwill by forcing an issue they are unlikely to win, or to conserve it for other affairs of life, including other possible ways of becoming land-holders, as individuals, or in some corporate sense.

There are some parts of Australia in which the situation is much more open. I will preface a brief discussion by recalling to mind some old matters which could still have point. There was a passage in Cook's instructions which read: 'You are also with the Consent of the Natives to take possession of Convenient Situations in the Country in the Name of the King of Gt Britain or: if you find the Country uninhabited take Possession for his Majy by setting up Proper Marks & Inscriptions, as first discoverers & Possessors.' It is a matter of history that he did not obey the instructions. He did not find the country uninhabited, and it was certainly not with the consent of the natives that he took possession of a part of New Holland. Phillip and all his successors acted as if the second part of the instruction had applied. They did so through the fiction that Australia was 'waste and desert' or 'waste and unoccupied'. Thereafter, the principle of the consent of the natives was buried at the very centre of the cult of disremembering. No more was heard of it until 1835 when John Batman made his abortive agreement with some Victorian Aborigines to transfer two very large tracts. It can at least be said for Batman that he acknowledged that the land *had* possessors; he also treated with them as principals; he came to agreed terms—an immediate consideration, and a yearly rent or tributes (two ideas which we have not heard of since); and he sealed the bargain by a sign the Aborigines understood—eight of them took up handfuls of earth and handed them to him. As far as I am aware, that was the first, last and only affair of its kind. Not the least interesting thing about it were the reasons given by that procrastinating Secretary of State, Lord Glenelg, for agreeing to disallow the conveyance. He would not recognise in the Aborigines 'any right to alienate to private adventurers the land of the colony', and went on to say: 'It is indeed enough to observe that such a concession would subvert the foundation on which all proprietary rights in New South Wales at present rest and defeat a large part of the most important regulations of the local government.' That is still the central rub.

As I said in my second lecture, within the 'Aboriginal reserves' of the north there are still many corporate groups living on lands which have never been 'waste' or 'desert' or 'unoccupied'. From having actually mapped just such lands, from having plotted agreed lines of demarcation, and from having tied identifiable groups to identifiable tracts, with the public agreement of all the groups, I myself am morally satisfied that in many places a form of title exists which could be recognised if we thought it proper or worthwhile to do so. One of the main troubles is that the concept 'Aboriginal reserve' does not mean what most Aborigines, and perhaps most of us too, suppose it to mean. Any piece of land in the 'reserve' category is in the first place Crown or Government land. Few Aborigines truly understand that this is the case. Being Crown land it is subject to a complex body of land law, which few Aborigines know anything about. It is an 'Aboriginal' reserve only in a rather elliptical sense, whereas the Aborigines take it in a candid and simple sense. The land is 'reserved' in the sense of being withheld from sale or lease under any Act dealing with Crown lands, but at the same time governments can and increasingly do create rights and leases over it without necessarily, up to the present, having to ask Aboriginal consent. They can add to, subtract from, or do away with a reserve altogether if they so choose, a fact by which some Aborigines are beginning to be increasingly troubled. What turns 'reserve' into 'Aboriginal reserve' is the purpose of reservation, which is that the land should be for 'the use and benefit of Aborigines'. The particular Aborigines for whom it is reserved are not and do not have to be specified. The reserves of the sub-tropical region of the Northern Territory may be in principle as open to any Aborigines as to those of the immediate localities. This could become a serious issue as the development explosion in the north continues. Further, the conception of Aboriginal 'use and benefit' is notably elastic. Apparently neither 'use' nor 'benefit' is thought to be affected adversely by the creation of mining and other leases. The Aborigines themselves are not fully persuaded. All leases contain a provision that Aboriginal 'rights and interests' will be protected but what these amount to has not been clarified. It is an interesting contrast with the 'rights, liberties, easements, advantages and appurtenances' which may be specified for leaseholders.

Under the law as it stands the Aborigines have no ownership rights, although they may think they do. They do not in our sense 'own' anything on the land, such as timber or water-sources, or anything underneath, such as oil and minerals, all of which may be subject to reservation. The payment of royalties on products marketed by leaseholders is a tacit recognition of interest in natural resources, but it is hard to say how far tacitness runs. The situation otherwise is that undesignated Aborigines, certainly those living on a reserve which is gazetted, but possibly others too, have rights of ingress, egress and regress; may camp and rove at will, or at least over those parts not leased subject to special restrictions; drink the water, catch and eat the game, make domestic use of the annual crops of vegetable foodstuffs, use the wood for fires, and exercise other such notable freedoms. There is apparently nothing to stop them marketing natural products if they know how and can afford to do so.

In recent years there has been a growing disposition to let them protect their more sacred places. I may have missed a point or two but that is the substance of the position as I understand it. It seems that an 'Aboriginal' reserve rather resembles a 'wild life' reserve until it becomes of interest to us and, when it does, portions of it may pass into our substantial possession as 'private adventurers', to use Glenelg's phrase, without consideration other than the payment of royalties for assets which are used.

Here then are the two extremes of the land question. At one extreme, history cannot be undone; at the other, it may yet be made; in between is a range of intricate and difficult problems of decision which are not, I believe, beyond composition by statesmanship.

It is an odd turn of history that brings us once again after 150 years to problems not unlike those of Batman and Glenelg, and it returns me to the point at which I began, which was the survival into the present of the older and in some cases the fossil structures of our racial relations.

I gave these lectures their perhaps strange-sounding title because the old Aboriginal philosophy of life, which I once tried to express through their conception of The Dreaming, took little account of futurity. So far as they thought of the long future at all they seemed to suppose that it would take care of itself as a kind of everlasting present, and the present was supposed to be very like the past. Having only a mythological memory of the long past they could allow convenient structures of life to attract an appropriate morality and grow into rigid forms which became too inelastic to respond readily at a time of necessary change. There are perils in analogy but from an anthropologist's point of view the Aborigines are not the only people to whom that kind of thing can happen. Mythologising and disremembering are part and parcel of each other. It would be the essence of mythologising to suppose that effects like those of the past will not follow if we continue to allow causes like those of the past to work, for example, within the development explosion that is now about to overrun the very last parts of Aboriginal Australia. Fortunately, for something like thirty years the content of modern Australian history in respect of the Aborigines has shown heartening signs of conforming to Acton's principle—'the emancipation of conscience from authority'. The process may be inconvenient, but I hardly think it is now reversible, and I like to believe that its terminal is not as far off as it used to seem.

1968

The Yirrkala Land Case: Dress-Rehearsal (1970)

There is a long story to cut short. The law says it should start in 1786 or 1788. I would prefer it to start about thirty millennia earlier, but I will have to compromise. I will start in March 1969 when the Yirrkala Aborigines applied to the Supreme Court of the Northern Territory for an interim injunction to restrain the Commonwealth and Nabalco from continuing with allegedly wrongful acts within the Gove region of the Arnhem Land Aboriginal Reserve.

This application was brought about by Aboriginal fears that time was running out for them. It was part of a more comprehensive action begun in the previous December, by which they had sought, in addition to the injunction, damages against Nabalco, a declaration of title to the lands intruded upon, a declaration that the Commonwealth had acted unconstitutionally in acquiring the lands without just terms of compensation, and a declaration that the agreement by which Nabalco is in Arnhem Land was unlawful. The application for the interim injunction was stood over until interlocutory summonses by the Commonwealth and Nabalco were heard. The hearing of the interlocutory summonses in some sense became a dress-rehearsal of the trial which is still to come.

The Commonwealth and Nabalco sought to persuade Mr Justice Blackburn to take a severe course, or rather one of several courses of descending severity. The most severe was to deal summarily with the matter of the interim injunction as a frivolous and vexatious abuse of the Court; or, failing that, to make an order for the trial of the main action without pleadings and on issues to be defined; or, failing that, to strike out the Aborigines' statement of claim in whole or in part. Later, I will review briefly the arguments which were put forward, because I think it important that we should keep in mind the positions that were being taken fourteen months ago (1969). But, at the moment, I hasten on to say that in his decision, which was given about two months later, Mr Justice Blackburn refused the Commonwealth's and Nabalco's main prayer for summary judgment. He did so in five sentences which, taken together, had, I thought, a delphic ring. He said:

> I have very carefully studied all the contentions of counsel and every authority to which they referred me. I am not satisfied that the issues are properly before me and I have not come to a clear and certain conclusion adverse to the plaintiffs [the Aborigines]. I say no more. In particular, I do not suggest that there is any point to which my consideration has tentatively brought me, on the wide range from complete satisfaction that the plaintiffs' contentions are sound, to (but stopping short of) complete satisfaction that they are unsound. All arguments are open.

His Honour can never know the sleepless hours his words have caused me. Why, having decided to 'say no more', at once go on to say more, and in particular to contrast a 'complete satisfaction' favourable to the Aborigines with something less than a 'complete satisfaction' adverse to them? Was there a hint that at that point he had excluded from the possible the complete unsoundness of the Aborigines' case, something which had been urged upon him most fervently and confidently by both the Commonwealth and Nabalco? Was he saying that, in a sense, 'all arguments' are not really open? I will come back to the point later, but, once again, hurry on to say that Mr Justice Blackburn also refused—as premature—the defendants' second prayer, that he should proceed to try the main action, without pleadings, on issues to be defined; he said the statement of claims should first be put in order. He offered some quite severe criticisms of the Aborigines' statement. He said that the Commonwealth and Nabalco were entitled to a clearer indication of the real nature of the issues, which had become clear only after Mr Woodward's address. This had about it a substantial degree of novelty. There were as well many defective elements in the statements of claim. Some were essentially legal, and I need not go into them. But among those he mentioned were some which, in the context of other remarks, have continued to cause me anxiety—failures to explain the use of words such as 'clan', 'possession', and 'proprietary interest', and to give particulars of sacred areas and objects and of the traditional manner in which the land was and is used. He struck out the statement of claims but—it seemed to me with great care to temper the wind to the shorn lamb—put the Aborigines at liberty to make another statement within 28 days, and gave them other liberties as well.

The new statement of claims was made, I think, on the 28th day. Anthropologically speaking, it was still not to my complete satisfaction, but I had no right to grumble. The management of the action is for lawyers, and it became abundantly clear in the Darwin proceedings that the case will turn upon points of law rather than on matters of anthropological fact. I came to understand, with difficulty, that there were twenty or more points of law to be agreed upon by both sides as being at issue before the trial stage could begin at a place and time agreed by both sides.

It has taken much discussion to bring about those agreements. I do not know all the circumstances and, if I did, probably I could not speak about them freely, but I think we would have to use both of the Shakespearean categories—'the law's delay' and 'the insolence of office'—to account fully for the slowness of movement. Had both sides been ready Mr Justice Blackburn would have heard the action in August or October of last year (1969). No one was ready in August. The Aborigines, though worried and mystified by the delay, have shown great confidence in their legal advisers, and deferred to the fact that their leading counsel, Mr Woodward, QC, was committed during and beyond October in a long drawn out arbitration case. The Crown itself was not ready. Of course in October a Federal election was in the very near offing. Could that have been a consideration? No: we heard then that the Crown now considered the case required much more research than had been realised earlier. That was my own impression: I recalled that in Darwin the only Aboriginal contention that the Crown appeared willing to admit was that George III had been on the throne 'in or about 1788'.

Towards the end of the year preparation of the proofs of evidence, for which I went to Yirrkala, were in their last phase. There was hope then for a trial in February or March. That work was knocked on the head a few weeks ago by the death of Mathaman, the elder whom the Rirratjingu people had named as their head and spokesman. It meant, of course, a new affidavit from his successor Milirrpum. I had met Mathaman during my brief visit to Yirrkala in November and, having heard him talking to Mr Purcell, the Aborigines' solicitor, I thought him likely to be an impressive witness in court. But he was plainly a dying man.

Everyone knew there would be a race for time. Something rather strange happened. Unknown to Purcell and me, a decision was taken to anticipate the mortuary rite partly, I think, for Mathaman's comfort—as I will show—but also partly, I think, to make Purcell and me understand the gravity of the things they had been saying to us about the claim to land. The older Rirratjingu men took Purcell and me to a secret place where we saw Mathaman prone on the ground. On his chest and abdomen they were painting the totemic designs which are the sole prerogative of Mathaman's clan. I am not sure, but I think, the act had something to do with the possibility that he might die away from home while he was in Darwin for the case. We were allowed to watch the act of painting, which was accompanied by singing. That done, we were told to sit, with our backs turned, while other singing went on in a hidden place a short distance away. We were then taken by the hand and led towards the singing. As we walked we were asked to look only at the ground and not to raise our heads until told to do so. We went into a patch of jungle, and then were given a sudden command to look. At our feet were the holy *rangga* or emblems of the clan, effigies of the ancestral beings, twined together by long strings of coloured feathers. I could but look: it was not the time or place to start an inquisition into these symbols. A group of dancers, painted—as far as I could see—with similar or cognate designs, then went through a set of mimetic dances. When it was over I heard Mathaman say: 'now I can die'. One of the men said to me: 'now you understand'. He meant that I had seen the holy *rangga* which, in a sense, are the clan's title-deeds to its land, and had heard what they stood for: so I could not but 'understand'. The Rirratjingu and the Gumaitj, the main plaintiff clans, intend to take their *rangga* into Darwin to show the court. They think the court will then 'understand'. I had the sense that, although they have been warned, they cannot conceive the possibility that the court will not understand.

When the hope of a February trial became unrealisable, there was talk of

March. Then something else happened. The Full Bench of the High Court gave a decision which knocked a hole through the middle of the last form of the Aborigines' case. It came about this way. The Full Bench had been asked to decide a fundamental question arising in a case concerned with the mining operations in Bougainville. The question was whether three New Guinea ordinances, vesting in the Crown or the Administration the power to acquire compulsorily minerals in the Territory, were invalid because they did not provide for just terms of compensation for the acquisition. In an immediate, unanimous and—as one senior counsel remarked to me—'contemptuous' judgment, the court said 'no'. The matter was approached and determined solely as one of constitutional law. The Court said that the question had its answer in Section 122 of the Constitution, which grants legislative power for the government of Commonwealth territories whether on the mainland or external to it. The legislative power, it said, is 'plenary in quality and unlimited and unqualified in point of subject matter'. The Court rejected the submission that s.122 is limited by s.51 (xxxi), which requires compulsory acquisition to observe just terms. The Crown or the Administration is thus not limited to the making of laws which provide just terms. Its power is akin to that of the States to make laws to acquire property without having to provide in those laws for terms of acquisition which can be seen in the circumstances to be just. Unhappily for them, the Aborigines in the Yirrkala case had been invoking the protection of s.51 (xxxi) against the Commonwealth and Nabalco. The High Court's decision is final. There is no appeal. Some of my legal friends say that the decision has puzzled them. The High Court chose one from at least three possible approaches to the question but did not explain its choice, although each approach could have been given eminent justification. Lawyers say they find a refreshing novelty in the unanimity and immediacy of the High Court's decision—usually, they tell me, they expect seven different decisions on any single question, and a long wait for them—but that is not my affair.

On 25 February [1970] the solicitors for the Aborigines, taking the High Court's decision into consideration, made a new statement of claims before the N.T. Supreme Court. I have not seen the statement but it must have changed considerably from the amended first statement made in May 1969. I have been told that both the Commonwealth and Nabalco objected to the changes, and that the matter was adjourned. But as far as I am aware the trial will take place on 18 May in Darwin, but after the experience of the last twelve months I am less than certain that everyone will keep the appointment. The unexpected keeps on happening. On the very day on which the last statement of claims was lodged, two of the leading Aboriginal witnesses, and a third man, were arrested at Yirrkala 300 miles away on charges of assaulting or obstructing or resisting the police in the execution of their duty. This was the affair mentioned in the newspapers and on the radio at the weekend. Things are not well at Yirrkala.

At this point, I think I should go back to the March 1969 proceedings to notice the arguments used, not towards compensation, which was barely mentioned, but towards title. I recorded the arguments from natural interest but also from a belief that in fifty or a hundred years' time people will want to study how we approached the complexities of the first case of its kind to arise in 180 years of settlement. What light does it throw on our mentality and institutions? What does it say about our ideas and conduct when events compel us to grasp both circumstances and principle at the same time? Which do we reach for with the stronger hand: principle or circumstance?

I remind you that when the Aborigines went to law they went into a forum of adversaries. Possibly they were puzzled by the fact that they were opposed both by the Company and the Commonwealth. I know that some of them brood on the matter and think it a conundrum. One of them asked me in November, 'does Government really think we do not own the land?' I had to say 'yes'. So in this summary I will run together the Commonwealth's and Nabalco's arguments. I think that fair, because in court they were Tweedledum and Tweedledee. They jointly saw the action as a remarkable, misconceived and most unsettling attack on the laws of property. They jointly said that the Aborigines' statement of claims did not disclose a true cause of action and indeed none could be alleged that could be sustained in law. If the Aborigines relied on establishing tribal rights to land, the answer was clear: the law did not recognise such rights. If they relied on adverse possession, the statement of claims was radically unsound. [I should interpolate here that until the afternoon of the second day both Crown and Company appeared to assume that the mainstay of the Aboriginal case would be a claim of adverse possession, and my impression was that they were flummoxed, though only momentarily, when it was revealed not to be so. Woodward QC for the Aborigines had used Wellesleyan tactics. He had put his guns well behind the crest-line, and for a day and a half watched while the

Crown and Nabalco skirmished rather vaguely towards and then tried to overrun his very secondary position. I will tell about it later.] So Crown and Company went jointly on. The law in Australia had never recognised any title in the Aborigines stemming from tribal rights in land. Aboriginal law and custom could not be applicable unless admitted as part of the law of the land. Common law never had done and did not do so, nor any statute. The Crown and the Legislatures had never taken any step on any basis other than that the land was entirely Crown land from 1786 or 1788 and that grants of unencumbered titles to it were within the Crown's prerogative. No statute could be read to suggest the least recognition of Aboriginal proprietary rights. The insertion in settlers' leases of 'reservations' in favour of Aborigines (e.g. rights to take game and water, and to live, on the leaseholds), and the formal creation of Aboriginal Reserves, did not amount to a recognition of Aboriginal property rights. They merely showed that the Crown had a paternal attitude to Aborigines. The fact that

Aborigines remained on granted land, or even on unalienated Crown land, did not constitute possession in law: the Aborigines were on such lands as permissive occupants; if not, they were trespassers. [I interpolate again. A great deal of time was spent building an ironclad defence against adverse possession. The essence of the defence was to show that since 1786 there had been no continuous period of sixty years—the period prescribed by the *Nullum Tempus Act* of 1769—during which Aborigines could claim to have been in effective possession of the Gove Peninsula and thus have possessed it adversely to the Crown. I must pass over the details, but I was lost in admiration of the patience and ingenuity with which the work was done. No German scholar has ever described an elephant more minutely. The Crown worked its way on from 1786. The Company worked its way back to 1786. Neither found a trace of the adverse. But they did find things which surprised me, including the fact that in 1839 the Gove Peninsula was really part of the New England and Liverpool Plains district.] But to resume: the arguments mounted up rather as follows. No period of sixty years could be satisfied. No possession at any time had been adverse. The Crown title had never been extinguished. Time had never run against the Crown. But if there had been adverse possession, it had been fatally interrupted by leases from as early as 1886. There was evidence of payments of rent by leaseholders or of occupation by the Crown from 1881 to 1958. But in any case, if there had been adverse possession, it ceased in 1931, when the Arnhem Land Aboriginal Reserve was created. Thereafter the Aborigines were there by the Crown's express permission. Any clan occupation changed to permissive occupancy by individuals. And the 'use and benefit' of the Reserve was non-exclusive to them: all the Aborigines of North Australia now had the 'use and benefit'. Any acts the Aborigines might rely on to constitute adverse possession were not inconsistent with the Crown's enjoyment of the land, even when it was unalienated. In any case they were acts of trespass rather than acts of possession. The wandering of nomadic or semi-nomadic people could not be acts of the class constituting adverse possession in law. The very most that could be said was that the Aborigines had some form of land occupation. What was this talk of Aboriginal 'proprietary rights'? Did the Aborigines have a freehold? No. A *profit à prendre?* No. No title could be claimed. Their acts did not amount to either type of interest. In law, an uncertain and fluctuating body, such as an Aboriginal clan, could not even acquire rights in land allowable under the *Nullum Tempus Act.* For good or ill, that was the situation in law.

I will make no attempt to bring in the wealth of legal authority which was cited. One counsel told me that the number of authorities far exceeded the number in any case of comparable length known to him. I seek to adduce the arguments only in order to show two things. One is the condign quality of the defence against the Aboriginal initiative. These were not arguments of an actual trial but arguments to prevent a trial: in other words, to have the Aboriginal application dismissed at the outset as frivolous and vexatious. The other is to show the neuralgic nerve that the case exposed. As Nabalco said, and as the Crown echoed: 'to accede to the aboriginal propositions would be to unsettle the property law of the continent'. This was almost identical with what Glenelg said in the reverse affair of Batman in 1837: 'It is indeed enough to observe that such a concession' (the right of Aborigines to alienate land to private adventurers) 'would subvert the foundation on which all proprietary rights in New South Wales at present rest and defeat a large part of the most important regulations of the local government.'

It was now Woodward's turn. I did not see how he could hope to demolish the Crown and Company arguments. Indeed, after he had been speaking for nearly five hours, I still thought the trend was against him. Then, late at night (the Court sat after dinner) he made his move, and I then saw that he must win. This is how it happened.

He began by trying to put a new complexion on the Aboriginal stand. They were not attacking the law of property. They were invoking its protection. They sincerely believed they were the owners of the land. Indeed, they knew they were the owners. As far as they were concerned, it had been given to them by their spirit ancestors, and they had held it ever since. For over thirty years they had felt secure in the knowledge that the Government had reserved the land for them. What they now feared was exactly what the Crown and Company had said in Court: that 'reserve' meant no more than 'permission to remain'. They were making legal history in asking the Court to declare their rights. These rights were of the same kind that had been recognised in every civilised country which had taken colonial possessions to itself. Of course in other countries the common law had been reinforced by legislation. It was not too much to hope that the same might be done here. But in the proceedings he must, and would, rely on the common law. (This was the first surprise: Crown and Company had barely mentioned the common law.)

He then went on to describe the nature of Aboriginal landholding and title in Australia generally, and in Arnhem Land in particular. These matters did not come into issue at the interlocutory proceedings, except to be pooh-poohed by Crown and Company. They may quite well become the crux of the full trial. But I pass over them now because I think it more important to dwell on the common law approach. The Aboriginal claim, he said, went to the very foundations of the common law, where basic questions of morality, justice and practice were important.

He put forward eight propositions. (i) Whatever the means of acquisition of a new colony—conquest, cession, mere occupation—the Crown acquired the radical, paramount or ultimate title to all land along with its other sovereign rights. (ii) This was the end of the matter as far as new settlers were concerned. To acquire any property in the land they must have been able to show a grant by the Crown or adverse possession for 60 years. (iii) But a mere change of sovereignty was not presumed to have disturbed existing native land rights. Indeed, the converse was to be presumed: that existing native rights were to be respected. (iv) These rights would be protected even when they were of a kind unknown to common law, as was usually the case. (v) Only the Crown could extinguish the native land rights. (vi) Except in time of war, the Crown could extinguish the rights only with the consent of the native owners. (vii) The method of extinction was by purchase or the payment of compensation. The amount of compensation should reflect the virtual ownership of the land, as in fee simple, and should not be reduced by the limited disposal available to the natives. (viii) The extinction of the rights required a statutory enactment, a 'new law'.

Woodward spent most of the afternoon elaborating these propositions. I had an uneasy sense that he was not making an impression. It all rang true but it seemed too far away from the market-place mentality of Crown and Company, unrelated to the raucous life of the Northern Territory. Then my depression lifted. He began to examine the Crown and Company thesis on Australian history, about which I had been muttering to myself, and had decided to fail. He took the Court through the salient facts of New South Welsh, South Australian and Commonwealth history as they had successively affected the Gove Peninsula. Between 1788 and 1863 there was no evidence of white settlement there, no attempted dealing with land. There had been no statutory enactment, relevant to the area, expressly or by inference extinguishing native land rights. The fact that native rights in other parts of New South Wales may not have been understood or not claimed had no relevance to the common law situation as it affected the Gove Peninsula. But in any event the law of New South Wales was set aside as from 1836, when the Northern Territory became part of South Australia. That stream of law then ran dry at the border. A new stream of law began to run from South Australia to the Northern Territory. Aboriginal land title was in fact recognised at the foundation of the Province of South Australia. The Letters Patent of 19 February 1836, erecting and establishing the Province, expressly did so. The 1838 Act to amend the Act of the previous reign (Victoria was now on the throne), which empowered the erection of South Australia into a British Province, recited the Letters Patent. (This fascinating fact, hitherto quite unknown to me, also caused Mr Justice Blackburn to look sharply over his glasses.) The fact again that native rights were not understood or claimed in South Australia was not relevant to the common law and Gove Peninsula. But in fact all the pastoral leases recognised Aboriginal rights, not in general terms, but by trying to spell out the most important incidents of those rights. This showed that native title could coexist with other forms of occupation. What really happened in the Territory was that there were two streams—that of the men of law who kept alive the common law as it affected native land rights, for example by the lease provisions, and that of the men of affairs, who knew they could ignore them. There was certainly no statutory enactment extinguishing native land rights. Such an enactment would have had to be very clear. The rights could not be extinguished by a side wind.

What of the Commonwealth period? He ran through this quickly and, I thought, decisively. In 1911 the Commonwealth inherited all South Australian laws relevant to the Northern Territory (*N.T. Acceptance Act,* 1910, s.7). There was nothing consequential for Gove until 1931, when the Aboriginal Reservation was proclaimed. Reservation was not inconsistent with native land rights. The definitions of 'waste lands' and 'crown lands' are sufficiently wide to cover such lands even though subject to native land rights. No conflict arises. The Arnhem Land Reservation was in fact a positive and deliberate recognition of those rights. Certainly the Aborigines so understood it. It set the land aside for the use and benefit of Aboriginal people. (Woodward here went into a point which I had got wrong in my Boyer Lectures. Crown and Company had made play with the non-exclusiveness of the Reserves to the Aborigines of the particular locality. They referred to the words of various ordinances—'use and benefit of

Aborigines', 'use and benefit of Aborigines of the Northern Territory'—and interpreted them as meaning 'all' Aborigines. Woodward pointed out that the word 'all' did not occur. It was realised that Aborigines of one clan or tribe went on the land of other clans or tribes by right or licence. The actual wording was the necessary wording. The ordinances were silent as to the regulation of interests between clans and tribes, thereby inferentially leaving them to be settled by Aboriginal law and custom.)

By 1931, then, the Gumaitj and Rirratjingu had a proprietary right in their land, which was clearly established. The common law presumed it to exist. No step had ever been taken to extinguish it. It has been protected against infringement by the reservations within the pastoral leases. It had received positive recognition in the 1931 Reservation, which was given without qualification. Since 1931, no valid act of prescription had occurred to detract from the established proprietary interest.

I think I can just about pin-point the stage at which the 'break' of trend occurred. Crown and Company had been contending that the Aboriginal claim was worthless. The words they chose to use surprised me: 'plainly bad', 'obscure', 'misconceived', 'obviously untenable', 'useless', 'vague and unsubstantial', 'embarrassing', 'no possibility of success', 'manifestly groundless', 'worse than demurrable'; all those and many others. One gem from the Company should not be withheld from history: to recognise the land rights of nomads as proprietary rights 'would be like saying of someone who has escaped the penalty for bigamy that bigamous marriage was recognised as the law of Australia'. By such rhetoric, and by the use of ominous phrases such as 'guiding lights to courts of first instance', they sought, with a heavy rustle of silk, to sway the Court to summary dismissal. The issue turned on two things. First a true reading of the rules of court concerning summary judgment. The Company said the Court needed only a degree of satisfaction, a 'comfortable reassurance' that the claim could not succeed. Woodward said that the Court must be satisfied beyond doubt that the claim was hopeless. That of course turned on values of facts and points of law. It was plain that Mr Justice Blackburn was dissatisfied. He quizzed Woodward closely. 'You are saying that native title to land is just as good as that of a person who has received an express Crown grant?'—'Yes. Once the rights are infringed they are "property" under the Constitution and "an interest in land" under the *Acquisition of Lands Act.* The only possible challenge is that we had no rights.' 'You are saying this issue was not met at all by what defendants' counsel had to say?'—'Yes, and said by their own choice; they were thoroughly familiar with all the authorities; it was their own election.' 'Has your statement of claim got a basis in law? Have you got a cause of action?'—'The only question is: do we have an arguable cause of action.' There was a great deal of this, and it went on for a considerable time. Much of it I missed. There were asides from Crown and Company. From Woodward: 'Right up to now our clients have had native title in these lands. That title is entitled to protection at common law'. From the

Crown: 'I put it to your Honour that the plaintiffs have no title'. From Woodward: 'Let us not forget where the onus of proof lies. If we have a weighty argument we are entitled to our day in court. This is the real question, leaving aside the epithets employed by the opposite side.' He went on hammering these themes. A summons for summary judgment should be reserved for absolutely hopeless actions. It could not be said he had not raised important and difficult questions of law. There was a presumption at common law that the native rights continued. This presumption could only be extinguished by legislation or similar action of a formal kind. No such extinguishment had taken place. Although 200 years had passed the natives should be given the opportunity to convince the Court of their just rights. The absence of time was no bar to the Court hearing such an action. Summary dismissal would deprive the natives of their opportunity.

The break came when Mr Justice Blackburn said: 'Mr Woodward, you have put to me an argument of very great weight and interest. If it is accepted a great deal of received doctrine has to be upset.' A little later, when he saw how Woodward has seized on this remark, he sought to qualify it, a little, but significantly. 'The case put by the defendants and the case put by you have proceeded on a different basis of doctrine. You have shown me a tenable argument on a different basis of doctrine'—at which point Woodward said: 'that must be the end of the matter. Once you have a difficult point of law, you must proceed.' And Mr Justice Blackburn said, I thought in a slightly nettled way, 'Mr Woodward, I do comprehend, but I do not fully agree.'

The main battle—against dismissal—was clearly over. The argument against trial without pleadings then took place. Woodward said he was unprepared; the full case would be long and involved; dismissal would be a misuse of summary proceedings; it would be unjust to his clients. The Judge was not very receptive to this contention but neither Crown nor Company seemed inclined to press objection. I think their troops, guns and banners had been too stiffly deployed elsewhere for the assault of the Aborigines' secondary position, adverse possession.

On this contention Woodward likened the Crown's effort to a pea-and-thimble trick. The Crown had tried to show that of the three periods 1788–1863, 1863–1931, and 1931–1969, the pea—sixty years—was not under the first, and that thereafter there could not have been any adverse possession because of 'implied permission'. Woodward attacked this proposition. How had it been deduced? From what? How different had Aboriginal occupation been from that of the squatters? The two necessary elements of adverse possession—exclusive occupation in a physical sense, and *animus possidendi* (the intention to possess)—had both been there for the Aborigines until 1863. Time had run against the Crown, the Crown title had been extinguished, over this period, and the Aboriginal people and their descendants in title had occupied the land ever since.

Native rights could not be destroyed inadvertently or accidentally. Where was the Act or Ordinance that had deliberately set out to destroy their rights? To pretend that any Australian action had destroyed Aboriginal title would be a confidence trick on a very large scale, and would everywhere be deeply resented. If Aborigines had brought an action in New South Wales in 1800, in South Australia in 1840, or in the Northern Territory in 1870, there could be little doubt of the outcome. The Yirrkala people had had nothing to sue about until the present attempt to take their land away. They should be permitted to come to Court.

Mr Justice Blackburn now remarked on 'two surprising turns' that the case had taken: the different doctrine that Woodward had revealed, which he thought at least arguable; and the procedural question of what his powers were—his inherent jurisdiction and his jurisdiction under the rules of court covering summary proceedings.

I will skate over what followed. Crown and Company edged apart a little in their replies. I thought I saw a fissure shaping, for example, an intimation that the Company would rely on the Statute of Limitations, even if the Commonwealth did not. The Company made about a dozen or more hard points. Whether native proprietary rights were recognised was solely for the Crown. The Crown was the sole arbiter of its own justice. No case could be produced to show that, without cession or conquest, the common law had looked at native custom as having any validity for purposes of recognition. There could be recognition only in cases of cession. Recognition presupposed an organised system with some ascertainable system of law. There had to be an ordered society, a settled law, an ability to make a deal or contract with a juristic person. None of them existed in Aboriginal Australia. There was no automatic recognition of native laws and customs. It depended on the state of civilisation. New Zealand? Simply 'an admirable exception'. Treaties of cession had a very important role. Without a treaty there was no springboard for doctrine. The courts had to administer, not to make, the law. Bending and stretching the common law introduced deleterious matter into a pure stream. To accept the Aboriginal submissions would be to unsettle the laws of property of the continent. The fact was that the Aborigines had been expropriated in the 19th century. It was simply pretence to say they had been expropriated in 1968. But as for native title: anthropology was not a closed science; later research might upset Berndt's and Stanner's views. Must it be assumed that there was only one kind of title? It might have been very variable throughout Australia. And how many of the overtones of our law had been worked into the submission? The law of England did not recognise the 'unbreakable', 'inalienable' and 'deeply spiritual' type of ownership alleged to exist among the Aborigines. If they indeed had a 'system' it was not compatible with the common law; not suitable for grafting on to it; not apt to be made acceptable to it. The relevant law had been settled for ever, unless altered by a further Act, by *Cooper* v. *Stuart* 1889, *14 Appeal Cases;* p.291. The Aborigines could not possibly surmount two bars: Privy Council judgments, and the *Nullum*

Tempus Act of 1769. Lastly, it must be remembered that there was a national project at risk. Had there been native title, which was denied, then the Company's licence in itself was a sufficient authority to terminate that title for the duration of the lease.

The Crown's reply was somewhat less frontal. It conceded that the matter must proceed to trial if the Court were uncertain as to the law, or if there were some other doubt, or if there were an arguable case. But there were 200 years of authority and legislation to say that Aboriginal rights in land were not recognised by common law or statute. *Cooper* v. *Stuart* was the law laid down by the highest tribunal: a bold, clear and inescapable exposition. The Aborigines' case begged the whole question from cases and principles not applicable in Australia. Things done when there had been a change of sovereignty did not apply when there had been no antecedent sovereignty. Pre-existent rights were protected only when there was a pre-existent, settled system of law. It was true that only the Crown could extinguish native land rights: *if* there were rights to recognise and extinguish. Woodward had kept on presupposing there was something to extinguish. There had not been. (At about this time a curious incident occurred. The Crown had made a long traverse of New Zealand, India, Canada, Africa and America to adduce cases to counter Woodward's submission that Australia was the only exception to a general rule of recognising pre-existing native rights at common law. Woodward protested at these tactics. How was it that the Crown had come equipped with multiple copies of all these judgments but had concealed them in chief and had used them only in reply? Why had they not been used in chief? The Judge rebuked him.) The Crown went on: recognition depended on three things. First, the fact of private rights before conquest or cession; second, the continuation after conquest or cession of a developed land tenure system; third, the existence of an autonomous, organised native authority system able to treat authoritatively for the Aborigines. None of these conditions existed. And occupation had to be discriminated from conquest or cession. For good or ill we did not conquer Australia. We occupied it. The native system was displaced. 'And that,' the Crown said in a memorable phrase, 'was that.' The colony of New South Wales was peopled only by native inhabitants who had no settled system of law. The anthropological evidence did not establish that there were private rights, or a system of land tenure, or an organised authority system. The most that could be said was that there was some form of occupation.

Woodward was given permission to reply to the reply, and to range more widely if he so desired. I will not go into the details of the ways in which he discriminated a large number of cases. But, having done so, he said that so far he had argued the case at its proper, that is, its highest level, but he thought it justified even at its lowest level. What was this? There were seven points. (i) The common law presumed that native land title would be respected, but in the final analysis the matter had to be decided one way or the other by the exercise of the prerogative or by legislation. This argument must succeed. (ii) In South Australia the prerogative had been established in favour of recognition of native title wherever it could be established. This was done by the Letters Patent which were recognised and impliedly adopted by Act of Parliament. (iii) This law was carried forward into the Northern Territory. (iv) The worst that could be said was that in the Northern Territory there was a different approach as between men of law and men of affairs. The approach of the men of law was exemplified by the form of the pastoral leases. The men of affairs found that the law could be ignored with impunity. That was all that occurred. (v) The law had remained in force unimpaired. The Crown had not attempted to allege that anything had extinguished native title. It had not pointed to a single instance. (The Crown broke in here to say that Woodward had not understood the argument, which was that all the legislation and other Acts had been inconsistent with there ever having been native rights. If there had been, they were extinguished by the legislation. To this, Woodward replied that it just wasn't so. There was nothing inconsistent with the continuance of native rights. There was absolutely no authority for the Crown's extraordinary submission. If what it said had been true there would have been an outcry from one end of Australia to the other. Nothing cited *could* have destroyed native title, and the South Australian Letters Patent had something of the nature of a constitutional guarantee.) (vi) If it required some legislative provision for compensation before it could be sued upon, then that was provided by the *Land Acquisition Act.* (vii) The fact that there were other Aborigines who could have claimed its protection, but failed to, is irrelevant to the case of the present plaintiffs. They had had no need to invoke the protection of the law until now. Woodward closed by saying: 'They come before Your Honour to invoke that protection. The only thing we have to establish is that we have a tenable case.'

I am not sure, because I do not know, but I think that right to the end

Crown and Company were reasonably sure of a summary dismissal of the case after a reserved decision. I have already dealt with the judgment. Perhaps I should add one thing: before the March proceedings terminated, the Aborigines' legal advisers made an open offer to Nabalco to settle the injunction proceedings in return for assurances. Nabalco said it could not accept any offer in terms expressly or implicitly making it appear that the Aborigines had any legal title to the land but undertook to act 'with goodwill and understanding'.

We now have to wait for 18 May. I presume, though I do not know, that the High Court decision removes any possible basis for a claim of compensation. That would leave the action substantially reduced to one for a declaration of title, whether original or prescriptive. Even so, there will be a round dozen issues of fact or law to be agreed for trial. It will not surprise me if Crown or Company attacks the validity or representative capacity of the so-called 'clan heads'. It is certain that the nature and incidents of the alleged clan-ownership of land will be searchingly questioned: it was plain at the hearing that Crown and Company had misunderstood the affidavits on the social and land systems of the Aborigines. I expect the anthropological evidence to come under a very severe attack: I have found widely in official life both hostility and derision towards the work and opinions of anthropologists, and I expect court tactics designed to make us appear mere wafflers of vocables, and to make the facts appear either uninterpretable or misinterpreted. The particular claims of the two main clans—the Rirratjingu and Gumaitj—and their interlocking with those of the nine other clans, will have to be determined, and I expect artificial confusions to be added to the real ones. There are some vexing questions of historical fact and the ensuing legal effects, mainly but not only from the South Australian period, to be considered, e.g. the legislative and administrative intentions and effects over a very long period, e.g. the recognition, if any, of native rights by the proclamation of reserves. There are also all the questions of common law, and the possible forms of titles that might be declared.

So much for the legal aspect. I now go outside the arms of the Court, and intend no reference to it. It is a pity that the historical context has to be the Yirrkala affair. A quieter time, a smaller scene, would have been better. A lot of heady stuff is being spoken and believed that partly blinds and deafens people to the racial, social and political aspects of the affair. For example, there is much talk about 'the national importance' of the bauxite-alumina venture, and of the 'risk' to which the case exposes 'the national interest'. The public is being encouraged to assimilate the affair to the model of the little old lady refusing to allow her tottering house to be pulled down in a slum clearance programme, or that of the backward farmer using his old Martini-Henry against bulldozers making a dam to help a drought-stricken countryside. What is 'the national importance'? The Gove bauxite is not a bonanza. The capital and workforce committed there could readily be used elsewhere on ventures as, if not more, useful and profitable. The decision to go ahead was taken before the mineral boom got under way. I have some doubt if it could be capitalised on the same basis if it were being undertaken *de novo* in 1970. The only people who stand to do excellently well are the Swiss partners of the consortium. They should get what they want: a dependable and very long-term supply of bauxite and alumina at a firm price for a very long-term production and marketing programme. If one took into account the *net* effect of the enterprise on the Australian balance of payments, i.e. after the expatriation of profits, and the forgone alternative investments which languish for capital, the 'national importance' might well seem very much smaller. I do not think that 'the national interest' would imperatively demand the immediate development of the Gove Peninsula. The 'national interest' is of course a judgment—often an evanescent judgment—about a bundle of interests, each of which is given a weight. There are two interests which have been given no weights in this calculation. One is the Aboriginal interest. The other is the interest of the public who will foot the bill for the very considerable direct costs and the larger social costs of the enterprise. These questions have been approached through the conventional wisdom of the 19th century.

It is bad luck for the Aborigines that their problems arise so acutely just as the mineral boom is reaching the phase of mania. My friend Gregory Bateson once said that a house falling down around one's ears is no place in which to study the laws of architecture. The Aborigines have picked a bad time to ask us to study the principles of racial justice and social costs. The draconic quality of the attempt to snuff out all talk of Aboriginal interests in land is related to this excited background, and to a deep commitment which has to justify itself. You have a very large commitment of private capital, well in excess of $300 million. It will work out at something like $100,000 per head of all the Europeans concerned just to bring the industry to the point of full yield. If you were to put a value of $1000 millions at present prices on the bauxite and the alumina from it you would be conservative. The venture is wholly in line with a posture maintained without legal challenge for 200 years. The Company is there by Crown licence; it has an agreement with the Commonwealth; and the agreement is covered by an N.T. Ordinance. It thus has a defensible right to fight tooth and nail and of course it will do so. I cannot detect anywhere in political Australia an impulse to reconsider Aboriginal rights or wishes at so basic a level.

I think that what has been happening since the 1950s—and is now happening in an intensified form because of the mineral boom—is a reinforcement of something already very old: an unwillingness to change the ethos and the structure of Australian society in respect of the Aborigines. Unwillingness is being reinforced into a self-assuring proof of incapacity. So that anyone who is in the simple mood of *fiat justitia ruat coelum* ('Let justice be done, though the heavens fall') is just not in touch with the world of politics, industry and commerce. The Australian thesis is not only that there is nothing in the Aborigines' claim: there never was. I can understand the Company's saying that. But what a way to begin a stay of forty, or possibly eighty, years in Aboriginal country! It is harder for me to understand the Crown's support of that position.

1970

Aborigines and Australian Society (1972)

My concern for many years has been to try, whenever possible, to use direct Aboriginal testimony to illumine their problems with us, not ours with them. My idea was to try to change our perspective in the belief that we might then find credible motives for going more than half-way to meet them. I have heard this called 'the scholar's fallacy' but, in all the circumstances, historical and contemporary, as I understand them, it seemed the best approach. It was, anyway, the thing I could do best because of the knowledge and experience I had gained from many years of friendly and rewarding association with Aborigines. It also let me express, through authentic material drawn from living people, a long-settled view that, in themselves, and as the bearers of unique and unrepeatable social forms and culture, they were and still are disvalued by our conventional European outlook; not just *under*-valued, but *dis*valued. And, in a sense, it allowed me to try to repay a debt of obligation.

Without having any particular plan, I set out to try by the spoken and the written word to convey more widely the understanding I had formed of Aboriginal life, ideology and values in their authentic past and their actual present. How best to do that was a problem in itself. It seemed to me that I had to choose between a direct and an indirect approach. The direct approach—by pamphlet, tract, demonstration or political pressure—had not produced many results up to that time. Nor could I persuade myself, on the evidence, that very many Australians felt wicked or guilty about what had happened to the Aborigines. That said nothing whatever about the 'ought' or the 'should' of the matter. It was no more than a personal judgment of fact, one man's reading of a state of affairs. Rightly or wrongly, I made the judgment that, for most people, the problems were just too old in time, too settled in history, and too remote from personal concerns, to signify greatly. Human history after all crawls with invitations to feel vicarious guilt. Only a robust common sense saves any of us from a sense of despair about it. No doubt I too would have subscribed to the comforting theory of 'long ago and far away' about Aboriginal conditions but for two things. They both came about in the routine experience of an anthropologist in the field. I got to know and lived with Aborigines who were the victims of things that had happened in their lifetime and mine: the injuries to their interests were visible, present and continuing. And I discovered that Aboriginal ideas, customs and values, when well arranged and transposed into words with meanings understandable to us in relation to familiar things, were enormously impressive in the human sense. You cannot be long in Aboriginal company without becoming aware of the passion and conviction with which they believe in their tradition, and of their dignity and honesty in instructing those who are interested to learn. What they have to say is educative to a degree which our schools and universities are the poorer for not trying to understand and teach. It is, in my opinion, true to a most lamentable extent that Aborigines are administered, controlled, educated and so on by people who know almost nothing about them and give a good appearance of believing that there is nothing significant to learn. Yet no one who took part in the Yirrkala land case came out of it without a heightened respect for Aboriginal life, ideology and values. What we all saw there were black men who, in the very process of failure, won white minds to a new point of view. Their only failures were against 18th century law, 'history' as we construct it, and some rather intractable European superstitions about land.

Perhaps what finally made me prefer the indirect to the direct approach was a conviction that in affairs of the human will internal change precedes external change. There have to be motives of credibility. I could not see us making any great changes in the external conditions of life we had imposed on

Aborigines unless and until we found credible motives for doing so. That, I thought, could come only from a changed perspective. It so happened that for professional reasons I also wanted to some extent to change the anthropological perspective. I am not sure exactly how it happened—there was certainly no fine-spun plan—but I found myself writing for public as well as professional readers. From today's vantage point it was clearly a case of a cork on a wave already starting to roll. The interest in Aboriginal art, music, dance, mime and theatre was already well established. In those circumstances it was easy and rewarding from time to time to write and speak about things which interested me professionally and also to some extent had a wider appeal—the conception of The Dreaming, the world-view of a society at almost the opposite pole from ours; the life-story of a great warrior; the religious cults and the syntax of their ritual symbolism; the territorial system; and other things of the kind. If some of my pieces reached and influenced a wider audience than I had in mind, I can only be glad of it.

When I was preparing this lecture someone said to me: 'Why not tell us what makes it so hard to do anything *for* the Aborigines? If we can judge by the results, nothing seems to work—in education, in health, in economic development, in social progress. What makes it all so difficult?'

The questioner was of course a European. The question itself would tell us that. So, I think, would its silent presumptions: the presumption that our measures and methods *should* work, and the presumption that there is something almost inexplicable in their failure or comparative failure. Was there also a presumption, on an unvoiced but deeper level, that the Aborigines are a main part of the trouble? In the end it often comes down to that: dark hints about their mentality, social habits and cultural oddities. I have never wanted to deny Aboriginal shortcomings, in their own life, or for life in our kind of world. But I like to invite people to make an act of imagination and to suppose, just for argument's sake, that Aborigines are, in every essential human respect, much of a muchness with us, and to put ourselves in situations like theirs. For example, take Yirrkala in Arnhem Land.

For several years Aborigines there saw strange Europeans coming and going on land which everyone supposed was Aboriginal land. The strangers measured or marked out the ground, dug into it here and there, and did some ambiguous things without saying why. No one seemed to know—at least no Aboriginal knew—what if anything portended. Eventually it became clear that there would be some kind of mining but the Aborigines—or so they told me—supposed it would be very small and short-lived. No one told them anything to the contrary. Then, virtually overnight, we sprang the huge bauxite venture. There had been ample time to prepare their minds, but no one did so. There had been no consultation. It was never intended that there should be. There *could* have been no true consultation because there had been no intention to give the Aborigines an option. The die had long been cast. We had decided what their interests were and what should be done about them. Their role was to conform. It sufficed for them to discover the truth later. They did, later, find out several significant truths. That the land was not theirs at all; that they had no say in what happened to it; that they had no bargaining or contractual power of any kind; that the town would need an hotel, the idea of which they particularly hated and feared; that the town would be built with further possible expansion in mind; that ancillary or supplementary ventures, such as a wood-chip industry, were in contemplation for still other land; and so on. I doubt if anyone on our side then thought or saw how unbearable all this would seem from an Aboriginal point of view. Now, by our act of imagination, we can admit that had we been in their position we would have thought the world a bit hard. We would have thought hints about our particular or general shortcomings hardly relevant. And I think we would have been likely to describe what had happened as an offer they knew we could not refuse. The Yirrkala affair was not so unusual. Indeed, it was so ordinary that we were surprised and put out when it blew up in our faces.

We have long settled into habitual routines which for ordinary human reasons produce some of the effects of which we complain. We put the Aborigines in situations in which they have no option but to do what we have arranged for them. We make for them the choices and decisions they would like to make for themselves. We do things in ways that do not give them what I called a 'half-way decent chance' to exhibit their own capabilities. We are justified in our hints about their shortcomings only after we have made proper allowance for the human responses to these continuing causes of trouble. There are others too.

One of the more recent roots of trouble is our obsession with time. There is always something because of which *we* cannot wait: a schedule to meet, a budget entry to complete, a date for a contract to be signed, a point on a graph where curves will intersect, or some other mysterious god to be placated. The Government, the Minister, the Director, the Board, the Superintendent must know by tomorrow, next week, next month: hurry! Many Aborigines think we are 'mad nor'-nor'-west' about time. In the old days we gave them plenty of time but very little else. Now, when we are more willing to give them material and other help, the one thing we are stingy with is time. We are too close to what we are doing to see how this preoccupation immeasurably worsens the effects of the older insensitive routines.

Of course the Aborigines, like us, can come to the point of rational choice and decision only in certain conditions. They need credible motive for having to choose and decide at all between This and That. They need information—all the information that bears on the choice and possible alternative decisions. They need time—all the time needed to work out the implications: how This will affect That and how That will affect Something Else; time to consider the alternatives; time to take into account new thoughts that did not occur to them earlier; time to strike balances between losers and gainers; time to make sure of consensus. They need high confidence in the worthwhileness of the yield from their decision. And so on. I do not know why we should suppose that choice and decision are any easier for them than for us, but it would not be difficult to cite suggestive evidence that we do. For one reason or another we seldom give them that 'half-way decent' chance of which I have spoken. Perhaps we should ponder the fact that it took us, with all our skills and resources, six years to choose and decide between the alternatives we were able to see in *our* problems with the Gurindji at Wattie Creek. I do not enter on the question whether these in any way resembled *their* problems with us.

Why *is* it so hard? There are many sorts of answers. The administrator, the missionary, the policeman, the doctor, the welfare worker, the pastoralist, the politician—all have answered differently for the times, places, problems and localities they know, and for the general problems universal throughout Australia. There is hardly time for me to categorise them, let alone list them, and were I to try to do so I would probably be saying more about us than about the fundamental troubles. Let me instead invite reflection on a particular matter which worries the Aborigines at least as much as it worries us. That is the problem of adolescent boys who, too widely and in too many cases, are on their way to becoming a lost generation of malcontent drop-outs, lay-abouts, delinquents and worse.

***

I will ask you to make another act of imagination, and to suppose you were with me watching what happened to a boy in an Aboriginal camp a generation ago. This boy was about ten years old. He was one of twenty or thirty people making up a local band of his tribe. All of them were relatives of a fairly close kind. The band was in camp for the night. The camp took the shape of a rough circle perhaps twenty paces in diameter. The circle was marked out by a ring of fires. The fires and the sexes alternated in an interesting way: if there was a man on one side of a fire there was a man on the other side; if there was a woman on one side, there was a woman on the other. The fire-pattern of the camp thus revealed an underlying social pattern. The fires were so arranged that they divided family from family so that persons of opposite sex but different families did not share the same fire. Different relatives placed themselves on different arcs of the circle. But I need not go into such details. I say this much to show that the camps had an intricate hidden structure. The day's work of hunting and foraging for food was over. Everyone had finished the evening meal. The fires were blazing; someone began to sing, and soon everyone joined in the singing or keeping time with simple percussions; one or two younger men began to dance. The corroboree went on amid jollity, laughter, and sometimes boisterous fun. There was at the same time a hum of gossip, tale-telling, and ordinary conversation, but with an emphasis on what we would call 'good form'—that is, manners, the common courtesies of conduct and conversation, the avoidance of rudeness or impoliteness, or words that might offend or shame. Everyone looked inward—to the centre of the circle, with backs towards the darkness of the surrounding bush—so that all sat more or less face-to-face. In between the phases of the corroboree children ran between the fires out, into and back from the darkness—but never too far into the darkness, because the night had terrors; no one liked to be too far away from the firelight for too long.

For the boy of whom I speak one thing—as we remembered, looking back in later years, when I talked with him about it—distinguished this night from all others. It was the last night of his careless childhood. He did not yet know that. Even next morning he did not guess it when one or two of the mature, older men flattered him by asking him to go hunting with them. He rightly thought this a privilege, and felt a little more grown up, which was exactly why it was done. Out on the hunt one of the men made an excuse for halting at a particular place. Other men and other boys of the same age suddenly appeared. The encounter seemed rather strange but the men passed it over off-handedly. Fires were lit, food cooked, and eaten in an ordinary way, and any sense of puzzlement the boys may have had came to an end. Then the men sang songs—wonderful, musical songs the boys had never heard before, because they were part of the men's secret cult of initiation. The singing went on until sundown. It was an unforgettable day. All the men were kind, but very, very firm. Each boy sensed something in the air: the force of impersonal authority concentrating on him as never before. Other men, not their fathers or very close relations, were in charge. In the dusk each boy was led back to the camp and told to sleep with the other boys between fires in the centre of the camp. A rift had been made between child and father and mother, with the parents' consent. By that sign everyone, without having to be told, knew that a boy was beginning to be 'made' into a man.

Note that phrase: being 'made into a man'. The Aborigines did not think or say that a boy 'grows up'. They said he was 'grown up' by men, or that men 'grew him up'. As they saw it, a boy could not make himself into a man: the men of the society in which he lived must do that for him. Of course he could 'grow' physically, and perhaps mentally too, by himself, but he could not by his own unaided talents or his personal resources, confer on himself the attributes of manhood according to the Aboriginal conception of what it was to be a man in knowledge, in discipline, in social personality, and in responsibility. This, they said, was work for society. You could not say 'I am a man' until *after* society had said 'you are a man by these public tests'. The initiation ceremonies were the tests. They were methodical social ways of carrying out and publicly proclaiming the 'making' of a boy into a man. Under the Aboriginal art of life, and it was a true art, they seized on natural stages of growth, which would occur anyway, and turned each one of them into a great public event. They often singled out as a first stage one of which we make little. That is, the stage when a boy had given up playing in mixed groups of boys and girls, and is starting to run around with a gang of boys of about his own age. At this stage Aboriginal boys had a good deal more muscle and animal spirit than sense. They were often rambunctious, troublesome, undisciplined, and on the whole a nuisance. For years they had been indulged by everyone. The older Aborigines were patient, calm and good-humoured about this. They were also perceptive and skilful because they made it serve one of their ultimate social purposes. In their understanding boys could not be made men until they had been freed from their mothers' apron-strings. From the time boys were five or six they were tacitly encouraged to become independent, even somewhat hostile to maternal influence, indeed, to all female influence, including that of their sisters. You could hear small boys shouting rude things at their womenfolk, with a certain approval by the men. It was not real hostility, only mockhostility, and must not go too far. It was a sort of make-believe, a form of symbolic behaviour, which pointed to the eventual need to cut the apron-strings. The older men kept their eyes and ears well open, and when they thought boyish rambunctiousness had had its term, they judged that the time was ripe for the first stage of initiation.

On the morning after the first rift with their families, and especially with their womenfolk, the leader again took the boys away. From this time, until their first initiation was over, they were not referred to by their names, but as 'wild dogs'. This was a double-barrelled symbol, a way of saying that the boys were 'non-human creatures of the wild', and for the time being 'outside' human society. They were led to the secret place for more singing. Later, on the pretext of a sudden faked quarrel among the men, a special guardian hurried them, nominally for their safety, to hide in a still more isolated place. Some of the men left behind now painted themselves with pipe-clay and ochre, and put on their bodies, which were covered with blood drawn from their own veins, striking decorations of wild kapok or feathers. Then they hid themselves in a thicket. The guardian now brought the boys back to the first place. On the way they had to bow their heads and keep their eyes fixed on the ground. The guardian was very stern with them about this, and promised heavy punishment if they looked up. As the boys came near, the undecorated men suddenly burst into a wild, boisterous display which overturned all the conventions of good and seemly conduct. This astonishing performance, which the Aborigines thought of as 'good fun', went on for a long time. A second group of men continued singing at the same time. The boys were bewildered by all these changes and contrasts. Then, quite suddenly, they were told to look to one flank. The hidden dancers sprang into view, ran to a central position, and danced spectacularly, as the boys had never seen men dance before, because the dances were also part of the men's secret cult. This went on throughout the afternoon. When sundown came, everyone returned to the main camp. But now a second rift was made: the boys had to wait outside, in the dusk, until full dark came. The men came out to escort them, with heads bowed, and in utter silence, to their sleeping position of the night before. They might not speak; no one might speak to them—no one, not even their parents, brothers or sisters. Late at night, older men stood and sang quietly over them before they slept, if their nervous excitement would let them.

Next morning, a sterner discipline was applied. Perhaps a boy had seemed to the older men to have the wrong outlook—as the Aborigines said, to have 'hard ears', that is, not to have shown willing, not to have listened, or to have been unresponsive. If so, he was made to sit in the sun, not in the shade, or to lie on his back and stare at the sky with open eyes. There were grades of discipline. A lesser offender might lie with his head in the lap of an older man. The singing and dancing—wonderful, theatrical dancing—went on all day until the night came. The pattern of the night before was then repeated. And so it went on for days.

On the seventh day, just when the boys were beginning to relax and to feel that they now had the measure of initiation, there was an abrupt, frightening change: two hideously disguised men, armed with spears, but otherwise barely human in appearance, suddenly sprang upon them, it seemed out of nowhere. These men were simulating the dreaded warlocks or sorcerers who often put the Aborigines under a reign of terror. They disappeared as quickly, and the tension fell again.

It would be hard to exaggerate the cleverness which the Aborigines poured into these affairs, which were, in a sense, natural theatre. But they were much more. They were highly educative, the work of teachers who were masters of their craft. The older Aborigines had much insight into the elements of human psychology. They worked on the boys' imaginations. They built up the sense of being prepared for an unknown and mysterious climax. Discipline and kindness, fear and reassurance, gravity and jollity, danger and protection, mystery and mundane things were blended within a wider plan to make the boys feel that all the time they were in good hands. All this was shown very dramatically towards the end of the ceremony.

For day after day the tension was allowed to fall. The last dance of the second last day was made by only a few men. Where were the others? No one seemed to know or care. The air was full of anticlimax, even of boredom. But secretly, some of the men were preparing the climax. In a special hiding place they transformed themselves by paint and masks into horrendous, brute-like figures. No one was recognisable. (The first time I saw them my own heart stood still.) When the last dance petered out the guardian showed sudden alarm. He told the boys that the absent men must be preparing for a fight. He urged them, anxiously and excitedly, to run to the one safe place—the camp, where the women and young children were. The boys felt real fear: a general spear-and-club fight is a most frightening and dangerous experience. They scurried back along the road to the camp, urged on by the guardian. As they came near the camp they were brought to a halt: a strange fire was burning on the path. The guardian sent one boy to pluck a burning brand. As he did, a masked figure rose out of nowhere and, with a peculiar grunting imprecation, such as an animal might give, threw a spear that missed the terrified boy by a whisker. The boys ran this way and than but, turn where they might, another and another and another monstrous figure rose and hurled a spear, a club, an axe, a heavy stick. Only one way was left clear: the path whence they came, back to the men's secret dancing ground. When they finally reached it in safety they were—as many told me—often beside themselves with fear. Then, marvellously, familiar faces reappeared and the fears were found to be baseless. The men calmed the boys with reassurance, real tenderness, and praise. All was made well again. And so, later, to bed, as on the other nights.

Next day they again went to the dancing ground. But the whole atmosphere had now changed. There was only singing, no dancing. The boys were made much of, made to feel that they had passed triumphantly through an ordeal, and had acquitted themselves well. They were painted brightly with red and white colours, and were festooned with special gifts, including firesticks. On their bodies secret signs were put whose meanings were known only to the men, not, as yet, to the boys. These signs led on to the later initiations, of which I have not time to speak. They were then escorted back to the camp, to be reunited with their female kinsfolk. But for a good month they might not speak to females and then only after the women had made a formal presentation of food to them. The last event was when the boys lit a fire with their own firesticks and cooked on it some food as a symbolic repayment of all the men who had played a special part in the ceremony which helped them over the first part of the long road of being 'made into a man'.

Let me try to sum up what I have been saying. In the olden days all the dynamic things—that is, the changing, active, moving things—of the world, even things with only a potential for change, activity and movement, seem to have fascinated the Aborigines: the motions of the planets, comets and shooting stars; the tides and the winds; thunder and lightning; the whirlwinds and bushfires; the silent growth of plants, the change of the seasons—and of course the growth of human beings. All were brought up and given recognition and place in an interesting philosophy of life. Boyhood was a stage on a longer, dynamic path of life, not just from birth to death, but from before birth to after death. The body went along part of this path. The soul or spirit went over the whole of it. Other people had duties to you all the way along it. Before birth they helped your spirit find a mother. After death they helped your spirit to return to the world of invisible spirits. In life they helped you to manhood and to all the higher stages of attainment and respect. Initiation was meant to create in a boy an understanding of all this, and to make him see that he had a need of others but could also count on them and, correspondingly, had duties towards them.

It would miss the whole point to make too much of the particular customs by which this was done. The grown-up men used shock, fear, terror, privation, isolation, and mystery in the customs, but they used them with care and discretion, as materials of teaching. But they also used the most spectacular theatricals, and the best art, music, singing and dancing of which they were capable, interspersed with jollity and humour. There was always, unfailingly, someone—a strong guardian, a friend, as well as a teacher—who was there to give a boy support and protection. When it was all over, and only then, a boy could stand up proudly in a new status.

The calling of the boys, when they were taken away to be initiated, 'creatures of the wilds', was a way of saying: 'man is truly man only within the companionship and the society of his fellows. Without them, he is not human.'

All that is now gone or going. Missions and governments did not care for it and saw no value in it. They thought they could do better by religious instruction and education in our style. It would be hard now to say on which sort of notion of people, culture and society they based their theories. They *were* theorists, though they might have denied it. But they could not find a way of making our religion and education part of Aboriginal ways of thinking and living, and they deepened their own instructional—and the Aborigines' learning—troubles by refusing to teach literacy in the native languages or use them for teaching purposes. The custodians of the old tradition, seeing their wisdom, teaching and language thus dishonoured, and sometimes ridiculed by their own young under our teaching, retaliated. They withheld knowledge and wisdom they would ordinarily have felt under duty to pass on to the young. The 'lost generation' of which I speak are products of that process, and of the pallid, unstructured, imperceptive sequel that we condone and perhaps even approve. They are permanently 'creatures of the wilds' with no one to guide them to a confident home or status or attainment or honour either in their society or in ours. Do not think of this as a sad accident or by-product. To rely on 'education' to bridge the gap between the old way of life and a new way independent of it, was our policy from 1954 onward. The Aboriginal future was to be one of 'development through individualism'. The new Aboriginal was to be made into an 'independent unit' in a life-system like ours. It did not matter if Aboriginal society and culture fell to pieces. We could fit them together again in a better way. Yes, there would be inevitable human costs but we would have to brace ourselves to be equal to the weight of the burdens carried on Aboriginal shoulders.

Almost every element in the Aboriginal tradition was undermined in this way—ecology, livelihood, language, patterns of residence, law, religion and the like. Breaking down was simple: building up was not. There are no known and proven methods for moulding into approved shapes the decay-products of a destroyed tradition. The idea that this is something which schools and education can do may well be hallucination. Where is the proof?

But we have pinned our faith, and the Aboriginal fate, to that idea to such a degree that I doubt if we now could bear to face the truth if we found we had been hallucinated. Miss Sommerlad reported to the annual conference of the Australian Association for Research in Education on a survey which she had made of adolescent students at Kormilda College in the Northern Territory. She reported that there had been an overall drop-out rate of more than 63 per cent before the completion of two years at the College. Indeed, only 17 per cent of post-primary students had finished a course. A large majority had been unable to resolve the conflict between their traditional way of life and that requisite in the College. A third had developed behavioural problems. Very few failed to show signs of tension—depression, tearfulness, headaches, stomach-aches, nightmares, and imaginary illnesses. Some ran away, others absented themselves without permission. Sleeping habits, food, clothing, discipline and language all made for difficulties. Now, I do not speak from personal knowledge of the school and I do not know what other facts could be set against those I have cited from Miss Sommerlad. But one wonders why it was ever supposed that adolescents coming from the background described would respond differently. One wonders too whether it might not have made a difference if the children had come to the school already literate in their own languages and thus have been able to write home, and to have had regular letters from home. It is nonsense to say that we cannot teach Aborigines to be literate in their own languages because of administrative difficulties. The real reason why we do not do so is some sort of philosophical or policy objection. If it is by policy that a homesick Aboriginal child has to be miserable in English before his troubles can be understood then there is something wrong with the policy. I hope this attitude to Aboriginal languages will soon come to an end. It is much more than bureaucratic philistinism. It is really a sign of fear that if we help Aborigines to write anything they can speak in their own tongues, and read anything that is written in them, we will somehow damage the peace and good order of the Queen's realm.

***

The life-conditions which Aborigines now enjoy, if that is the way to put it, are the product of measures and methods which no doubt appeared rational and appropriate in their day. We now see them as wrong in concept or approach or scale; or as applied in conditions insufficiently analysed; or as pushed too feebly, sometimes only in disingenuous token; but we cannot be sure that the same may not be said some day about what we are now doing. Those of us who are seeking to introduce a new philosophy of policy and action feel nevertheless that we can hardly be wholly wrong, and are likely to be more right than wrong, in the main assumptions we are making.

We see the Aborigines as a distinctive people, with their own traditions, their own social forms, their own cultures, and their own values. We think that where it is still possible it is for the Aborigines, not for us, to make up their own minds in what respects and to what extent they wish to try to maintain or to adapt their distinctiveness. We see our obligation as being to make possible for them the conditions in which they can make their choices and decisions as of right, not under our compulsions, gross or subtle.

There are three arguments to urge that philosophy upon us. The Aborigines now widely ask us to accept it. A rational and honest appraisal of our actual skills, as demonstrated, strongly suggests that we would be wise to do so; because, wherever we look over the face of the continent, we see unvarnishable evidence of the failure of our approach, our measures and our methods in the past; that, at least, is one unarguable induction from the facts of poverty, ill-health, confusion and discontent in the Aboriginal scene. There is a third argument which to me has particular force. We are only now starting to understand the true quiddity of the Aboriginal system of life, the things which made it what it was and, in some parts of Australia, still is. Speaking quite seriously, I would liken our state of knowledge to the understanding of biological evolution before the principles of genetical science were worked out. Until Mendel, Darwin was a maker of hypotheses. It was through the geneticists that the biologists were able to demonstrate the mechanics of the evolutionary process and, in turn, move to some understanding of the biological bases of primate and other animal behaviour. I make the comparison for two reasons. One is to suggest that for some at least of our past and continuing measures and methods towards the Aborigines there was no scientific basis. The other is to suggest that we have not yet tested, under conditions which would allow it to disclose itself, the possible potential for development that may lie within the Aboriginal people.

It is going to be enormously difficult for us to entertain this as a conceivable possibility and to give it a fair test. Every vested interest in the country will be against it because the whole of Australian society was built upon an assumption that it was not conceivable. Most of our histories, letters and commentaries confirm that view. The whole picture which has come down to us from the past suggests that the Aborigines were a people without potential. The older literature depicts them as only intermittently active in the food-search, only occasionally taking part with enthusiasm in ceremonies, often brawling and bloodletting over grievances but, for the most part, living an unambitious, slothful and earthy life which made them incapable of conceiving or striving after higher things. Roving, sensate and feckless, they lacked what the Victorians called 'industry'—a diligent application to useful and improving purposes of life. A potential for development was just not in them. They were never going anywhere.

You will find a very characteristic picture given in the Reverend J.G. Wood's *The Natural History of Man* (1870). He was a reasonably good scholar who tried to be objective. He saw many admirable qualities in the Aborigines but was quite clear that they had no future; more, he hardly thought they deserved a future, because they had 'performed badly half their duties as men'. They had inherited the earth, but had not subdued it and did not replenish it. They left it in exactly the condition in which they found it. In fact 'they occupied precisely the same relative position towards the human race as do the lion, tiger and leopard towards the lower animals and suffered in consequence the same law of extinction'. The coming of the white man was not a curse: it was a benefit. It offered them a means of infinitely bettering their social condition. But they could not appreciate the means. As a natural consequence, they had to make way for those who could. Their imminent disappearance from the face of the earth to him was, quite simply, a case 'following the order of the world, the lower race preparing a home for the higher'. Looking equably through his bifocal spectacles, Christian and Darwinist, he came to his peroration.

> I am persuaded [he said,] that the coming of the white man is not the sole, nor even the chief, cause of the decadence of savage tribes ... We can introduce no vice in which the savage is not profoundly

versed, and [I] feel sure that the cause of extinction lies within the savage himself, and ought not to be attributed to the white man, who comes to take the place the savage has practically vacated [and indeed nearly depopulated by his] everlasting quarrels, irregular mode of existence and carelessness of human life ... (p.105)

I would hardly have thought it worthwhile to set out this old point of view were I convinced that we had done with all of it for ever. But I am not convinced. Something very like parts of it lingers on, alive and powerful, but in another dress.

We may not now look on, say, the Aborigines of Yirrkala as 'a lower race preparing a home for the higher'. But it is obvious from the whole debate that some amongst us look on them as a backward, ignorant and ungrateful people irrationally, indeed unlawfully, making it needlessly hard for us to prepare a home and livelihood for some thousands of our people on land which is ours, not theirs. We may not claim the sanction of Christ, as Mr Wood did, but we are as sure as he was that the 'national interest', the Holy Ghost of today, is on our side. So there is still an 'order of the world' to which we ask them to bow. We may no longer define that order in the words used by the Victorian philosophers of 'progress' but we do so in terms of a philosophy of continuous economic 'growth', which is progress minus the moral element. The debate does leave a distinct impression that to allow a few hundred imperceptive Aborigines to hold up development or thwart growth seems to many moderns as reprehensible, as much against 'the order of the world', as Mr Wood thought it would be to allow a few sinful Aborigines to hold up or thwart progress. We are using precisely his arguments. The Yirrkala Aborigines did not and cannot use the land productively; they overlook or waste precious resources; they do not see or cannot appreciate the benefits we offer them; they must make way. There is a smack of the ineluctable and the inevitable about all this which has in it something of religion. It could even be described as a secular religion. It is certainly believed in as deeply, practised as devotedly, and justified with as little regard for social costs, as some religions we have known.

I spoke earlier of the need of motives of credibility. This applies to both sides. I wonder what the effect on Aboriginal minds will be when they read some of the observations made in Parliament recently by Senator Little. On several occasions the Senator has sought to persuade Parliament that only the coming of Europeans to Australia saved the Aborigines from extinction. He argued that at the end of the 18th century the Australian continent was ceasing to be capable of sustaining either human or animal life. It would soon, possibly by now, have become a desolate, uninhabited and uninhabitable desert but for the arrival of Europeans with their agricultural and pastoral skills to farm and stock it. That and that alone rescued the Aborigines from the grave. He did concede later that perhaps some Aborigines might have been able to hang on in the more lush areas but, as I followed him in Hansard, he did not shift from his main thesis which, he said, was supported by scientific evidence. I know of no scientific evidence which could imaginably be interpreted in that way. The professional colleagues I have asked cannot suggest any. What evidence there is suggests the opposite of his contention. For several millennia before 1788 much of the continent was becoming more rather than less habitable by man and beast. There had of course been fluctuations but the trend was clear. The Senator's thesis therefore is not history, nor is it myth, because both have some relation to actuality. It is not science; it is not even science-fiction. Perhaps its best place is in a hagiography of Australian saints. It is memorable only for what it says unconsciously. To say to the Aborigines 'we saved you from extinction' is the same as saying 'we are as God to you'. To go on to say 'we alone made Australia what it is' is the same as saying 'anything you have of our Australia is by our gift, grace and favour'. One might as well say: 'you are lucky people to be alive and to have anything at all'. I do not know if that kind of reasoning is at all general. If it is, I do not see how we can hope to carry the Aboriginal people with us in what we try to do for them or to help them do for themselves. What little credibility we have left for them would be gone.

***

This year, 1972, has some claim to be remembered as The Year of the Blackfellow. Within these twelve months his life-affairs became the subject of explicit undertakings by the governing and the opposition parties and the undertakings became in some sense an issue at a national election. Aboriginal affairs are thus now in all probability irretrievably political.

At all times in Australian history, go back as far as you will, there were always a few men who found intellectual and human interest in the Aborigines and their plan of life. The interest had its ups and downs; it reflected the ethnic knowledge and social preoccupations of the day, so much so that on occasions you have to dig for evidences of it beneath a thick overburden of indifference, dislike or contempt; but there is no period in which it cannot be found, somewhere. The story that began with Collins, Tench and Dawes in the first years of settlement may have thinned out here and there but it was never wholly broken. Nevertheless, the numbers of such men, and the amount they left on the written record, were of no great account until the second quarter of this century. I would think this is the general pattern of all scholarly writing about the Aborigines. It fits quite well with the facts given by Dr Moodie and Dr Pederson in their valuable bibliography of writings on Aboriginal health. Of a total of some 2000 titles only about a quarter came from the long period between 1788 and 1930—500 titles in 142 years! Another 500 were written in the next twenty years. The remainder—a good 1000—were written after 1950. That progression seems to continue. In the eleven years since the Australian Institute of Aboriginal Studies was founded (in 1961) no less than 653 research projects have been approved, extended or assisted through it alone. The range is very wide—human biology, social anthropology, linguistics, ethnomusicology, material culture, prehistory, ethnobotany, and dance notation, apart from ethnographic expeditions, archival research, radio-carbon dating, the making of musical discs and cinema films, and the support of academic positions including the use of research assistants. That range is certainly going to widen still farther, for example, into studies of Aboriginal religion, ecology, ethology, territorialism, law, art, and heaven knows what else. Meanwhile, the steady flow of more popular writing and talking will continue and the unremitting attention of the media to Aboriginal affairs of all sorts is bound to go on. I have not tried to form an opinion whether this avalanche of information, good and bad, caused or followed or simply accompanied the politics of Aboriginal affairs. But I am sure that its full effect has by no means yet made itself felt. It may not be felt until the first fully-trained generation of Aboriginal scholars and critics arrives, which should be in another five or ten years or less.

I have no doubt that they will soon have their Richard Wright, James Baldwin and Ali Mazrui, and I have no doubt that their will to survive, which brought people of their stock and line successfully through more than 30,000 years, will continue to make itself felt increasingly in our affairs. We may have over-rated ourselves in supposing that our presence over .005 per cent of the time they have been in Australia has made all that difference. Consider the many challenges to survival which they have overcome, any one of which, for all we know, may have affected their society more severely than we have. We can now document a large miscellany: glacio-eustatic, climatic, faunal, vegetal, ethnic, technological, demographic, social and no doubt psychological and spiritual challenges all successfully surmounted long before Europeans arrived. The successive maps of Australia between the late Pleistocene and the present, could we but draw them—and we yet may be able to do so—would be alive with evidences of successful behavioural adaptations. I can see no reason why we should suppose that their well of inspiration has run dry.

1972

Aboriginal Humour (1956)

A life by flood and field is a hard one and Aboriginal life was very hard indeed. Unknowledgeable Europeans have thought it joyless, but this was far from being the case. The Aborigine's culture was materially simple, but it was adequate to his needs; his social organisation was exceedingly complex, but it allowed him a life of great satisfaction when not too much interrupted by Europeans; we are slowly discovering that he had a rich aesthetic capacity and an interesting metaphysical conception of life and world; and I can testify from much acquaintance that he added to these a very marked sense of humour. He had, in short, fundamentally all that we have. At least he once had. He was fully equipped to meet life on even terms and, with humour, to get a little the better of it in passing. To understand and appreciate his humour is one of the best ways of rounding out an estimate of him as a human personality.

Much of what I shall say amounts in the end to a roundabout statement that the Aborigines found amusing much the same kind of things which we find amusing. In other words, we are dealing with human universals. It is therefore, perhaps, as well for me to begin by saying that there were of course major differences.

We find a certain amusement—kindly, but still amusement—in much Aboriginal custom. This is parochialism on our part, but it is well matched: the Aborigine felt (and feels) much the same way about European custom. Much of our scheme of life does not 'make sense' to him. A quick handful of things that baffle him about us, and for which he laughs *at* us behind our backs, would include our inexplicable passion for unremitting work; the fact that men willingly carry things where there are women to carry them; that we actually thrash small children; that we accumulate, and hold in perpetuity, stupidly large amounts of goods instead of dispersing them to gain reputation; that we have no apparent rules of marriage—I could give many such instances to show how the two schemes of living lie across each other. It is remarkable, in the circumstances, that the universals of humour show through so strongly. Sometimes, of course, all communication breaks down, and blackfellow and European look helplessly at each other over an uncrossable frontier.

Several years ago I was making some psychological tests which required the Aborigines to repeat, days and weeks later, a story I had told them. Many of the recalls broke down, the blacks being overcome with laughter at the same point. The story was about two brothers who had quarrelled over a girl. As the blacks began to tell me how one brother sneaked up and killed the other with one stroke of a stick, their self-control failed and they hooted with mirth. Something about the idea seemed to them quite risible. I suspect it may have been the connotation of romantic love. I saw too late that this kind of theme suffused the story. Sexual passion of course they know and understand, but the sensible thing for Aboriginal brothers to do if they like the same girl is to *share* her favours. The cult of romantic love, as far as they can comprehend it, possibly seems to them a sort of lunacy, very much as some of us look on tooth avulsion, the cutting of bodily cicatrices, or widow-strangling.

You will appreciate the difficulties. I have to rule out of my discussion a certain amount of Aboriginal humour since it rests on—indeed, only makes sense within—the context of their own outlook and customs. But I cannot go to the other extreme and propound a general theory of laughter to account for what I call 'the universals'. One of the most distinguished of anthropologists, Bronislaw Malinowski, once said that 'anthropology is the science of the sense of humour'. That is not the impression you would derive from a study of the standard texts. I am simply telling the truth when I say that humour is not a subject to which the discipline of anthropology has given much serious thought. I find this, on reflection, a curious matter. I know of only one anthropologist who has written on the subject—Professor Ralph Piddington, an Australian; but he did so when he was still a professional psychologist; and he subsequently had to go to New Zealand. The only 'theory' I have is that 'humour', as we ordinarily use the word, is a way of looking at things or situations. The 'humorousness' is first of all *in* the things. Laughter is a sign of acknowledgment, our way of relating ourselves to 'humorousness'.

The underlying philosophy of Aboriginal humour is likely, therefore, to baffle a European mind. This is not surprising. The philosophy of all humour is baffling. If it were not, we should not have had wit likened by Burton to 'the rust of the soul', and we should not have had Ogden Nash advising us that

> It is better in the long run to possess an abscess or a tumour than to possess a sense of humour.

There are, I know, delicate souls to whom the idea of fingering the anatomy of humour is repulsive. The anatomy of melancholy, they feel, is a fit subject. Men's sadness has a wistful fascination. It also often allows the sad to live very comfortably writing about their almost incommunicable sensibility. But they make an examination of why men laugh seem to be a kind of morbid hepatoscopy. True, there is some kind of affinity between humour and tragedy, an affinity which is almost too painful for many minds to wish to know too much about.

> O, unseen jest, inscrutable, invisible,
> As a nose on a man's face, or a weathercock on a steeple.

But this is no reason for not studying it. Anyone who thinks or reads is aware of the affinity, and of a strangely concealed antinomy within it. What is it, Horace asked, that forbids us to speak the truth, laughingly? The paradox which humour forms with truth is one of man's oldest insights into himself and his situation. I think I have recognised its evidences among the Aborigines.

An Aborigine of whom I was fond was once discussing with me the extinction of his tribe. He was being dispassionate about it—I thought too dispassionate, for the area was one in which there had been violence, betrayal and murder. Many of his countrymen had been translated to a higher place by European marksmanship, disease and the genial use of strychnine in the waterholes. My old man had observed much and had thought much. Perhaps because his thoughts went too deep for words, perhaps only from good manners—his were impeccable—he parried my questions and showed some amusement. I said: 'In a few years you will all be dead; there will be no blackfellows left; but you laugh about it. Why do you laugh? I see nothing amusing.' He would not be drawn for some time. Finally he said, 'Bye-and-bye, altogether blackfellow dead. Plenty white man sit-down this country. White man walkabout longa bush. Him losim himself longa bush. Altogether white man try findim. Altogether white man losim himself longa bush. No blackfeller. Can't findim. Whitefeller dead. Blackfeller dead.' And he smiled sardonically.

This is Lancashire humour. *'Wit's nowt, till it's dear bowt.'* There is a good deal of dear-bought Aboriginal humour, pointing to their insight into the 'gravity concealed behind the jest' and also to their courage to proceed, nevertheless, to make the jest. At a mission station which I know, a certain conflict was raging. The issue was between what the old Aborigines wanted to do, and what God wanted them to do. The matter was not at all clear to the Aborigines. They *knew* what they wanted. There were being told what God wanted. They thought there was something second-hand about the instructions. The questions turned on *how* their instructor *knew* what God wanted. Some said the clergyman just knew; others that he only said he knew; both these unreasonable theories failed to convince them. One man finally volunteered: 'might-be him got telephone longa God'. I was appealed to. Did he or didn't he? I said I did not know, but that I had always found the clergyman truthful. I also said that he had a lot of tea, sugar, flour and tobacco. This argument appealed to the Aborigines. One of them said: 'That man, him good man, y'know. Him got plenty everything. Plenty tucker. Plenty *wian* [i.e. tobacco—the word also means human excrement]. Plenty mouth [i.e. words]. Might be him got plenty savvy-belong-himself [i.e. private knowledge or wisdom].' I said that this might be so. I was then asked if I had a telephone. I said that I had; but it was only a small one. 'You savvy belong God?' I was asked. I said that I sometimes thought I heard a voice, a long way away. I was asked what the voice said. I replied that I could not quite make out the words. My inquisitor said: 'That's what blackfeller reckon.' I then said: 'Well, what are you going to do?' My friend said: 'Today, tobacco. Sunday, God.' We both laughed.

    I do not feel called upon, or indeed competent, to prove anything to you about Aboriginal humour. I can simply narrate some of the things they say, describe some of the things they laugh at, and add a sort of minimum glossary. The main point to keep in mind is that the Aboriginal scene is in most respects the universal scene. Humour wears familiar garments, but with a twist all its own. There is coarse buffoonery, salacity, punning, practical joking, and all the rest. I would not mention them were it not that a perfectly intelligent European once asked me, quite seriously, if the Aborigines laughed and cried 'just like other people'. It made me wonder what image of savage life many Europeans can possibly have in mind to suggest such idiocies. The hammer on the thumb, the slip on the banana peel, the sudden loss of dignity—all these 'reversals', the basis of a universal class of humour, evoke much the same responses among the Aborigines as among Europeans. Perhaps the principle is carried a little far: I have seen Aborigines roaring with laughter at another chased by a crocodile, or at an old man trying to climb a slippery tree to escape a rogue buffalo. The sentiments of pity and compassion are, on the whole, a little on the weak side, a fact which itself requires another kind of explanation. But it is not of this level of humour that, I imagine, you would wish me to speak. I myself would rather try to bring out, if I can, the aspect of humour we call wit, which Aristotle described as 'cultured insolence'. For it is a capacity which the Aborigines unmistakably have. At least, we can recognise a certain pawky vein of wit in spite of the surrounding crudity.

I was once building a bush hut as a shelter from the wet season. I was putting on the ridge-pole when an old blackfellow called out to me to come down. He said that he would fix it himself. He was twice my age and very authoritative in his manner to me, as Aborigines frequently are when they know you well. He said: 'Bye-and-bye you fall down, breakim leg.' I told him to mind his own business. 'You,' I replied, 'have one leg in the grave anyway.' 'No matter me,' he said, 'you come down, like I bin tellem you. Straightaway. Me blackfellow. Supposim you fall down, breakim leg, every policeman from Darwin race up longa this country, chasim up altogether blackfellow. Full up humbug. Plenty trouble. You come down. Straightaway.'

Then there was the day my old bush friend Charlie Dargie and I went hunting. We did not see a lizard all day. We came home out of spirits and rather grumpy. Charlie suddenly found a solution. 'We'll go and *shoot* a barramundi,' he said. The barramundi is the best-eating fish in Australian waters, fresh, salt or mineral. We walked some miles to Bamboo Creek, a slack tributary of the Daly River, where barramundi often lie sunning themselves a foot below the surface. We stood on the top of the steep jungle-covered bank and sought our quarry. Charlie soon pointed to a fine fat fish faintly swishing near the surface. He shot like a Bisley marksman, swift and true, and the stunned fish floated to the top. We had it, in imagination, almost sizzling in the pan when a shrill *'yackai'* came from a nearby bush and the face of Jarawak, a Madngella man, thrust out. 'What-the-matter you Charlie,' he cried, 'you try stealim fish belonga me?' We had touched the depths. To *shoot* a *caught* fish *tied up* to the bank by a *string.* Jarawak saw that the tale spread. The blacks never forgot it. To this day, half a lifetime later, they still laugh. When I go fishing with them, someone is sure to say in an innocent tone: 'You got plenty bullet?'

On a nearby station they were breaking-in some rough colts in the horseyard. One mankiller threw every stockman and black 'stockboy' on the place until only the manager and Jacky were left. The manager said: 'Come on, Jacky, your turn now.' Jacky, slouched on the top rail, looked in turn at the wild-eyed and perspiring colt, at his dishevelled companions, and back at the colt. He seemed lost in thought. 'Well, come on,' the manager snapped. Jacky gave him an under-the-eyebrows look and said 'No-more,' which meant 'nothing doing'. He then added: 'You better go first-time, boss. Plenty more white man. Blackfellows getting scarce round here just now.'

But these, after all, are but episodes. They may make us smile but they do not necessarily help us to understand what humour is. There is another and very distinct kind of Aboriginal humour which, I think, to some extent does: it can be spoken of as 'formal' humour. That is to say, there are certain well-known situations in Aboriginal life which, in their understanding, have to be *signalised* and resolved by a kind of banter, half-serious, half-humorous.

I shall draw a parallel with a situation which we will recognise in European life. Among a close company of friends, some occasion arises—say, the departure of one person to live elsewhere, or a retirement from active life—and the occasion is thought appropriate for him to be entertained in a rather formal way: perhaps a presentation, perhaps a dinner. At such times a certain embarrassment is felt, especially perhaps among men. Their feelings, and what they are met to do, lie a little across each other: it is embarrassing to appear sentimental, but they desire and are expected to express emotion; they wish and are expected to say words of praise but feel self-conscious about doing so. Their relations with the guest of honour are 'ambivalent': they are pulled one way, pushed another. Not uncommonly, men solve this little social problem by a very patent conversion. They praise, but they praise mockingly; they show affection, but tinge it with malice; they make use of what we may call the venomous endearments; they may use bad, even indecent language. Everyone knows and understands the convention and few take it amiss. No one 'means' to be really offensive. It is a symbolic way of dealing with ambivalence.

When an Aborigine meets his wife's brother, he utters (in certain tribes I know) a very odd expletive sound (by forcing air between his lips)—a sound which, to European ears, is extraordinarily vulgar. He will sit or stand some distance away and, in a high-pitched voice (quite unlike the voice he ordinarily uses) will call out a long series of insinuating epithets, vulgarities and sometimes obscenities about his wife's brother. They are our 'venomous endearments'. He doesn't 'mean' any of them. The tone and pitch of voice show this—both are consciously stylised. A chorus of appreciative laughter from the audience, if he thinks of something really outrageous, also shows the presence of formal convention. The men often say astonishing things. The anthropologist calls this the 'joking-relationship'.

The ambivalence here comes from the common interest of the two men in one woman, wife to one and sister to the other. The Aborigines have the idea that there is something embarrassing in such a relationship between men. Anthropologists are not agreed as to the precise way in which they should describe or examine the nature of the embarrassment. I mention it for several reasons. One is to show the common form, between Aborigines and Europeans, of dealing with a comparable situation. Among the Aborigines, to avoid *showing* embarrassment, the two men act *as if* they were not being embarrassed. They pretend there is a different *kind* of situation. They act *as if* to say that two men who can say such things about each other cannot possibly be embarrassed. As if no tension could possibly exist between them—for, look!—they are laughing at each other, taking liberties with each other. *As if* the relationship had no ambivalence at all. The symbolisms—laughter and mock hostility intermingled—are the means of this *as if* solution. They are expressive and symbolic means of dealing socially with feelings resting on ambivalence.

Anthropologists are so used now to this kind of custom that they tend to take it for granted: there is a good and, on the whole, satisfying theory about it; but the theory explains everything except the humour—the 'joking' in the 'joking-relationship'.

The embarrassment a man feels in the presence of his wife's brother is a modified form of a man's feelings towards his wife's mother. The Aborigines have the idea that there is something excessively shameful, even dangerous, in the mother-in-law relation. An Aborigine cannot bring himself to mention her name. If he is compelled to do so, it seems to cause him an agony of embarrassment. Since he cannot avoid all reference to her, he speaks of her as *aiyanimbi*, which means 'the stinging hornet'. But he goes out of his way to avoid meeting her. If by chance the two encounter one another on the same path, the man makes a wide detour through the bush.

In camp, he always faces away from her. He sleeps on the opposite side of the camp circle, as far away as possible. He never hands things to her direct, but always through a third person. If some emergency compels him to say something to her, he turns away and shouts at the top of his voice. This is a way of suggesting that, in actuality, the two are really an immense distance apart, and are not having any close relationship.

The analysis of what lies behind this 'shame' relationship (as it is called by the blacks) is very complex and it concerns my paper only in one respect: the connection between humour and shame in the particular relationships mentioned. The only way to make the connection is to consider briefly the use of expressive symbols or signs in human affairs. It is part of the vastly larger question of the communication of meaning by signs of all kinds. The expressive symbols or signs I am speaking of are those which communicate states of feeling about the 'significance' of things, as the Aborigines have been taught to see them.

They regard the bullroarer as so 'significant' that they treat it with something very close to 'reverence'. They keep its whereabouts a secret; they smear it with human blood; they give it names which only initiated men can hear; they kill women who stray near its hiding place; when they show it on formal occasions they sing certain songs, dance certain dances, use certain musical forms, and wear certain bodily decorations which call forth their highest capacity for visual, plastic and mimetic art. The word 'reverence' is a piece of shorthand for all these activities. We have to interpret the activities as 'signs' symbolic of the significance, worth or value which the Aborigines attribute to the bullroarer. The bullroarer itself is a sign of almost ineffable and immensely significant meanings: it 'points beyond itself', as any sign or symbol does. What it points to is the metaphysic of The Dreaming. The Aborigines use songs, dances, music, secrecy and so on as a means to convey and express their grasp of these larger significances.

Anything—literally anything—which can stand for, or represent, or designate, or indicate something about something else can be a 'sign': a mark, a word, a number, a gesture. The signs are gathered up into different kinds of systems. The Aborigines have hit on the device of using aesthetic means—song, music, dancing, art—as one signsystem for expressing their grasp of and attitudes to the significance of the most important things in their life. This will seem strange only to people of other cultures who use different types of symbolic idiom.

If one studies Aboriginal life closely, one can see several gradations in their system of significances. Some things are treated with 'reverence'; other things with 'respect', i.e. something less than reverence; other things with 'formality', i.e. a little less than respect. It is possible to range the signs in a perfectly logical series, strange though the idiom may seem to be to Europeans. The 'strangeness' simply means we are too wrapped up in our own sign-languages. The signs are simply the means of outward expression of inward sentiments in some convenient idiom. The Aboriginal idiom is part of the mystery of their past. The peculiar significances they see in particular things and situations are not always easy to grasp.

Some of the signs, or sign vehicles—music, songs, dances, art—belong, as I have said, to an aesthetic order. But bodily movements and gestures of all kinds can also be used. Laughter and the display of shame, in the circumstances I have described, are both 'signs' belonging to the large and complex class I have outlined.

By laughing *at* the brother-in-law and showing shame *in the presence* of the mother-in-law, the Aborigines are *expressing* attitudes or sentiments towards the relationships in which they stand, not towards the individual persons themselves. And the expressions are *formalised,* i.e. they are socially stylised, set in form and pattern for everyone. But they belong to what we may call the negative signs—that is, they fit in the same group as the signs which indicate grief, disrespect, irreverence, informality, hostility and so forth.

The signs used between brothers-in-law are, as I have said, a mixture—partly signs of hostility, partly signs of levity and jocularity. The signs of hostility (criticism, depreciation, mocking) can be traced to the fact that an Aborigine is never fully reconciled to the loss of his sister by marriage. But women *have* to marry and, because of exogamy, they have to marry out of the group; they *have* to be 'lost' to their brothers; yet brothers cannot forget. The only solution is to do what the blacks do. They couple two sets of signs—one positive (good humour), one negative (hostility) and, in a way, reverse them. They use humour to convey hostility. The symbolic signs are turned, as it were, inside out.

This custom is a perfect model for the analysis of much that lies within humour. If we study the 'humour' of things or situations, we will see that it nearly always consists of some incongruity, paradox, contrast or antinomy which our minds perceive. Hobbes said the perception was due to the passion he called 'sudden glory'. Leigh Hunt saw the nature of humour in 'the clash and concealment of incongruities, the meeting of extremes around a corner'. One revealing epigram was attributed to Montesquieu: 'wit consists in knowing the resemblance of things which differ and the difference of things which are alike'. The 'humour' of things is external to us: laughter is the sign we make towards what is humorous. It reconciles us to the humorous. But the sign can also be put to many other uses—some of them ambivalent, some hostile. European life is filled with equivalents of the Aboriginal 'joking-relationships'. We are all familiar with the humour—at least with the smile or laugh—of malice, of inner superiority, of condescension, of concealed hatred, of emotional falsity. So are the Aborigines. They can laugh and dance on the graves of their enemies about as well as we can. The only difference between us is that we make the savagery worse by doing so politely. Behind the ghastly 'social' smile is the image of the painted savage.

I have mentioned Horace's question: 'What is it that forbids us to speak the truth, laughingly?' There are clearly some truths, personal and social, which we cannot ignore, cannot solve by laughter—even insincere laughter—and from which we can only turn away.

The 'shame' felt between an Aboriginal mother-in-law and her son-in-law—felt actually on both sides—is, I think, of this kind. It has not, in my opinion, a sexual basis, although this has been attributed as a reason. I do not think any single reason can be attributed. But if I were asked to find a single reason I would say that in my opinion it is due to the fact that, typically, a brother's loss is less than a mother's loss. One can find other possible explanations from Aboriginal society, but this comes somewhere near the heart of it, in the sociological sense—i.e. the sense in which one looks for 'general' explanations. A mother-in-law and son-in-law simply cannot come to terms, yet if they are to associate they must come to terms. Brothers-in-law can: the tie between each man and the girl is a degree less intense than between mother and girl. The Aborigines draw an arbitrary line and 'formalise' the relation of mother-in-law and son-in-law by actually preventing the characteristic clash which often disfigures the counterpart relation in European society. I would argue that the Aborigines tag the relation with the sign of 'shame' because the relation is irreconcilable, and that this is why they 'show' shame. The brother-in-law relation is irreconcilable, but it can be solved partly by an *as if* fiction—the fiction that no hostility exists; partly by humour; and partly because it *has* to be solved. By rule brothers-in-law exchange sisters in marriage, by convention they are trading partners, and (in a small community) they have many other necessary relations, being of the same sex and usually of the same age. But the mother-in-law and son-in-law relation is thought wholly irreconcilable. Its solution, however, has a logically equivalent form: there is an *as if* fiction—the fiction that they never really meet; complete avoidance so that in most circumstances they do not meet; and a logically compatible sign, 'shame', if they do meet.

This has taken me rather far afield. But only in a sense, for it reveals as clearly as any situation can part of the social background in which any humour is to be understood. When Tacitus said that 'a bitter jest that comes too near the truth leaves a sharp sting behind' he may not have had marriage in mind; but our mother-in-law jokes are truly his 'bitter jests'. Understood, they tell us something very important about the inward anatomy of 'the humorous' and the logic as well as the pathos of the human sign-language. I must not be supposed to be attacking marriage; I think that every family should have one; but, as Radcliffe-Brown used to say, one aspect of every marriage is, fundamentally, that it is an act of hostility. It creates for one set of people a kind of incongruity—inevitable loss, lamented loss; for another set a different incongruity—the eating and being eaten in marriage. I simply point out that the Aborigines recognise one of these situations more clearly than we do. Our means of dealing with the incongruities is to raise the value of marriage itself, or each person in it, to so high a value that the 'signs'—respect, love, obedience, deference, dignity—ennoble it. Our way of dealing with the perpetual antinomy of love and notlove within marriage is to make it a sacrament, as permanent as baptism, though not as one-sided; as necessary as penance, though not as just; and as final as extreme unction. The Aborigines do not sacramentalise marriage: but they formalise a different set of relations from those which we stress. Their sign-system avoids one set of clashes and treats another set with humour, as far as possible.

Luckily, laughter does not only antagonise: it also ameliorates and heals. It is the good angel of enmity. I think the story that best illustrates the gift is that of one of my Aboriginal companions who had an unconquerable passion for tinned milk. In other ways he was thoroughly honest, but he stole milk at every opportunity. His conscience pricked him, especially as he had the complete freedom of my few bush stores, but he always lost his battle. I gloomily watched a carefully hoarded case of milk dwindle day by day. Now and then it irritated me, but I usually took the view that he was just a crazy mixed-up septuagenarian. Finally I found *every* tin except one empty, but all carefully repacked in the case. I looked at him and he looked at me. We both knew it was a crisis. I gave him the last tin, and with the true feeling which makes the martyr, said: 'Go on, you like milk.' He took it in silence (there is no Aboriginal word for thank-you and perhaps anyway it would hardly have been appropriate) and with great dignity. Then he went to the case of empty tins, and held up one or two so that I could *see* the tiny holes through which he had sucked them dry. He held one tin speculatively, poked at the hole, looked across at me, and said: 'Rust.'

I shall close with the story of a patrol—one of Stanner's Irregulars—in the war. The patrol was out looking for Japanese visitors. The men were crossing a plain and the track skirted a vast cluster of termite pillars in such a way as to create the illusion that the plain was in two halves, one covered with ant-beds, the other wholly bare. A soldier asked the detachment commander for the explanation. He could think of none, and put the question to an Aboriginal tracker. 'What name, boss?' the blackfellow asked in a puzzled way, not catching the drift of the question. The officer said: 'You puttim eye longa track.' *'Yowai* [all right, will do, OK]', said the tracker, all discipline. 'I puttim eye.' 'Now you look,' said the officer, 'One side, nothing ant-bed. Ain't it?' *'Yowai,'* agreed the tracker. 'Well,' enquired the officer, 'how did it all come about? *Why* were there so many ant-beds on one side and none on the other?' The tracker grinned impishly. 'That side,' he said, gesturing magnificently towards the ant-beds, 'plenty ants. That side, no ants.' This seems to fit Pope's 'midwives' phrase' concerning humour—a perfect conception, and an easy delivery.

1956

Concluding Thoughts from 'Aborigines in the Affluent Society' (1973)

I do not try to gloss or burke my opinion that some of the most difficult problems for [the Aborigines] and for us are still ahead. We shall all be doing very well if we keep them in focus as true lifesize, not make them smaller or larger than life. For that reason I believe we should reject two extremes of outlook that already have had some effect.

On the one hand there is a rather heady and facile optimism which brushes aside all mention of limiting conditions as irrelevant or, worse, as a prospectus of excuses for poor performance in the future. I can understand this view, although I cannot share it.

On the other there is a settled pessimism about the outcome of all and any efforts that we might make, alone or in unison with the Aborigines. This I neither understand nor share.

The contrasts are very reminiscent of the utopian–realist dualism that has worked a great deal of mischief in our own intellectual and social history.

I am against both extremes, but I am much more against the pessimists than I am against the utopian visionaries. This at least can be said for them: they may simplify unduly: they may live and work for what turn out to be illusions; but as Mannheim, one of my teachers, pointed out, 'illusions' begin as visions; they can be a powerful instrument of social struggle; a hard, working tool to re-shape the very situation in which the impulse to reform arises; and a brightly-lit goal for the will. The vision of a new Aboriginal possibility with Professor Elkin and others had more than forty years ago was then an 'illusion', but it had much to do with maintaining the struggle over the years and with the attainment of new national principles. There is still some work for the visionaries to do; in particular, to guard the new principles.

The pessimists seem to me by far the more dangerous. They would probably prefer me to speak of them as 'realists', and that I will do, although, being myself of a realistic turn of mind, I allow them no monopoly: I hold, with Herbert Read, that we are always free to try to make a new reality. They on their part seem to feel entitled to read with the utmost confidence from a history that has not yet happened. They purport to be able to stand 'over' or 'outside' history, and from some privileged knowledge, or natural insight, or inborn wisdom, or secret doctrine, to assure us (which I do not mind) and the Aborigines (which I do mind) that what we are doing is a waste of time: they say that nothing will work because nothing ever has worked.

Carr put the matter, some time ago, rather better than I can. I quote from him:

> The utopian, fixing his eyes on the future, thinks in terms of creative spontaneity: the realist, rooted in the past, in terms of causality ... The complete realist,

unconditionally accepting the causal sequence of events, deprives himself of the possibility of changing reality. The complete utopian, by rejecting the causal sequence, deprives himself of the possibility of understanding either the reality which he is seeking to change, or the processes by which it can be changed. The characteristic vice of the utopian is *naïveté:* of the realist, sterility.

Realism of this kind, having been maintained over a long period, and having exhausted all its possibilities, led to the terrible sterility which can still be seen in many arrangements we are trying to sweep away. I think it was my friend and former colleague, John Barnes, an Englishman coming here with fresh eyes in the middle 1950s, who first made me see how inveterate a gloomy outlook had become amongst us. It still persists. There is more than a touch of it in at least the title of Andreas Lommel's recent book *Fortschritt ins Nichts—Advance* or *Progress into Nothingness,* which is his description of the end awaiting the

Aborigines, their society and their culture. There may be other anthropologists of the same outlook. I would think that the very last thing in the world needed, or likely to be appreciated, by a people increasing at a rate of 3.4 per cent annually, is an anthropological lesson on eschatology. I could warm to this theme, but I will simply assert that there is no one amongst us with, as I said, the 'privileged knowledge, the natural insight, the inborn wisdom or the secret doctrine' that allows him credibly to say that the Aborigines are wasting their time in an effort to make a new reality.

I believe I interpret rightly, as against an indulgence in *Weltschmerz*—for that is really what it is—at Aboriginal expense, the evidences of a new dynamism of outlook, a new vitality of effort, and an adventurous new response to new conditions, occurring in some Aboriginal communities. I do not think that anyone who has read comprehendingly the recent works by Schapper, Rowley, Moodie, or Broom and Jones would ask them to believe in any magic-wand doctrine of improvement. But I do not think that anyone privileged to have talked to the Aborigines concerned would feel intellectually entitled to use the past to foredoom them under the very different conditions of the future.

In the past we were wrong—in some respects grotesquely wrong—about the Aborigines. We thought that they could not possibly survive; that they had no adaptive capacity; that there was nothing in their society of other than antiquarian interest; that there was nothing of aesthetic value in their culture. We could be as wrong about the future. There are few Aborigines who now seem to want, as I seem to recall Bertrand Russell having said, 'to sit down with folded hands to wait in dumb adoration of the inexorable'.

1973

Publication Details & Acknowledgements

PUBLICATION DETAILS

Each of these essays with the exception of 'Aboriginal Humour' was published in W.E.H. Stanner, *White Man Got No Dreaming: Essays 1938–1973,* Australian National University Press, Canberra, 1979.

'Durmugam: A Nangiomeri' was originally published in *In the Company of Man: Twenty Portraits by Anthropologists,* ed. Joseph B. Casagrande, Harper and Bros., New York, 1960.

'The Dreaming' was originally published in *Australian Signpost, An Anthology,* ed. T.A.G. Hungerford, F.W. Cheshire, Melbourne, 1956.

'"The History of Indifference Thus Begins"' was originally published in *Aboriginal History* 1(1), 1977.

'The Aborigines' was originally published in *Some Australians Take Stock,* ed. J.C.G. Kevin, Longmans Green and Co., London, 1938.

'Continuity and Change among the Aborigines' was originally published in *The Australian Journal of Science* 21, 1958–59.

'Boyer Lectures: After the Dreaming' was written for the Australian Broadcasting Commission and first broadcast in 1968.

'Aborigines and Australian Society' was originally published in *Mankind* 10(4), 1976.

'Aboriginal Humour' was published in *Aboriginal History* 6(1), 1982.

'Concluding Thoughts', an extract from 'Aborigines in the Affluent Society', was originally published in *Search* 4(4), 1973.

ACKNOWLEDGMENTS

The editor and publisher thank Mrs Patricia Stanner for permission to republish these essays and the back-cover photograph of W.E.H. Stanner.

Front-cover photograph reproduced with permission of Patricia Karui, the daughter of Walain (also known as Nadjik), of the Yak Madjilindi country.

Thanks to Helen Haritos and Romany Tauber, from the Northern Land Council, and Linda Barwick from the University of Sydney, for their assistance.

Back-cover photograph provided by the Australian Institute of Aboriginal and Torres Strait Islander Studies (AIATSIS).

'The History of Indifference Thus Begins' and 'Aboriginal Humour' are republished with the permission of Ingereth Macfarlane, Managing Editor of *Aboriginal History*.

Back Cover Material

"Bill Stanner was a superb essayist with a wonderful turn of phrase and ever fresh prose. He always had important things to say, which have not lost their relevance. It is wonderful that they will now be available to a new and larger audience."—Henry Reynolds

"Stanner's essays still hold their own among this country's finest writings on matters black and white."—Noel Pearsoni

W.E.H. Stanner's words changed Australia. Without condescension and without sentimentality, in essays such as 'The Dreaming' Stanner conveyed the richness and uniqueness of Aboriginal culture. In his Boyer Lectures he exposed a 'cult of forgetfulness practised on a national scale' regarding the fate of the Aborigines, for which he coined the phrase 'the great Australian silence'. And in his essay 'Durmugam' he provided an unforgettable portrait of a warrior's attempt to hold back cultural change. 'He was such a man,' Stanner wrote. 'I thought I would like to make the reading world see and feel him as I did.'

The pieces collected here span the career of W.E.H. Stanner as well as the history of Australian race relations. They reveal the extra ordinary scholarship, humanity and vision of one of Australia's finest essayists.

With an introductory essay by Robert Manne.

Index

A
Abaroo, *207, 211*
abidingness, *117, 118*
Aboriginal culture, *139, 140, 143, 507*
  undermining of, *529, 532, 534*
Aboriginal labour, *23, 25*
  dependence on, *265, 276*
Aboriginal society, see traditional society,
Aboriginal thought, *91, 93, 100*
  contrasted wiTheuropean thought, *318, 320*
  metaphysics, *110, 111, 114*
  related to social organisation, *107, 110*
Aborigines,
  appreciation of, *389, 390, 393, 395, 399, 400, 402, 404, 406, 409, 411*
  attitudes to, see attitudes to, Aborigines
  character, *411, 413, 416, 422, 425*
  early European encounters, *129, 133, 134, 136, 143, 145*
  European knowledge of, *124, 125, 128, 129, 133, 134, 136, 139, 140, 143, 145, 147, 151, 153, 155, 156, 159, 161, 164*
  phases, *124, 125, 128*
  and European values, *309, 312*
  as farm labourers, *23, 25*
  future prospects, *576, 579, 580*

intellectual interest in, *393, 409, 544, 545*
  by historians, *302, 304*
  by the young Stanner, *355*
  early colonists, *161, 225, 229*
interest in, *241, 298, 299, 404, 406*
lacking, *362, 363, 366, 368, 371, 373, 375, 377, 380, 382, 383, 387*
lack of political influence, *239, 241, 243*
origins, *139, 140, 387*
pattern of rhythm and mobility, *387, 389*
popular folklore about, *387, 389, 390, 416*
population decline, *232, 234, 275*
society, see traditional society,
see also bush people; city dwellers; Dreaming; outback people,
absorption of mixed-bloods, *265, 267, 270, 275*
Alligator Ngundul, *68*
Angamunggi, *37, 312, 314, 317, 334*
antitypes, see types,
Arabanoo, *207, 340*
Arnhem Land Aboriginal Reserve, *426, 429, 431, 484*
assimilation policy, *299, 304, 306, 309, 312, 440*
  effect on Aborigines, *58*
  impossibility of achievement, *70, 284*
  origins, *368*
  related to customary law, *61*

see also absorption of mixed-bloods,
Association for the Protection of Native Races, *357*
attitudes to Aborigines, *275, 302, 352, 355, 357, 539, 541*
Augherton, W.V., Taking Stock, *373, 375*
Australia (Crawford), *373*
Australia (Rawson), *373*
Australia: a Social and Political History (Greenwood), *375*
Australia in the Making (Harris), *373*
Australian Civilisation (Coleman), *375*
Australian Institute of Aboriginal Studies, *382, 409*
Australian Native Policy (Foxcroft), *371*
Australian People, The (Fitzpatrick), *373*
Australian Way of Life, The (Caiger), *373*
authority structures, *118, 120*

B

Banks, Sir Joseph, *133, 143, 170*
Barij, *42, 43*
Bateson, Gregory, *501*
Batman, John, *451*
Belweni (Malboiyin people), *81, 83*
Belweni (Wagaman people), *16*
Bennelong, *210, 211, 213, 217, 340, 343*
Black Australians (Hasluck), *371*
Blackburn, David, *170, 178, 200*
Blackburn, Sir Richard, *458, 460, 462, 484, 487, 490*

Botany Bay, *143, 170, 173, 175, 178, 180, 189*
Bowes, Arthur, *178, 182*
Bradley, William, *185*
brothers-in-law, *562, 563, 568, 570, 573*
bullroarers, *42, 53, 566*
bush people, *438*

C

Caiger, George, The Australian Way of Life, *373*
Calvert, Albert F., *134, 302*
Carstenz, Jan, *129*
child mortality, *249*
children, *72, 75*
city dwellers, *438*
clans, *153, 155*
Clark, Ralph, *186*
Colby, *210, 211, 215, 217, 340, 343*
Coleman, Peter, Australian Civilisation, *375*
Collins, David, *145, 180, 198*
colonists,
  early interaction with Aborigines, *185, 186, 189, 191, 194, 195, 198, 200, 203, 204, 207, 210, 211, 213, 215, 217, 220*
  lack of understanding, *185, 186*
  see also settlers,
Conference of Protectors (Canberra1937), *261, 263, 265, 299*
conflict limitation, *422, 425, 426*
confrontation, *411, 413, 416, 418, 420, 422, 425, 426, 429, 431*
congeries, *145*
Cook, James, *143, 170*
corroborees, *515, 519*
Crawford, R.M., *366*
  Australia, *373*
creative drive, *100, 107*
Cunningham, Peter Miller, *134*
customary law, *54, 58, 59, 61*

see also polygyny,

D

distinct views, *136, 139*
  of early settlers, *161, 164*
  inattention, *371, 373, 375, 377, 380*
  indifference, *362, 363, 366, 505, 507*
  see also Little, John A.; Wood, J.G.,
Daly River region, *347, 352, 353*
  farms, *21, 23, 25, 28*
  see also Durmugam,
Dampier, William, *129, 133*
Dargie, Charlie, *559*
Dawes, William, *215*
de Brosses, Charles, *133*
depressions,
  northern Australia, *267*
  see also Great, Depression
development explosion, *431*
  see also mining leases,
Dingiri, *12, 236*
diseases, effect on Aborigines, *30*
Djarawak, *16*
Dreaming, The, *86, 89, 91, 93, 95, 97, 100, 102, 105, 107, 110, 111, 114, 117, 118, 120, 318, 320, 334*
  central meaning, *86, 89*
  as cosmogony and cosmology, *93, 95, 97, 100*
  elements, *89, 91, 93*
  subtlety of the concept, *86, 89, 91*
  tales, *95, 97, 100*
Durmugam, *2, 4, 7, 9, 12, 14, 16, 18, 21, 23, 25, 28, 30, 33, 34, 37, 39, 42, 43, 45, 48, 50, 53, 54, 58, 59, 61, 64, 66, 68, 70, 72, 75, 77, 79, 81, 83, 84, 418*
  killings, *39, 42, 43, 45*

origin of the name, *7*
wives, *54, 58, 61, 64, 66, 68*

E

Eearth,
  see land,
Easty, John, *170*
education, *265, 439*
Eldershaw, Barnard, My Australia, *371*
Elkin, A.P., *357, 576, 579*
European settlers,
  see settlers
  exogamy, *155*
extermination, *139, 225*
extinction, *30*

F

fights, *2, 4, 7, 413, 416, 422, 524*
First Fleet, *166, 170, 173, 175, 178, 180, 182, 185, 186, 189, 191, 194, 195, 198, 200, 203, 204, 207, 210, 211, 213, 215, 217, 220, 222, 225, 228, 229*
Fison, Lorimer, *395, 399*
Kamilaroi and Kurnai, *393*
Fitzmaurice River region, *291, 293, 295, 298*
Fitzpatrick, Brian, The Australian People, *373*
Flesh Creepers, *306*
Foxcroft, E.J.B., *371*
funding, *275, 278, 383*
  for medical services, *252*
futurity, *318, 455*

G

Gillen, Frank J., *353, 355, 399, 400*
Glenelg, Charles Grant, Baron, *451, 455, 475*
Grattan, Hartley, Introducing Australia, *373*
Great Depression, *23*
  effect on Aborigines, *37*
Greenwood, Gordon, Australia:

a Social and Political History, *375*
Gumaitj people, *467*
Gurindji people, *418, 513*

H

Hancock, Keith, *362, 363, 371, 373, 402*
Harris, H.L., Australia in the Making, *373*
Hartog, Dirk, *129*
Hasluck, Paul, *371*
health, *252, 254, 256*
Henderson, John, *373*
Herodotus, *140*
Hewitt, A.W., *395, 399*
   Kamlaroi and Kurnai, *393*
high culture, *37*
Home, Edward, *178*
humour, *439, 548, 550, 552, 554, 556, 559, 562, 563, 566, 568, 570, 573, 574*
Hunter, John, *189*
hunting, *16, 18, 21*

I

Indigenous Australians, see Aborigines,
initiation ceremonies, *72, 75, 515, 519, 521, 522, 524, 526, 529*
   Daly River region, *9, 12*
integration, see assimilation policy,
Introducing Australia (Grattan), *373*
isolation, *114, 156*

J

Jansz, Willem, *129*
Jarawak, *559*
joking relationship, *562, 563, 568*

K

Kaberry, Phyllis, *118*
Kamilaroi and Kurnai (Fison and Hewitt), *393*
Karwadi, *37*

Kendall, Henry, *139*
   The Last of His Tribe, *439*
King, Phillip Gidley, *170, 173*
   first encounter with Aborigines, *178*
   first interaction with Aborigines, *175*
Kormilda College, *532*
Kunabibi, *34, 37, 75*
Kunabibi–Karwadi cult, *37, 39, 327*
   and Durmugam's killings, *42*
Kunapipi,
   see Kunabibi,

L
La Pérouse, Jean-Françoise de Galaup, *170, 185*
Lamutji, *42, 45*
land, ties to, *147, 155, 156, 298, 416, 418*
land rights, *447, 451*
   see also Yirrkala, Land Case
languages, *95, 105, 153*
Last of His Tribe, The (Kendall), *439*
Laves, Gerhardt, *28*
le Guillon, Élie, *134*
leisure-time activities, *117*
Little, John A., *541, 544*
Lommel, Andreas, *579, 580*
low culture, *34*
Lyons, Joseph, *363*

M
McEwen, John, *363, 366*
Macquarie, Lachlan, *304*
male–female social principle, *107, 110*
Malinowski, Bronislaw, *550*
malnutrition, *249, 252, 254*
Mannheim, K., *576*

Maringar people, *9, 14, 30*
  Durmugam's hatred, *48*
  and Kunabibi–Karwadi cult, *37*
Marithiel people, *14, 30, 45*
  Durmugam's hatred, *48*
  and Kunabibi–Karwadi cult, *37*
  see also Lamutji,
Market, the, *320*
Mathaman, *464*
Mathews, R.H., *399, 400*
Melbyerk, *14, 48*
M'Entire, Philip, *213, 215, 217, 343*
Midgegooroo, *418*
Milirrpum, *464*
Milirrpum v Nabalco Pty Ltd,
  see Yirrkala Land Case,
mining leases, Aboriginal response, *426, 429, 431*
Land Case mixed-bloods, *265, 267, 270, 275*
Mongers of Aborigines, *306*
Morgan, Henry, *409*
  Systems of Consanguinity and Affinity of the Human Family, *393*
mortuary rites, *464, 467*
mothers-in-law, *563, 566, 568, 570*
Mulluk Mulluk people, *14*
  relations with Marithiel and Maringar, *48*
Mulvaney, John, *302*
Munn, Nancy, *334*
mural art, *325*
Muri, *43*
Murinbata people, *7*
Mutij, *43*

My Australia (Eldershaw), *371*
myalls,
  Daly River region, *28, 30, 352*
  Fitzmaurice River region, *295*
mythology, *97, 100, 118, 312, 314, 317, 318*
  unrecorded, *236*
  see also Dingiri,

N
names, *91*
Nanbaree, *207, 211*
Nangiomeri people, *30, 33*
  relations with Marithiel and Maringar, *48*
  see also Durmugam,
national importance argument Yirrkala Land Case, *499, 501*
native title, *380, 382, 451*
  see also land rights,

Natural History of Man, The (Wood), *539*
Noble Friend of Aborigines, *304, 306*
northern Australia, *265, 267, 270*
Northern Territory Acceptance Act 1910 (Cwlth), *455*
Nullum Tempus Act 1769 (UK), *473*

O
oneness, *91, 93*
oral history, *377*
Our Southern Outcasts (Hasluck), *371*
outback people, *438*

P
Palmer, Thomas Fyshe, *164*
Parkhill, Robert A., *363*
pastoral industry, *395*
Phillip, Arthur, *186, 304*

Aboriginal policy, *191, 194, 195, 198, 200, 203, 204, 207, 210, 211, 213, 215, 217, 220, 222, 225, 228, 229, 338, 340, 343, 345, 347*
  abortive expedition into the bush, *191, 194, 195*
  first interaction with Aborigines, *173, 175, 178*
  instructions from London, *166, 170, 229*
  lack of understanding, *143, 145, 185, 186, 228, 229*
philosophy,
  in the Dreaming, *97*
  of life, *111, 114*
Piddington, Ralph, *552*
place names, *236*
Polehampton, A., *134*
policy,
  see public,
policy polygyny, *61, 64, 66, 68*
popular folklore, about Aborigines, *387, 389, 390, 416*
population drift, *256, 259, 291, 293, 295, 298, 439, 440*
Post-War Reconstruction, Department of, *366, 368*
poverty, *352, 353, 420*
power,
  see authority structures,
powerlessness, *418, 420*
primitive peoples, European attitudes, *128, 129*
protectors, *254*
public policy on Aboriginies, *243, 246, 249, 252, 254, 256, 259, 261, 263, 265, 267, 270, 275, 443, 445, 447, 510, 513, 515*
  Arthur Phillip, *191, 194, 195, 198, 200, 203, 204, 207, 210, 211, 213, 215, 217, 220, 222, 225, 228, 229, 338, 340, 343, 345, 347*

change of attitude, *366, 368, 371, 373, 375*
development, *259, 261, 263, 265, 267, 270, 275*
optimistic philosophy, *298, 299, 302*
see also assimilation policy; selfdetermination; land rights,
Pundjili, *61, 64*
Purcell, Frank, *464*

Q
quittance rites, *81, 83*

R
Radcliffe-Brown, A.R., *28, 336*
Rainbow Serpent, *284*
rangga, *464, 467*
Rawson, Geoffrey, Australia, *373*
Reality, in the Dreaming, *95, 97*
referendum (1967), *404*
religion, *102*
  and ties to land, *156*
reserves, *256, 259, 275, 451, 455, 475*
  see also Arnhem Land Aboriginal,
Rirratjingu people, *464, 467*
Roheim, Géza, *336*
romantic love, *550*
Ross, Robert, *191*
Roth, Walter E., *336, 399, 400*
Russell, Percy, *225*

S
sameness, *114, 117*
Scullin, J.H., *363*
segmentary principle, *320*
self-determination, *534, 535*
settlers, Aboriginal perspectives, *182, 185, 440, 443, 548, 550*

association with Aboriginal women, *25*
confrontation with, *411, 413, 416, 418, 420, 422, 425, 426, 429, 431*
impact on Aborigines, *75, 77, 161, 164, 295, 298*
  see also colonists,
shame (emotion), *64, 66*
shame relationship, *563, 566, 568, 570*
shovel spears, *16, 18*
signifi cancies, *566, 568*
Smiler,
  see Durmugam,
Smith, Bernard, *302*
Smyth, R. Brough, *393*
social conditions, *246, 249, 252, 254, 256, 259*
social organisation,
  see traditional society,
Social Science Research Council of Australia, *382*
Sommerlad, Elizabeth, *532*
Southwell, Daniel, *134, 170, 173, 178*
Sowden, W.M., *134*
Spence, W.G., *380*
Spencer, Baldwin, *34, 304, 336, 353, 355, 399, 400*
Split-Lip Mick, *66*
Sydney Cove, *180, 182, 185, 186, 189, 191, 194, 195, 198, 200, 203, 204, 207, 210, 211, 213, 215, 217, 220, 222, 225, 228, 229*
  see also Phillip, Arthur,
Systems of Consanguinity and Affinity of the Human Family (Morgan), *393*

T

Taking Stock (Augherton), *373, 375*
talion, *42, 45*

Tasman, Abel, *129, 133*
Tasmanian Aborigines, *243*
technology, *117, 156, 159, 161*
Tench, Watkin, *189, 191, 200, 204*
Tennant Creek, *357, 359*
terra nullius, *380, 382*
territorial system, *145, 147, 151, 153, 155, 156*
Th ompson, George, *220*
time concept, *110*
Tjimari (Wagin), *12, 14, 21, 50, 66*
Tjinimin, *312, 314, 334*
totemism, *110*
trade routes, *117*
traditional society, *102, 105, 107, 110*
    breakdown, *34, 37, 53, 54, 58*
    change and development, *323, 325*
    decline, *293, 295, 298*
    see also tribal,
    decline male domination, *118, 120*
    as society of kinship, *110*
    see also Aboriginal culture,
tribal decline, *232, 234, 236, 239, 259, 261*
    attitudes to, *234, 236*
    northern Australia, *270*
tribal reserves, see reserves,
tribal structure, *105, 107, 145, 147, 151, 153, 155, 156*
tribes, extinction, *30*
Trollope, Anthony, *134, 139, 225*
types, *317*

U

under-nourishment, see malnutrition,

V

venomous endearments, *562, 563*
voluntary migration,

see population drift,

W

Waduwiri, *61, 64, 66, 68, 79*
Wagin,
  see Tjimari,
walkabout, *387, 389*
Waluk, *42, 43, 45*
wards of State, *286*
Warramunga people, *359*
Watling, Thomas, *217*
Wattie Creek, *411, 418, 513*
White, John, *182, 191, 210*
Wileemarin, *213*
Wistful Aboriginal, *306*
women, *118, 120*
  in clans, *153, 155*
  Durmugam and, *54, 58, 61, 64, 66, 68*
  and Kunabibi–Karwadi cult, *39*
  and settlers, *25*
  see also male–female social principle,
Wood, J.G., The Natural History of Man, *539*
Woodward, Edward, *462, 473, 475, 480, 481, 484, 487, 490, 492, 494, 497*
Worgan, George B., *182*
working conditions, *246, 249*

Y

Yagan, *418*
Yirrkala Land Case, *458, 460, 462, 464, 467, 473, 475, 480, 481, 484, 487, 490, 492, 494, 497, 499, 501, 510*
  arguments towards title, *473, 475, 480, 481, 484, 487, 490, 492, 494, 497*
  national importance argument, *499, 501*

www.ingramcontent.com/pod-product-compliance
Lightning Source LLC
Chambersburg PA
CBHW052040290426
44111CB00011B/1567